How to Ra[illegible]

AMERICAN

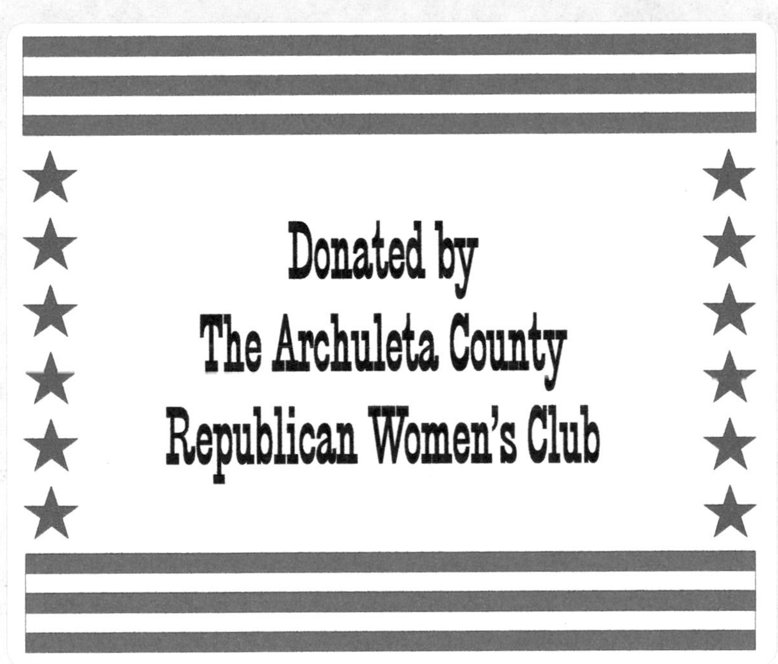

How to Raise an AMERICAN

1776 FUN AND EASY TOOLS, TIPS, AND ACTIVITIES TO HELP YOUR CHILD LOVE THIS COUNTRY

Myrna Blyth and Chriss Winston

THREE RIVERS PRESS
NEW YORK

Published in the United States by Three Rivers Press, an imprint of the Crown Publishing Group, a division of Random House, Inc., New York.
www.crownpublishing.com

Three Rivers Press and the Tugboat design are registered trademarks of Random House, Inc.

Originally published in hardcover in the United States by Crown Forum, an imprint of the Crown Publishing Group, a division of Random House, Inc., New York, in 2007.

Library of Congress Cataloging-in-Publication Data

Blyth, Myrna.
How to raise an American : 1776 fun and easy tools, tips, and activities to help your child love this country / Myrna Blyth and Chriss Winston.—1st ed.
p. cm.
1. Child rearing—United States. 2. Patriotism—United States.
3. Civics—Study and teaching. 4. Socialization—United States.
I. Winston, Chriss Anne, 1948– II. Title.

HQ769.B6366 2007
649'.510973—dc22 2006034136

978-0-307-33922-5

Printed in the United States of America

Design by Meryl Sassman Levari

10 9 8 7 6 5 4 3 2 1

First Paperback Edition

To the parents raising
America's next great generation.

CONTENTS

PART ONE

WHAT PARENTS NEED TO KNOW

1

THE PATRIOTISM GAP

"We want to make our children feel that the mere fact of being Americans makes them better off. . . . This is not to blind us at all to our own shortcomings; we ought steadily to try to correct them; but we have absolutely no grounds to work on if we don't have a firm and ardent Americanism at the bottom of everything."

—THEODORE ROOSEVELT

What does it mean to be an American? That's what *USA Today* wanted to know one Fourth of July, and their readers told them.

For Jeff Stark of Dublin, Ohio, being an American is "to live in the hometown of hope and dreams . . . where one hot dog stand can turn into two . . . where a second chance always follows a first . . . to live in the land of eternal promise for a better day . . . the Wrigley Field of nations."

Another Ohio patriot, Mel Mauer, says, "To be American is to be uniquely free."

Kathleen Butler of Wichita, Kansas, loves America for its diversity, "We are as American as apple pie, or stir-fried rice, or enchiladas or curried chicken. And because of that we are the luckiest people on the planet."

Being American? "It's about appreciating my country, loving it deeply and doing what I can to make the USA a better place." That was how World War II veteran Ezio Moscatelli of Columbia, Missouri, put his patriotism into words.

Opportunity, freedom, diversity, and duty. Four Americans . . . four patriots . . . four different ways of loving their country.

How about you? Do you love America? Are you the type who gets a lump in your throat when the flag passes by on the Fourth of July? Do you get goose bumps when "The Star-Spangled Banner" echoes in an Olympic stadium? Does a lemonade stand manned by a determined eight-year-old on a hot summer day make you smile? Do America's unique history and values make you proud of your country?

If you said yes to these questions, congratulations! You're probably a patriot.

But here's a much harder question. Do you believe your children, deep down, love this country and what it stands for, just as you do? You might be surprised to find out how your kids really feel about America. This wake-up call of a statistic shocked us. It may shock you, too.

> **If given the chance, almost one in four young Americans under thirty say they would rather live in another country.**

That's what an Independence Day poll on patriotism taken by Fox News in 2005 found when it asked Americans: "All things being equal, would you prefer to live in the United States or would you prefer to live in some other country?"

Most of us probably feel like almost 95 percent of the respondents over thirty who said they preferred the good old USA. No big surprise there, but *nearly a quarter* of our young people—the very Americans who are supposed to fight the war on terror, beat back the economic challenge of China and India, and keep our country strong, safe, and prosperous—would hightail it out of here if they could!

And an even higher number of our young teens are pessimistic about America's future. In a 2005 *Time* magazine cover story about thirteen-year-olds, the editors themselves were surprised at how gloomy young teens have become about America: "In a shift from just five years ago, when the new millennial teens were generally optimistic about the future . . . almost half, or 46 percent, believe that by the time they are their parents' age, the U.S. will be a worse place to live in than it is now."

A startling percentage of our youngsters have little or no hope for America's future. Almost half, it seems, have no confidence in their own abilities to ensure that our country will remain a good place to live when they are ready to bring up their own children.

Here's another somewhat startling statistic: In a 2006 *Scholastic* magazine poll, 80 percent of the kids said that they didn't want to grow up to be president. The fact that our country was a place where a youngster from the humblest of circumstances could become the country's leader was once very much part of the American dream. But thirty thousand children in grades 1 to 8 who participated in the *Scholastic* survey, said, "Thanks but no thanks" to the most important job in the world. In 2004, more than 80 percent of teens in an ABC/*Weekly Reader* survey also said they didn't want to be president. Over 54 percent, both girls and boys from all ethnic backgrounds, thought they could be president, but they'd rather not. The primary reason? They just weren't interested.

Most families in our country have experienced a better lifestyle in recent years than Americans have enjoyed at any other time in our nation's past, so these statistics are more than a little confusing. How can some kids today seem to be so negative or apathetic about the country that gives them so much? Why are some so downright uninterested and disillusioned they neither believe America is a special place with a special role to play in the world nor feel a responsibility to be the shapers of America's destiny as their parents and grandparents were before them?

It's not all kids, of course. Talk to any group of U.S. Marines or soldiers on a Baghdad street, and you'll see what America's young men and women can be and can do. But there's a disturbing gap separating far too many of our young people from the vast majority of Americans who believe that we are the most privileged people on earth to live in this great country. Call it the Patriotism Gap.

If we, as a nation, allow this growing cynicism to continue to infect our youngest generations, we put them and our country's future at risk. And the truth is your children could be next to "fall into the Gap."

This book aims to help parents bridge the Patriotism Gap by instilling a healthy love of country in our children. After all, it is part of our responsibility as Americans and as parents to teach our kids what this nation stands for. To teach them to be grateful for all our country gives to her own people and to people around the world. To teach them about the heroes and the history that will make our children proud to be Americans once again.

We should also help them build the backbone they will need to stand up to those who would harm our country from afar as well as those critics in schools and in the media who tell them and teach them over and over again a dark, negative story of America. Our enemies have been using vast resources to misrepresent our way of life and to indoctrinate their children, whenever and wherever they can, to hate America. Certainly, the least we ought to do is teach our children to value our nation. To put it quite simply: America's existence as "the shining city on the Hill" really does depend on it.

But how can we bridge this growing Patriotism Gap in very practical ways? First, to understand it, we've got to understand "us," who we are as Americans. Then, we've got to understand what's causing this disconnect, the "Bad Influencers," as we call them, who are turning our kids off to America. And last, parents need to know what they can do about it.

In this book, we provide real-world ideas and resources, including Dinner Table Debates to have with your family and 60-Minute Solutions that can help you find time in your busy schedule to help your children learn to love America.

We know that today it's not easy to raise a child to be a proud and patriotic American, especially one who understands what has made our country both different and special.

What They Don't Learn in Schools

Once upon a time, American children were taught in the classroom from the early grades onward about our country's great achievements and greatest achievers. In history, civics, and social studies classes,

Chriss Tells a Story: Is Patriotism a Dirty Word?

A couple of years ago, I attended the National Conference on Citizenship in Washington, D.C., a nonpartisan organization that has been working to encourage an active, engaged citizenry and to increase citizenship education for more than half a century.

It was held, appropriately enough, in the ballroom of the Ronald Reagan Building, honoring one of our nation's most unabashedly patriotic presidents who spoke often of our country's proud history and its unique values. He would have been as surprised as anyone by what was said that day or, more importantly, what wasn't said.

At the conference, I sat through thoughtful speeches and panel discussions on citizenship and civic engagement. But by day's end, I realized that I had not heard the word *patriotism* uttered by a single soul, nor had anyone mentioned love of country or military service as key elements in how we, as Americans, define citizenship today.

Being a bit of an outsider in this room full of historians, civics and history teachers, and national leaders in government, education, and the Congress, I decided to bypass the politically correct niceties of the moment and get to the point. Cornering a university professor, I told her that I had found the conference interesting and even enlightening in many respects, but that it seemed to me that something was missing.

"So, what's happened to the word *patriotism*?" I asked her.

The professor's answer typified the responses I got from everyone I asked the question of that day. With a slightly horrified look, she told me, "Patriotism really isn't a good word to use these days because it's been co-opted by the Right."

After scooping my jaw off the floor, I'm thinking, "Let me get this straight. Patriotism is out and discussing love of country is a little like having a crazy aunt in the attic. Everyone knows she's there. She may be part of the family, but no one really wants to talk about her because it makes people uncomfortable."

Instead, I discovered that citizenship is defined by many as community service. A good thing, to be sure, that ought to be part of every citizen's life. But patriotism, love of country, and military service didn't even rate a mention by a single speaker at the nation's premier citizenship event held in the shadow of the Washington Monument in the middle of a war. I was confused, so I'm not surprised our kids might also be a little confused. If university professors who train the teachers who teach our children the story of America reject patriotism as a value, we may be far worse off than merely confused.

★ ★ ★

America was held up as what it is: the world's oldest democracy that has a unique place in the world. Not only did kids recite the Pledge of Allegiance, but they were taught the truth beyond the Pledge's simple words. As Americans, we do live in the country unlike any other, one that offers hope and opportunity for all and has a long and proud history of sacrifices made for the freedom of others.

Washington, Jefferson, and Lincoln were portrayed, not as the deeply flawed, neurotic, or hypocritical human beings they often are today, but as heroes, extraordinary men of wisdom, courage, and vision—men who were able to change the course of history because of their character and their extraordinary actions. Yes, for decades, learning about our history, admiring our heroes, and developing good citizens were fundamental parts of American education, as important as learning those three R's. But not anymore. The awful truth is that kids learn too little at school about American history, and much of what they do learn is more likely to contribute to the problem of the Patriotism Gap rather than solve it. Equally troublesome, far too many youngsters suffer from this lack of positive civic education from the earliest grades through their college years. Too often, they learn what's wrong with America before they are told what's right.

Perhaps many social studies teachers seem to lack perspective because they have actually studied very little history themselves. That sad fact leaves them little choice but to rely almost exclusively on textbooks that espouse such a politically correct view of America's past it's no wonder our children's view of their country is so negative. New York University professor Diane Ravitch in *The Language Police,* her critique of current history textbooks, found so many examples of anti-American bias in the books she reviewed, she wrote that it often seems "every culture in the world is wonderful except for the United States." Yes, these are the textbooks your children's teachers could be relying on. Check your child's book bag and find out what textbook he or she is using. Later on, we'll give you tools to help you get involved in your child's history education. We believe learning about America's past is too important to leave in the hands of biased teachers and textbooks. For when it comes to the education establishment, sometimes it seems citizenship and patriotism have become as politically incorrect as the Founding Fathers.

One parent complained at a meeting we attended, "I spend $40,000 a year sending my son to college. Then he comes home putting down everything I believe in and everything that makes it possible for me to be able to send him to that school."

Dealing with Downers

Since 9/11 it's become especially tough to bring up kids who feel good about America. The threat of terrorism has been a concern for all Americans, young and old, and the battle against it is a long hard slog. Add to that the fact that for many kids, their first experience with our political system has been the 2000 and 2004 presidential elections—two of the nastiest, most cynical presidential campaigns in recent memory. And the 2008 election doesn't look like it will be any different. Most kids today know only two presidents—one who was impeached for lying to a grand jury after misbehaving in the Oval Office and the other who is more often than not portrayed by the media as incompetent, dishonest, or a warmongering cowboy or all three.

Let's face it. The media has been a driving force in creating the Patriotism Gap. When the Abu Ghraib scandal gets more than fifty front page stories in the *New York Times* while the liberation of more than twenty million women in the last three years by the U.S. military in Afghanistan and Iraq is all but ignored, the Gap grows. When the enormous human relief efforts our military has provided from Baghdad to Bali to Biloxi consistently gets second billing to scandals and screwups, what's an American child to think of his or her country today?

When the generation of children that we are raising hears little but rampant anti-Americanism trumpeted on the evening news night after night, we should hardly be surprised that teenagers are cynical or downright critical about the place they call home.

When our kids' favorite late-night TV comedians or the hottest celebrities ridicule our leaders, our traditional American values, or any notion of American exceptionalism, there is a cause and effect on our kids. It pushes them toward the Patriotism Gap, to the indifference and cynicism they think is cool and sophisticated—and there's nothing funny about that.

You can bet your teenager probably knows vile, angry rap song lyrics that use extreme and inflammatory language to insult and degrade America. Unfortunately, too many teenagers will remember the irresponsible invective spewed out by some celebrities in the days after Hurricane Katrina far longer than the pictures of courageous Coast Guard personnel rescuing storm victims from the rooftops of New Orleans or the hundreds of other stories of Americans helping Americans in the weeks after that calamity. Sadly, most of our kids probably also know more about Michael Moore's or George Clooney's distorted take on American current affairs than they know about American current affairs.

One concerned father, a decorated Navy fighter pilot who says he wants to raise his son to be as patriotic as he is, told us that he's more than a little discouraged, especially by the effect the media can have. "My son is a good student. Reads the papers, watches the news. But there are so many naysayers, so many people who think the best way to show they are smart is by bashing America. It influences him."

This father is right to be worried because there really isn't much to counteract this media tide of mean-spirited commentary or the daily diet of anti-American celebrity sarcasm.

Fighting Back

So what's a parent to do?

We say—fight back—and think positively. Because the good news is that unlike so many of the challenges we face, from the war on terror to our nation's social ills, raising your kids to love their country is one challenge that parents can do something about—up close and personal.

- Our first step back from the Patriotism Gap, then, is to be honest and admit the problem exists—that today most American kids enjoy our country's many benefits but are not as grateful for these gifts as they should be.

How Do You Feel About America?

We know how some celebs and some in the media and academic elite feel about our country. They are the ones who say, of course, they love America—not for what the country is, but for what it can be. Sort of like a man who says he wants his wife to be the best she can be, so he will love her more if she loses weight, has a face-lift, and, just maybe, gets a better personality. Does anyone really want to be married to a guy like that?

Well, here are some questions that will test your feelings about America and your attitudes about what it means to be an American. In the next chapter, you'll find out how most Americans responded.

1. Are you proud to be an American? ____Yes ____No
2. Do you think America stands for something unique in the world? ____Yes ____No
3. Do you think being an American is a big part of who you are? ____Yes ____No
4. Are you proud of our troops? ____Yes ____No
5. Are you proud of our achievements in science and technology? ____Yes ____No
6. Do you believe people who work hard in this nation are likely to succeed? ____Yes ____No
7. Do you think it is essential that everyone has the right to their religious beliefs? ____Yes ____No
8. Do you think there should be equal opportunity for all people regardless of their race, religion, or sex? ____Yes ____No
9. Do you think the United States has the best system of government in the world? ____Yes ____No
10. Do you think it is important to donate your time or money or both to community organizations that help those in need? ____Yes ____No

★ ★ ★

• The next step is to acknowledge that we, as parents, may be contributing to the problem. The truth is that most kids are generally clueless when it comes to understanding that the protected and privileged lives they lead are possible, to a large degree, because they are young Americans.

• But are we, as parents, all that different? We also have to acknowledge that we often forget that the hopes and dreams we have for our children and grandchildren depend on the fact that they are Americans.

Before we started writing this book, we spoke to a lot of moms and dads. Most of them tried to do everything they felt they should for their kids, from overseeing their homework and keeping tabs on their grades and ferrying them to soccer games and sleepovers to making sure they had the "right" embroidered jeans or the hottest video game. Yet most of these parents admitted they didn't talk to their kids about the uniqueness of our country and the importance of its history and how that directly impacts their young lives.

Shouldn't instilling a love of country in your child be just as important as a good school and piano lessons, a safe neighborhood, and a pediatrician you can trust? Absolutely. And raising a patriot doesn't mean you have to cut out any of those things from your life. We'll show you how taking a moment on the way to Little League to discuss why the field is named "Veterans' Memorial Park" or steering the discussion over dinner toward the upcoming local elections will quickly raise your children's awareness of the great country they live in.

Beginning at Home

Too many good parents assume that a love of country in their children will develop along the way like permanent teeth and puberty, a byproduct of Fourth of July barbecues and Presidents' Weekend ski trips. But it doesn't happen that way. Not anymore. Not with so many forces in our schools and in our culture that may be working far harder than you to influence your sons and daughters to be critical and negative about America. In a recent poll, 85 percent of parents said that in order to graduate from high school, students should be required to understand the common history and ideas that tie all Americans together. A darn good notion and one that parents have a right to expect from their child's school. But, trust us, it isn't happening in many classrooms; and unless you get involved, it won't.

But perhaps even more alarming, 80 percent of parents said that school is the best place for kids to learn what it means to be an American. Wrong. Dead wrong. Chester E. Finn Jr., head of the Thomas B. Fordham Foundation and a longtime expert on American education, says, "School is 9 percent of what kids learn. But 91 percent of what they learn, they learn at home."

Former secretary of education Bill Bennett, who has devoted years to improving school history curricula, agrees. "It is the family that teaches kids the right things to believe." And Ben Shapiro, author of *Brainwashed: How Universities Indoctrinate Youth,* which he wrote when he was a college student, offered this advice. When asked what parents should do if their son or daughter comes back from college suddenly spouting a newfound anti-Americanism, he said it was probably too late by then. The parents' job, he advised, is to "make sure they have the right ideas and can defend them before they are sent off to school."

Yes, as parents it's up to you! And there is nothing more important that you can do. Your kids probably spend a couple of hours a week playing soccer or taking dancing or skating lessons. They may spend hours playing video games. Well, they are probably not going to grow up to be professional video game players or Olympic skating champions. But they are going to grow up to be Americans. It is vital for you to spend some time each week to make them appreciate that. Especially when others, who once shared the responsibility of raising each

Blaming America

Even in post-9/11 class discussions, there were teachers in our classrooms who gave more than equal time to America's supposed "faults" to explain the acts of nineteen cowardly terrorists who murdered nearly three thousand innocent people.

In those dark days, the most-distorted-lesson prize just might have to go to a Maryland teacher whose young student shared this account with the *Washington Post*: "Why do some people hate America? Why did they do it? . . . 'Because we're bossy.' That's what my teacher said. She said it is because we have all the weapons and we think we can boss other countries around."

Obviously, this teacher wanted her class to learn one lesson in the aftermath of the terrorist attack: America only had itself to blame.

★ ★ ★

generation of new Americans, may be teaching your children what you don't want them to learn or constantly reinforcing a bleak picture of America that you don't share. Knowing what they should about our country teaches children who they are. And giving them a sense of patriotism and a commitment to our nation is also the best way you can do your part to keep America safe.

Dig into the Toolbox

We want to help you do this.

We've designed this book as a toolbox that can help you in a variety of ways, a toolbox of information and inspiration, stories and advice, and lots and lots of ideas and resources to help you mold your child into a proud American through teaching, sharing, and inspiring. Yes, we will tell you why it is hard to raise an American today, why there are forces working against it, but more important, we will show you how easy it is for you to make sure your children know what they should about our great nation.

- We identify the Bad Influencers that could be affecting your children and give you the best advice we could find to deal with them.
- We arm you with facts about our country and stories about remarkable Americans to share with your kids to make them proud of our past, grateful for our present, and enthusiastic about being the next generation who will shape America's future.
- We outline 60-Minute Solutions for raising a patriot. These Patriot Projects focus on everything from election day events to holiday parties to crafts you can do at home. Encouraging your children to love America doesn't have to be another burden in an already hectic schedule. We'll show you how to seamlessly instill patriotism into everyday life and have fun doing it.
- We give you lots of ideas to help you interest your children in our nation's history as well as include suggestions for books to read, DVDs to watch, websites to investigate, and great family trips to take.
- We provide topics for Dinner Table Debates with your family. Whether it's about current events or Revolutionary history, get to know what your children think and make sure they understand that their opinion counts.
- Most important of all, we ask you to sign the Patriot Pledge (see p. 126) and let your children know that you have signed it. Do it, and we guarantee it will become an important and wonderful way to enrich your family's life.

A Wise Farewell

This book can help your whole family better understand our American values, our national strengths, and the challenges we may face today and in the future. But before we begin, we want to remember and reflect upon the wise words of one of our greatest presidents, who sensed that the Patriotism Gap was developing nearly two decades ago. He was worried about that and had some right-on advice on how to bridge this Gap. In his Farewell Address to the nation from the Oval Office, Ronald Reagan wondered:

> Are we doing a good enough job teaching our children what America is and what she represents in the long history of the world? Those of us . . . who grew up in a different America . . . were taught very directly what it means to be an American. And we absorbed, almost in the air, a love of country and an appreciation of its institutions. If you didn't get these things from your family, you got them from the neighborhood. . . . Or you could get a sense of patriotism from school . . . and from the popular culture.
>
> But now . . . things have changed. Younger parents aren't sure that an unambivalent appreciation of America is the right thing to teach modern children. And as for those who create the popular culture, well-grounded patriotism is no longer the style.

He went on:

> I'm warning of an eradication of the American memory that could result in an erosion of the American spirit. Let's start with some basics: more attention to American history and a greater emphasis on civic ritual. And let me offer lesson number one about America. All great change begins at the dinner table. So, tomorrow night in the kitchen, I hope the talking begins. And children, if your parents haven't been teaching you what it means to be an American, let 'em know and nail 'em on it. That would be a very American thing to do.

We hope and we trust this book will make sure that your kids will never nail you!

No TV, No Trash Talk Dinner Table Debate!

Following President Reagan's advice, we agree there's nothing like a spirited debate over the kitchen table to get kids interested in important questions. Here's our suggestion. Pick a regular night every couple of weeks for what we've nicknamed a "No TV, No Trash Talk Dinner Table Debate" with your kids—attendance required.

You choose the topics. Make them think about the big issues they see on TV every night, but don't limit the discussion to current events. There's a lot we can learn from history that applies to what is happening today. Set up some guidelines to keep the discussion civil, but encourage everyone, young and old, to speak up. After all, it's the American way.

Besides giving your kids a chance to weigh in on issues that are important to every American and to the country, one recent study found that regular family discussions may help them keep their grades up and stay away from drugs and alcohol.

Don't expect miracles at first. Accept the fact that anything that doesn't involve text messaging will probably get you a roll of the eyes from your teenagers. Translation: You're not cool. But don't give up. If you can get them past that initial resistance, they may surprise you and themselves, too.

There are "Dinner Table Debates" in every chapter. Keep reading and find a good one to get you started on the next page.

When Do You Feel Most American?

A couple years ago, the radio show *Morning Edition* asked its listeners to describe when they "felt most American." They got a lot of interesting answers. One listener said it was when she rode the New York City subway, seeing the "melting pot" of America. Another said it was when she watched the one-block-long bike parade to celebrate Flag Day in her Illinois hometown, a place so small it doesn't even have a real Main Street.

What about your family? What makes them feel American? Find out over your kids' favorite dessert (we recommend chocolate cake and ice cream) by asking each of them to answer the question: "When do you feel most American?"

Is it when they learn about a past American achievement? When they read about the courage of our military? Maybe it's a patriotic holiday that brings out their American spirit. Or when your teenage daughter hits the shopping mall, does she make a connection between the endless shelves filled with products and America's unrivaled economic system?

Then ask them: Do they think it is important to feel American? Do most of their friends feel American?

Even ask them what makes them feel "un-American." You may be surprised by their answers. They might be, too.

★ ★ ★

60-MINUTE SOLUTIONS

Play Hometown History Detective

In this book you will find lots of ideas to help get your children interested in our country and our heritage. For starters: Make them understand that American history is all around them, all the time. We have already suggested you tell them why the local Little League field is called Veterans' Field. Here are some other ways to turn your kids into history detectives. Ask them to:

- Find out who their school is named after and why. Then, read a biography of that person. You'll find a list of recommended biographies of outstanding Americans for kids at different ages in the "Red, White, and Blue Grab Bag" section (pp. 267–277).
- Visit the town's war memorial for those who have served. See if the names of any of their relatives are on the memorial. Get many more ideas on teaching your children about the extraordinary sacrifices the U.S. military makes to ensure our freedom in Chapter 7, "All-American Year" (p. 137).
- Check out the local history museum or other nearby historical sites to visit on a weekend family excursion. There are lots of interesting and fun places to visit in your state listed in "250 Top Spots Your Kids Will Love" in Chapter 8, "Let's Take a Trip" (pp. 188–203).

★ ★ ★

2

WHO WE ARE

"They attacked us because of who we are."

—SECRETARY OF STATE CONDOLEEZZA RICE, TESTIFYING BEFORE THE 9/11 COMMISSION

Conservative or liberal, red state or blue, we all should be red, white, and blue when it comes to the love of our country. Unabashed liberal Norman Lear, producer of the hit television comedy *All in the Family,* had a rare opportunity to help demonstrate that during the past few years.

Lear is now one of the most successful and richest men in Hollywood. But as a child he lived for a time with his grandparents in a fourth-floor tenement building walk-up. He says that those years with his grandparents were the greatest influence on his life.

His grandfather always took him to parades—Fourth of July, Veterans Day, Presidents' Day. He remembers his grandfather, who loved this country, holding his hand very tightly when the martial music played and the flag went by. Often, his grandfather had a tear in his eye.

Lear's grandfather was also an inveterate letter writer to President Roosevelt. "Every letter," he remembers, "started off, 'My dearest, darling Mr. President: Here's what I think you should do.' " Lear recalls running down those three flights of stairs in the building where they lived to the letter box and how excited he would be when he found a small white envelope imprinted with the words *The White House.* It was a formal reply, but his grandfather always got a response. "When I asked my grandfather why he wrote the president, he said because everything the president was responsible for was very important to those he loved."

Years later, Lear found out that an original copy of the Declaration of Independence was for sale. It was discovered in 1989, tucked into the backing of a tattered painting that was sold for $4 at a flea market in Pennsylvania and was later authenticated as an original copy of the Declaration that had been printed the night of July 4, 1776, to be read aloud in town squares throughout the colonies.

Lear walked over to see the copy of the Declaration, since it was only three blocks from his office. "I was surprised at my own reaction. I looked at it, and I cried—like my grandfather had cried when the flag went by—and I knew in an instant that I would want to buy it."

In an online auction, Lear paid $8.1 million for the Declaration. Lucky for us, he has not kept it for himself. Instead, he has sent the document on tour around the country, so thousands have now seen this particular copy of the Declaration. Lear says, "Everywhere I've been where it's been shown I've been so amazed the way people will stand in line for an hour to spend a couple of minutes with it." And they react just like his grandfather did at those long-ago parades. "They walk away from it and you can still see tears in their eyes."

Who Are We?

Americans should be deeply moved by what is, in reality, our nation's birth certificate. Right now, in fact, there are more than 300 million of us lucky enough to call ourselves Americans because of that Fourth of July Declaration: about 260 million native born and more than 35 million first-generation immigrants from nearly every country in the world.

That's a far cry from where the country started. In 1776, there were only about two and a half million people living in the colonies. When Thomas Jefferson put pen to paper and wrote the words of the Declaration that would separate us from mother country England, most of the colonial population had British roots, was overwhelmingly Protestant, and came from lower- and middle-class backgrounds. The Founding Fathers would probably have a difficult time even recognizing the vibrant crazy quilt of American heritage today.

Seventy-five percent of us are white, but, now, 14 percent are also Hispanic, 12 percent are African American, and a little more than 4 percent of us are of Asian heritage. And there are lots of other folks with family backgrounds that reflect our country's increasingly diverse makeup, all living examples of the American melting pot.

What Values Define an American?

That's a very abridged version of who we are demographically, but that's only half the picture. If we really want to know who we are, it's equally important to ask, what are the values that define us as Americans? And do they set us apart from other nations? Of course, thinking about who we are is a very introspective and personal question. But it's also a very important question for the future of our country. So, as you begin to use this book, first, please, get your own bearings. Ask yourself how *you* would define America and Americans. Could you explain who we are to your kids, as they used to say in advertising contests, in just twenty-five words or less?

The overwhelming majority of ordinary Americans have a very positive view of this country. Unlike the constant critics at large in the academic, celebrity, and media worlds, as well as our critics overseas, Americans believe that there are many reasons to be proud of our nation's values and our fellow citizens.

In another survey taken in the spring of 1999, the Pew Research Center found that America's technological progress, especially the pioneering U.S. space program, was the largest source of pride for

Americans. When asked to name America's greatest achievements of the twentieth century, victory in war or economic superiority didn't top the list. Instead, Americans think the scientific breakthroughs and medical advances that have helped humankind over the decades are our nation's biggest and best accomplishments. Doesn't that say a lot about who we are?

Who We Are—What People Say

In the first chapter, we asked you a series of questions about how you think and feel about America. These were the questions pollsters have recently asked Americans in a number of national surveys. Do you agree with what your fellow Americans say about "who we are"?

1. Are you proud to be an American? YES! 95%
2. Do you think America stands for something unique in the world? YES! 84%
3. Do you think being an American is a big part of who you are? YES! 91%
4. Are you proud of our troops? YES! 93%
5. Are you proud of our achievements in science and technology? YES! 93%
6. Do you believe people who work hard in this nation are likely to succeed? YES! 79%
7. Do you think it is essential that everyone has the right to their religious beliefs? YES! 89%
8. Do you think there should be equal opportunity for all people regardless of their race, religion, or sex? YES! 88%
9. Do you think the United States has the best system of government in the world? YES! 89%
10. Do you think it is important to donate your time or money or both to community organizations that help those in need? YES! 80%

★ ★ ★

And what do most of us believe are the reasons behind our country's extraordinary success? In that same Pew survey, Americans credited the pillars of our democracy: first, the Constitution (85%), then free elections (84%), and, finally, the free enterprise system (81%). There is no question that most Americans think the Founding Fathers got it right.

Even though other polls show we don't know as much as we should about the important dates, documents, and debates of our past—and we are going to discuss why we should know a lot more about our country's history later on—Americans still seem to understand, through instinct and experience, the fundamentals of what makes this country both different and special.

An Idea First

Unlike every other place on earth, America was not created by an accident of history or geography. Our existence didn't depend on either a tyrant's dream of conquest or on the length of an army's supply line.

America, and only America, was an idea before it was a nation—an idea that all men are created equal with an inalienable right to "life, liberty and the pursuit of happiness." At our country's birth, Thomas Jefferson came up with that revolutionary phrase as both the justification and rallying cry for our new nation. Our Founding Fathers were able to brilliantly transform that democratic vision into an effective, workable government.

Eleven years after the Declaration of Independence was signed, the Constitution created an even more perfect union—a republic limited by law and respectful of private property that guaranteed a set of basic rights to its citizens. Though it may be the most powerful prescription for individual liberty ever written, our Constitution is the shortest constitution in the world—only four and a half amazing pages. We've read VCR manuals that are longer than that! (The constitution the European Union is still trying to pass is more than four *hundred* pages long!) The American Constitution remains a truly extraordinary framework for democracy that still governs our lives every day.

For Americans, freedom isn't an abstract principle found in dusty history books. Unlike millions around the world, we enjoy freedom as an integral part of our daily lives. A mother from Dayton, Ohio, told pollsters from Public Agenda what she—along with a majority of American parents—cherishes most about our country is personal freedom. She said, "I don't have to be the same or conform. . . . I can be what I want to be, or work to be what I want to be. And if you choose to take a different path, then that choice is up to you."

Americans: The Facts

- A new American is born every 8 seconds.
- An immigrant arrives every 26 seconds.
- Americans have the highest per capita income of any large industrial nation.
- We're homeowners—more than 68 percent of us own our own homes—the highest rate of home ownership in the nation's history.
- Americans are better educated than ever before. Eighty percent of Americans are high school graduates. Twenty-three percent are college graduates. Since 1995 more women than men have graduated from high school and college.
- Nobody works harder than Americans. An average U.S. worker puts in 70 hours more per year on the job than a Japanese worker, and nearly 350 hours more than Europeans.
- We're a religious people; 94 percent of Americans say they believe in God.
- We're a generous people. More than 64 million Americans offered their time as volunteers in 2004, and Americans give over $248 billion a year to charities.

★ ★ ★

Americans also seem to value opportunity, the opportunity that has always been available and that most of us believe still abounds in America. Jefferson put it so eloquently when he said, "We must dream of an aristocracy of achievement arising out of a democracy of opportunity."

The Lure of America

From the time of the very first settlers, who eked out a difficult existence in Jamestown or stony Massachusetts Bay, there has been a "push" and "pull" that brought millions to these shores. Many were "pushed" from their homelands because of political or religious persecution, overpopulation, unemployment, or famine. Others were "pulled" here by an availability of land, jobs, opportunity, and religious and political tolerance.

At one time many newcomers believed that the streets of America were paved with gold. Italian immigrants with a sense of humor used to say, "When I got here I found they weren't paved at all . . . I was expected to pave them."

Genevieve Gwei, who came to America from Cameroon in 1991, told the Voice of America, "When you're back home, you watch TV, you watch *Baywatch,* you watch *Dallas,* you think everywhere looks like that. You think there's milk and honey just flowing down the street. But when you arrive here, that's one of the first things you learn, that it's not like that."

Disappointed as they may be that Americans don't spend most of their time in bikinis at the beach, immigrants are still able to get an education, find a job, work hard, and climb up the social ladder. Former secretary of state Henry Kissinger came to America at the age of fifteen with his family, fleeing the horrors of Nazi persecution just before the Second World War. Young Henry worked in a shaving brush factory during the day and went to school at night. "Although life was hard," he recalls, "everyone I knew was confident of a better future and was convinced that he could reach it by his own efforts." Genevieve Gwei agrees. "I've found out that if you work very hard, if you set goals for yourself and put your mind to it, things will get better for you." Fifteen years after coming to America, Genevieve now works as a computer programmer and her daughter is finishing law school.

Over the past two centuries, immigrants have changed America for the better, and immigrants have been changed themselves by living in America—a transforming process that has been a part of the American story from our earliest days.

We Believe in Hard Work

Building the new American nation required grit, determination, and lots of hard work. Just as Americans share values, we also seem to share some characteristics. The very first Americans were characterized by a willingness to work hard, in part because so many had come from closed societies in which opportunity for the average man or woman was as rare as kingly compassion. Since those first hardscrabble years of early America and the settling of the West, our belief in the value of an honest day's work has become as much a part of the American character as our faith in the principles of freedom and democracy.

In many surveys, people say that to be an American, you really must subscribe to the work ethic. But Americans, in general, don't see work as a grind or a punishment. An overwhelming majority of us say our work is important to us. Most Americans are satisfied with their work, which many see as a way to express or define themselves and as a means to benefit their families and their communities.

The World's Best Tinkerers

Another American characteristic? Yankee ingenuity that some of our best and brightest have had in abundance. The book and PBS television series *They Made America* chronicles some of our country's most extraordinary people: well-known inventors such as Thomas Edison, who modestly explained his success by saying "There is no substitute for hard work," and the Wright Brothers, as well as lesser-known innovators like Lewis Tappen, an abolitionist who also dreamed up the idea of the credit rating, and Ida Rosenthal, who got women out of corsets and into her Maidenform bras.

The book's author, British journalist Sir Harold Evans, an admirer of our inventiveness, said, "Time and time again innovators proved to be democratizers. They turned America's political ideals into economic realities." And they did it less often for personal gain than from a sheer love of invention, that peculiarly American spirit that mixes our respect for hard work with our optimistic belief that we can do anything if we put our minds to it and make full use of our "God-given talents."

You've Gotta Have a Dream

Our belief in the opportunity our country affords us has been the driving force behind the extraordinary success of millions of our countrymen for more than two centuries. In fact, according to a survey conducted by the National League of Cities in 2004, nearly two out of every three Americans believe that they are presently living "the American dream." Moreover, 62 percent believe that it is achievable for most Americans, and 65 percent think their children have a good shot at it.

Americans Are Believers, Too

The American dream, however, has always been about more than just financial security. We are also a deeply faith-based people. And we have been since the first colonists arrived on our shores seeking the freedom to practice the religion of their choice. Not much has changed in the ensuing four hundred years when it comes to how Americans feel about their God.

Not only do 94 percent of Americans today say they believe in the Creator; perhaps even more important, according to a Pew Research poll, nearly two-thirds of people in the United States say religion plays a very important role in their lives. Ninety percent said they prayed at

An American Tale: Seven Girls, One Big Dream

Here's a story of American ingenuity that we loved, and your kids might, too. In 2001 in Petaluma, California, seven girls had a dream—kind of a crazy dream. Though Petaluma, population 55,000, was the scene of the 1970s coming-of-age classic *American Graffiti,* thirty years later the nearest movie theater was miles away. For the girls, that meant their parents had to drive them, and they all agreed: "When you are almost a teenager, you don't want your parents to have to take you to the movies."

The solution? Their own version of the American dream: build a movie theater in downtown Petaluma—a movie theater within walking distance and one that could revive the downtown as well.

With encouragement from one of their moms, the "Superb Seven," as they nicknamed themselves, got together for sleepovers every Wednesday night to brainstorm and make plans for their theater. They picked the brain of a small-theater owner to learn how to order movies, splice film, and, vitally important, make good popcorn. They talked to the vice president of finance of a large theater chain to learn more about the economics of the business and put together a professional business plan for a moneymaking theater in Petaluma. The girls then wrote Hollywood's heavyweight George Lucas, the director of *American Graffiti,* and, before long, they were selling their dream to four LucasFilm executives, who were impressed.

"It was one of the best business plans we had ever seen," said Gordon Radley, then president of LucasFilm. The LucasFilm executives agreed to let

least once a week—unless, of course, you're a Cubs fan or play the lottery, then your number's probably higher. And that makes us different when compared with others in the developed world. The importance of religion in the majority of Americans' lives is roughly twice the percentage of self-avowed religious people in Canada (30%), and an even higher proportion when compared with Japan and western Europe.

the girls screen *American Graffiti* on the side of an old building downtown to work up enthusiasm in Petaluma for their idea. Radley also called several theater owners and asked them to listen to the girls' ideas and take them seriously.

Next, the Superb Seven took on "city hall," lobbying the town council and talking to developers. When it came to promoting their plan, the girls were determined professionals, but they were still junior high schoolers and sometimes it showed. Sometimes, it worked, too. When one developer did not return their calls at first, the girls didn't take no for an answer. They sent him Girl Scout cookies to get his attention.

Matt White, the developer who finally agreed to make their dream come true, said, "They were very persistent with me. A lot of us tried to dismiss them. They would never go away." Like many American dreams, the girls' theater plans had a real domino effect and led to a $100 million downtown redevelopment project that now includes new housing and office space as well as shops and restaurants.

When the twelve-screen Boulevard Cinema opened its doors in May 2005, the girls, dressed in evening gowns, were the guests of honor as gold stars embedded in the sidewalk with their names on them were unveiled. Then, they were presented with $2,500 college saving bonds, plaques from the city, and, best of all, lifetime movie passes. "Without the theater," declared White, "we never would have taken the risk on the whole project." One of the Superb Seven, Noelle Bisson, said, "We decided to step it up and make a difference in our town. Maybe we inspired others to do the same."

★ ★ ★

The Power of Belief

Over the past two decades, Americans have grown more, not less, religious. And Americans practice what they preach. Six in ten Americans attend religious services at least once a month, while 43 percent attend at least every week. According to a recent Pew poll, those who attend weekly services are the happiest of all Americans. And many volunteer or donate to charity through activities related to their churches, synagogues, and mosques. And though it might seem surprising, strong majorities who support both political parties believe in the importance of religion. Nearly 70 percent of both Democrats and Republicans say religion is very important to them. Most Americans continue to define themselves, at least in part, by their faith and believe that religion has an important and appropriate role to play in the civic life of our communities and our nation: For many people, faith is more than a matter of individual morality. It is part of who they are as Americans, too.

Faith and a strong commitment to community continually spur Americans to help their neighbors in need. From the Pilgrims of Plymouth to the thousands of people across America who volunteered their time and money in the aftermath of Hurricane Katrina, Americans of faith have a tradition of helping those less fortunate.

Building an All-American Generation

Historian David McCullough has said, "A good society, it seems to me, ought to believe in teaching children generosity of spirit, a willingness to help and especially to help those in the most need." But maybe John Adams said it best when he urged that civic engagement is "not just doing good to other individuals but thinking as a whole how the country can be better."

In truth, that is why we wrote this book and why you're reading it. We all want to know how we can create a generation of patriots. How

An American Tale: Angels in Straw Hats

In April 2002, an F4 tornado cut a sixty-four-mile path across southeast Maryland, leaving three dead, more than a hundred injured, and $100 million in damages. La Plata, Maryland, a small nineteenth-century town of old Victorian homes and pretty streets lined with thirty-foot oaks, found itself in the deadly tornado's epicenter. In a matter of minutes, La Plata looked more like a war zone than a prosperous county seat. Few of the city's homes and buildings were undamaged, and many were destroyed.

The next morning, however, God answered a lot of prayers when groups of Amish men, farmers and carpenters from nearby St. Mary's County, began arriving to pitch in. They put up tarps on battered roofs and cleared away the remnants of the town's once towering trees that now blocked the main roads and side streets. The town would have been lost without their help in those first few days, but the biggest challenge lay ahead.

Despite the terrible destruction everywhere else, in the center of town, one of the local landmarks was still standing proudly—the more-than-a-century-old Christ Episcopal Church. And though the old stone walls had inexplicably withstood the 158-mile-an-hour winds, most of the church's Gothic-timbered roof was gone. That was a big problem. Replacing it was going to take a small miracle because the hundred-year-old timbers that were needed required special milling—a bit of a lost art in the age of Home Depot.

When the time came to rebuild the church roof, it was the Amish, once again, who came to the rescue. They still knew the old ways, and within a few weeks these quiet men had milled the special timbers and rebuilt the roof better than before. When offers of payment were made, not one of the "angels" would take a dime. Instead, they simply said, "Pass it on."

★ ★ ★

can we instill the kind of values in our children that have defined the people of our country for almost four hundred years? Values like generosity, resiliency, courage, caring, hard work, and innovation, all with a deep faith that will sustain them and their country in the years ahead. How can we make our children proud to call themselves Americans?

When a *New York Times* reporter asked California businessman and affirmative action opponent Ward Connerly, "What are you?" he replied, "I am an American."

The reporter objected to his answer, "No, no, no! What *are* you?"

Connerly responded in kind, "Yes, yes, yes! I am an American."

The journalist tried another angle. "That is not what I mean. I was told you are African American. Are you ashamed to be African American?"

Connerly replied, "No, I am proud to be American." He then went on to explain that he was part African, French, Irish, and American Indian.

"What does that make you?" the reporter then asked. Connerly answered, "That makes me all-American."

Keep reading. In the following chapters we provide you with the tools to raise an all-American generation and to help ensure a better America in the future.

DINNER TABLE DEBATE

Is This a Great Country or What?

Here's another family debate that should get your kids talking, thinking, and arguing—which is just what you want. This time try to find out what they think about "Who We Are" as Americans. You can help them along by throwing out words that others have used to describe Americans—some good and some not so good:

Freedom-loving	Materialistic
Idealistic	Arrogant
Hardworking	Aggressive
Independent	Unsophisticated
Traditional	Rebellious

Which words do they think best describe us? Do they wish Americans were described in other ways? If they could only describe America with three words, what would they be? You can also ask them during this discussion:

- Do they think America is still a special place?
- Do immigrants have more or fewer opportunities than they once had?

Many of our enemies abroad say America is a force for evil in the world. And many liberals here at home, including some outspoken Hollywood celebrities, seem to agree.

- But then why are millions of people still trying so hard to come here?
- Isn't this a contradiction? What do they think?

★ ★ ★

Who We Are—Make It Personal

Here are some ways to help the kids understand and appreciate their American identity.

- Take a look at "America's birth certificate." On page 219 we tell you how you can find an original of the Declaration of Independence at the National Archives, read a transcript, download it, and, best of all, let the kids sign their own copy.
- Also check out the Constitution, as well as the Bill of Rights, which protect the freedom all Americans enjoy. On page 259, there's a great game on the Constitution Center's website that will let them "Save the Bill of Rights!"
- Does your son or daughter demonstrate "American inventiveness"? We bet they sometimes do. They can learn how to come up with ideas for new inventions and even submit them for awards. See Chapter 9, "Patriot Projects," and the section on young inventors on page 246.

★ ★ ★

3

LESSONS TO LEARN

> "I believe with all my heart that America remains 'the great idea' that inspires the world. It is a privilege to be born here. It is an honor to become a citizen here. It is a gift to raise your family here, to vote here and to live here."
>
> —GOVERNOR ARNOLD SCHWARZENEGGER, AUSTRIAN IMMIGRANT

In October 1950, the dark and difficult early months of the Korean War, thousands of Red Chinese forces ambushed American troops hunkered down at Unsan, North Korea, in a massive nighttime assault. With the enemy bearing down, a lone rifleman with the Army's Eighth Cavalry stepped forward to man a 30-caliber machine gun position, putting himself squarely in the enemy's crosshairs. Three soldiers had already been killed at this post. For twenty-four hours, Ted Rubin held the enemy back, allowing what was left of his unit to retreat southward to safety. He was wounded and captured.

Ted Rubin was twenty-one years old, and his real name was Tibor Rubin. Tibor was born in Hungary. At age thirteen, when Nazi troops rounded up the Jews of his village, he was sent to the infamous Mauthausen concentration camp. Ted survived the next fourteen brutal months, but most of his family perished in Buchenwald and the gas chambers of Auschwitz.

Like thousands of survivors across Europe, young Tibor was liberated by American GIs. "They were so nice to us," he recalled more than sixty years later. "They fattened us up; they took care of us." In gratitude, Tibor made a promise. He would go to America and thank the country and the soldiers who had freed him by joining the U.S. Army.

After working his way to America and learning just enough English to pass the army's entrance examination, Tibor—now calling himself Ted—took the soldiers' oath and soon found himself on the front line in Korea.

Perhaps Ted's greatest heroism came after he was captured and marched along with hundreds of American GIs to Pukchin POW camp, nicknamed "Death Valley" by its inmates. The prisoners of this brutal camp were cold and hungry, and disease was rampant. "It was hardest on the Americans who were not used to this," Ted said. "But I had a heck of a basic training from the Germans."

For thirty months, he drew on his experience as a Holocaust survivor to take care of many of his fellow prisoners. He stole food from the guards' supplies and cared for the sick. Fellow POW Sergeant Leo Cormier, who met Ted on the long march to the camp, says, "If it wasn't for Ted, none of us would have made it out alive."

Because Ted had originally come from Hungary, by then a Communist satellite, the Chinese offered to send him back to his native country. But this brave U.S. soldier, who wasn't technically even an American, refused to be a pawn for Cold War propaganda and turned them down flat. "I wouldn't leave my American brothers because they needed me," he says today. "I was in the U.S. Army. I stood by my oath."

At the time he was freed, his immediate superiors recommended him for the Medal of Honor. But a sergeant, charged with sending up the paperwork, refused because Ted was Jewish. "Not on my watch," he said.

When Ted returned to the United States, he received his American citizenship, but still there was no talk of medals. Years later, in a ceremony at the White House in September 2005, President Bush gave Ted the Medal of Honor and the long overdue recognition he deserved. About his medal, Ted says, "It's a dream come true. This can only happen in America. The highest honor from the best country in the world!"

The story of Tibor "Ted" Rubin is a perfect tale of courage and resiliency, faith and compassion, and most of all love of America. Few of us could ever equal his bravery and character. But, as we read his inspiring story, it occurred to us that in many ways, this single man embodies those Americans who today are often the most patriotic among us. He is an immigrant, a man of deeply held faith, and, of course, he was a soldier.

Three Important Lessons

Trying to understand how to raise an American turned us into a pair of detectives, and our investigation led us to politicians, teachers, academics, think tanks, and even a talk-show host or two. While there are millions of patriotic Americans, we began to realize that there were three groups of citizens that seemed to stand out when it came to love of country: Americans of faith, immigrants, and members of the military and their families. From them, we learned three very important lessons on our journey to discover how to raise good Americans, our "3 C's":

- From religious Americans, we learned that part of being a good American means **counting our blessings,** something most of us don't do enough of.
- From immigrants, we learned that those who have lived under other forms of government with less freedom and opportunity have a unique ability to **compare America to the rest of the world,** in ways we natives never can.
- From our military and their families, we learned that **core values are important.** The core values of honor, duty, and courage are instilled into every sailor, soldier, Marine, airman, and member of the Coast Guard.

Lesson One: Stop Whining and Start Counting

"When I see the American flag, I go, 'Oh my God, you're insulting me.' " That was Janeane Garofalo, part-time comedian and full-time critic, sounding off, like a lot of celebrities do, about the country that has given them so much. Like many of her Hollywood pals, she's been given more opportunities and enjoyed more success than most people dream of. Maybe Janeane and many like her, who can't seem to find anything good to say about this country, ought to learn, as we did, an important lesson from Americans of faith: Stop whining and start counting—your blessings as Americans, that is. People of faith look for what is positive in their lives; they focus on the good, and they ap-

America's Blessings: Our Top 10 List

To develop our own gratitude attitude about America, here's our list of America's Top 10 Blessings. What would you include on yours?

1. **The Declaration of Independence.** Did you know that George III wrote in his diary on July 4, 1776, "Nothing memorable happened today"?
2. **The Constitution.** The shortest constitution in the world but still the best. It starts with those three most important words: "We the People."
3. **The Bill of Rights.** Thomas Jefferson argued for it, saying, "A bill of rights is what the people are entitled to against every government on earth."
4. **The All-American hamburger.** Of course, we think the list must include small pleasures as well as great accomplishments. Thanks to Oscar Weber Bilby of Tulsa, Oklahoma, who, his relatives claim, cooked up the idea of burgers on a bun.
5. **Jazz.** Jazz has been called the purest expression of American democracy, a music built on individualism and compromise, independence and cooperation—"Let freedom swing."

preciate what they have. And what better place in the world to find things to appreciate than right here in the USA?

Though some would like to separate religion from the public life of our nation, claiming a constitutional "wall" that must segregate our belief in God from our attempts to build a just and equal society, for many Americans a commitment to their religion and a commitment to America are not only compatible but closely joined. In fact, our belief in God has been a driving force behind most of the major political battles in our history. Revolution, independence, slavery, suffrage, the social reform movement of the early twentieth century, and the civil rights movement of the '50s and '60s—these were all great political debates, but they also represented both collective and individual

6. **Baseball.** "Whoever wants to know the hearts and minds of America had better learn baseball," said historian Jacques Barzun. The seventh-inning stretch, the pipe organ belting out everyone's favorites, hot dogs and beer, peanuts and the pennant race. It doesn't get any more American than that.
7. **The Statue of Liberty.** "Give me your tired, your poor, your huddled masses yearning to breathe free. . . ." The Lady in the harbor is the first great welcoming sight of America.
8. **Blue jeans.** Yes, we designed the pants that the whole world wears—a symbol of the American lifestyle of freedom, equality, and independence. Thanks to Levi Strauss who sold them first.
9. **National parks.** "From the mountains to the prairies to the oceans, white with foam," the natural beauty and historic sites of America—390 areas covering 84 million acres.
10. **Old Glory.** Isn't it a Grand Old Flag? But it was a New Jersey congressman, Francis Hopkinson, who probably designed it, not Betsy Ross, and then submitted a bill to the new government for a "Quarter cask of the public wine" for his efforts.

★ ★ ★

crises of conscience. Fiery preachers and ministers often led these controversial causes, which were cast as great moral dilemmas that the nation and its citizens, as people of faith, were required to address.

Little has changed. Today, Americans of faith are involved in many of our country's most controversial and morally difficult issues, but while they strive to make their country a better place, they are also grateful to call themselves Americans.

Now we're not suggesting that you have to share someone else's beliefs to be a good American, but every one of us, and especially our kids, can learn a lot from those who are religious. They can help us teach our children about a basic tenet of patriotism—to have what Oprah Winfrey calls a "gratitude attitude."

Lesson Two: Shop and Compare

Lev Sviridov is a graduate of City College of New York. But Lev isn't your average American college grad—not by a long shot. In fact, that might be a good way to describe Lev—a long shot. When he was eleven, he came to America with his mother, a Russian journalist and human rights activist, who was doing a brief teaching stint.

While they were here, there was yet another political upheaval in the Soviet Union, and his mother decided to stay, moving them to New York City. Lev says he learned English playing baseball in Central Park. Because his mother had difficulty finding work, the pair were literally homeless at times. As he tells it, "If we couldn't find a place to sleep, we would spend the night wandering around."

A brilliant student, Lev came to the attention of Fieldston, an elite private school, which offered him a full scholarship. He went on to City College of New York, as he says, "because I could afford it," where he studied computational biophysics and was president of his class. His mother urged him to do community service as well, and Lev tutored at a Bronx community center along with volunteering at the United Nations.

Lev Sviridov went on to study inorganic chemistry as a Rhodes scholar at Oxford, a stunning achievement. This twenty-four-year-old immigrant who has faced so many difficulties in his young life says with great passion, "I will never go back to Russia. It is a country that doesn't cherish its people. It's worse than a caste or a class system. There is no opportunity. They don't know what freedom or liberty is for."

Like Lev, most immigrants are characterized by their ability to contrast America's culture with their past experiences. They see the difference between a system that encourages and rewards individual achievement and one that doesn't. But far too often, too many of us and our children just take the opportunity and the freedom we enjoy for granted. We see them as entitlements. Immigrants don't.

Myrna's American Tale

Unfortunately, I only know the broad outlines of the story of my immigrant grandparents' arrival in America. What I do know is that my father's parents came from Hungary and arrived in this country at the end of the nineteenth century. My grandfather became a pants presser who worked very hard in a garment factory, six days a week. My grandmother raised four sons and one daughter. My father was the youngest.

They soon bought some land and had a small farm on Staten Island, which is still the most rural of New York's five boroughs and then, truly, was the country. Living in Manhattan today with its skyscrapers and endless traffic, it's hard for me to imagine that one set of my grandparents were farmers just a few miles from here.

My father started work when he was thirteen, just after finishing eighth grade. He worked for a fabric company and, eventually, after saving enough money, started his own small business and became quite a successful businessman. He never complained about having to leave school early, and he did go back and get his high school degree later. But it was just expected that he would work and so he worked and worked hard.

My mother was born in England and came here as a young girl. Her father had come to America first, like many men did at the time, and he later sent for my grandmother and their six children, four girls and two boys.

After high school, my mother worked as a secretary at the Boy Scouts Association and met my father on a New York subway. And he was so taken with my mom that he went home that night and told his mother that he was sure he had met the woman he was going to marry.

In some ways, my family's story, like so many others, is not very special. My grandparents came here and worked hard. My parents worked hard. They were always very grateful that they had the opportunity to work and achieve what they wanted—a home of their own, cars, the ability to put their children through college, a comfortable retirement.

In 1995, I was one of the delegates to the UN Conference on Women in Beijing. As I sat there surrounded by delegates from around the world, I thought of my immigrant grandparents, and my father who had gone to work so young. I knew how proud they would have been. I also knew that nowhere else but in the United States could I have had, in one generation, the opportunity to be the official representative of my country at a world conference of women.

★ ★ ★

The Great American Melting Pot

"It is no accident that all the immigrants I know are passionate patriots," Henry Kissinger once said. Lev Sviridov would probably agree. Today, there are differing views about how immigrants should become Americans. At one time, during the end of the nineteenth and the beginning of the twentieth century, public schools energetically "Americanized" the children of immigrants and encouraged them to then go home and teach their parents how to be Americans, too. It seemed to work. For millions of immigrants, each succeeding generation became more and more American, learning to speak English, keeping their Old World customs in the family but also melting into the predominant American culture, which continued to reflect the background and beliefs of America's first English settlers.

And America is the better for it. We can thank German immigrants for both the Christmas tree and the Easter bunny. The Irish brought us St. Patrick's Day, which was first celebrated in 1737 in Boston, and corned beef and cabbage, of course. Early French explorers first celebrated Mardi Gras on the banks of the Mississippi way back in 1699, and New Orleans ended up the American home of Mardi Gras.

Every time we order out Chinese, we have Cantonese immigrants who settled in California in the mid-1800s to thank for a whole new kind of cuisine along with the Transcontinental Railroad. And it was nineteenth-century immigrants from southern Italy who gave us the one and only pizza pie no self-respecting American teenager could exist without.

We could go on and on about immigrants' contributions to American culture, small and large, but you get the picture. As immigrants adapted to their new country, their new country adopted some of their Old World traditions. Assimilation gave us one of the most diverse cultures in the world, but even as we embraced the best of each new wave of immigrants, it was their acceptance of America's basic values and beliefs that made the melting pot work and made America one strong and united society, setting us apart from Europe and the rest of the world.

But that may be changing. Many cultural critics today are promoting an entirely different approach. They believe that our country should be less a melting pot than a multicultural "salad bowl" in which each "ingredient" retains its integrity and merely adds its flavor to the final dish. These multiculturalists argue against the traditional melting pot concept, claiming it is little more than an instrument of intolerance that forces third world peoples, especially, and other immigrants to abandon their cultures in order to be accepted into mainstream America.

Assimilationists (as proponents of the melting pot theory are called), on the other hand, assert that multiculturalism will destroy the fabric of American society through ethnic divisions much as we are seeing in Europe today. Supporters of the melting pot argue that multicultural policies such as bilingual education actually keep immigrants and their children at a disadvantage, unable to live the American dream that drew them to our shores in the first place.

Chriss's American Tale

I know very little about my mother's Irish roots other than that her family came over in one of the earlier Irish migrations in the middle of the nineteenth century. My grandfather, James O'Brien, was a boxing promoter in Fort Dodge, Iowa, and owned the local pool hall; but strangely enough, he apparently was also one of the town's most respected men. Perhaps that was how he captured the heart of a "Lace Curtain" Irish lass. It was a love match, the kind that was supposed to have a happy ending. It didn't. Both my grandparents died very young, leaving five children behind, my mother the oldest at fourteen. Still, Mom was able to graduate from college, and no one was prouder of her Irish roots than Peggy O'Brien.

My father's father had a rough time of it, too, emigrating to America from eastern Germany by boat, not to Ellis Island, but by a path less traveled—through Mexico. The family's emigration was plagued by disaster. When they reached the Mexican/U.S. border, half of their eleven children were found to have an eye disease and were denied entry into the United States. Papa Horst decided to stay with the ailing children, assuring his wife, my great-grandmother, he would join them later in the States when the rest of the children were well. Sadly, none of them were ever to see each other again. Today, we have an entire branch of the family in Argentina we've never met!

What Parents Want

It's not surprising, then, that immigrant parents are often the most opposed to bilingual education, as a survey conducted by Public Agenda showed. Like most parents, they think it is important for children to learn to speak and read English. The attitude of most immigrants and their children remains close to that of former secretary of state Colin Powell, whose parents were immigrants from Jamaica and who grew up in a multiethnic neighborhood in New York, playing with boys from different backgounds. A friend from those days has said

My grandfather, who could neither read nor write, settled with his mother and the rest of his siblings in Iowa where he went to work first as a farmhand plowing, seeding, and picking vegetables instead of going to school. Later, he worked in a canning factory, as a short-order cook, and after years of savings, he bought and ran his own small restaurant specializing in the best German chicken and noodles you ever tasted.

It was my grandmother who finally taught him to read and write English; and over the years, Grandpa became part of that great melting pot, enthusiastically embracing his new country and its culture. His was a classic "only in America" kind of success story. He began with nothing and saw his son, my father, graduate from both college and then from law school thanks to the GI Bill. And though he didn't live to see it, in just two generations, the first grandchild of this once illiterate fieldworker became the first woman to head the White House Office of Speechwriting and serve as a senior White House official. For me, I'll never forget the look on my father's face as I introduced him to President George H. W. Bush in the Rose Garden of the White House. Only in America.

★ ★ ★

that on the "melting pot" streets of Washington Heights Powell picked up "a little Yiddish, a little German, Spanish, Italian. We all did in those days."

Powell has said about his background that his family's story is "a common one," like millions of other Americans'. His parents met and married in New York, and "By their hard work and their love for this country, they enriched this nation and helped it grow and thrive. They instilled in their children and grandchildren that same love of country and a spirit of optimism." He also said that he found when he traveled the world as secretary of state, "People still want to come here. . . . Refugees who have no home at all know that America is their land of dreams. . . . You see, I believe that the America of [today] is the same America that brought [my parents] to these shores, and so many millions of others. An America that is still the beacon of light to the darkest corner of the world." Most Americans would agree and not just because most can claim immigrant roots. They know immigrants, seeking a better life for themselves and their families, have made this country what it is today.

Many family stories, including our own, are living proof that assimilation works—for immigrants, for their families, and for America—and that's what makes the American melting pot so wonderful. One mother told the pollsters of Public Agenda about an experience she and her teenagers had: "We recently took a friend to the Statue of Liberty. He was an immigrant from China whose family is not allowed to leave, and he fell to his knees and kissed the ground. And it was the most moving thing I ever saw in my life because I realized the basic things we take for granted. . . . My children were awed, just absolutely dumbstruck. And you know teenagers are hardly ever without something to say."

Lesson Three: Core Values Create Patriots

For much of his fifty years on this earth, writer Frank Schaeffer was a part of the intellectual elite that often has little appreciation for the military—that is, until his son, John, a prep school senior, decided to enlist in the Marines instead of going to college. Talk about culture shock!

As Frank put it in the book he wrote with his son called *Keeping the Faith*, ". . . in the circles we moved in—on the Volvo-driving, higher education–worshipping North Shore of Boston, a son or daughter going into the Marines was something unheard of." Talking about the Marines, one parent actually asked him, "But aren't they *terribly* southern?"

Twelve weeks after John left for basic training, Schaeffer and his wife, Genie, watched proudly from the stands of the Parris Island parade grounds as their son officially became a Marine. They realized he was much changed . . . tougher, proud, determined, not to mention thinner. He was no longer a boy; he had become a man of strength, values, commitment, and character. As his son went through those grueling months of training on Parris Island, however, Frank Schaeffer discovered he was changing, too, and realized something shocking. He loved America. As he put it, "I felt fortunate to be a small part of her. If any nation in history was a worthy cause, America was." Later as they toured the island, Frank was overwhelmed with his new feelings, "I watched several platoons march past through the glimmer of tears. . . . I felt small, an alien to all the selflessness around me. . . . What had I ever done for my country that made me worthy to be defended by these young men and women? . . . I was standing on the footprints of forgotten men who went forth from this place who laid down their lives so I could go to my town hall without fear, speak my piece. They had gone forth . . . to protect my way of life."

Sadly, many members of America's intellectual and media elite may not see it this way. They are still lost in the antimilitary fog of the

1960s when campus professors along with much of the media began taking an adversarial position toward the military and even their own country over the Vietnam War. This divide was the beginning of the Patriotism Gap we see today. That Gap has only widened over the past thirty years, infecting many of America's most powerful, prosperous, and educated people with an antimilitary bias, often, the very people who should be most grateful to our country. It is taking a toll on our children as well.

But not all of our children. Thousands of young men and women continue to step forward every year to serve their country. We wanted to know why, and we wanted to know how the U.S. military trains and teaches its young recruits to not only fight for their country but love and respect it as well. We posed those questions to a number of members of the military as we tried to learn their secret to creating men and women willing to defend their country even at the cost of their own lives, troops who seem infused with a sense of duty and destiny that rises far above even the most patriotic of us civilians.

Here's what we found.

Living by the Code

Behind all the basic training, behind the influence of parents and teachers, behind the kind of place they call home, the men and women of the U.S. military aren't driven by some kind of shallow super patriotism or inspired by clever jingoism. They aren't brainwashed "robotons" as some would have us believe. Quite the contrary. Talk to soldiers or sailors for five minutes, and you'll understand that, first, they do love their country. Second, they want to be part of something bigger than themselves—part of a noble mission and a great team. In truth, many are idealists driven by a desire to make this a better country and world.

At the heart of all they do is a set of core values that demands a higher standard of conduct and instills a sense of mission and teamwork in new recruits, a code that transforms and strengthens.

- For members of the U.S. Army, "loyalty, duty, respect, selfless service, honor, integrity, and personal courage" are what being a soldier is all about.
- "Integrity first, service before self, and excellence in all we do" is the common standard of conduct demanded of those who wear the wings of the United States Air Force.
- Marines and sailors pledge themselves to be warriors of character through "honor, courage, and commitment."

The "Code" asks our young men and women volunteers to "be all that they can be." And every child in America can benefit from that example.

The Making of a Marine

How does what some parents call "the Transformation," from sometimes slacker teens to men and women of courage and commitment, occur? How do the Marines turn out dedicated, brave, and responsible men and women in just twelve short weeks? Here's what the officers to whom we spoke said:

- By emphasizing, over and over, those "core values" and demanding that a Marine's every action reflect those values.
- By teaching recruits to follow orders as long as they conform to "core values" and to care for one another without thought of self.
- By setting the bar high—very high—because the military has learned that when challenged, most young Americans will push harder and meet that challenge. The higher the goal, the harder they push themselves to succeed.
- By insisting on respect for the long, proud traditions of the Corps, understanding that they are part of something larger than themselves. Talking about the importance of tradition, Marine drill instructor Keith Burkepile likened it to civilians telling their children

What Military Families Say

When we asked iVillage, the popular women's website, to poll visitors to their home page about patriotism, the first question the site posed was whether it is hard to raise an American today. One of our favorite responses came, appropriately, on the Fourth of July from a military mom who answered the question with her own American tale.

"I don't find it very difficult to teach patriotism to my daughter. She knows to respect the flag and what it stands for. We've always lived on military bases since she was a very young child," the mom explained. "She knows that at the end of the duty day when the National Anthem is played to stop whatever she is doing, turn to the nearest flag, and salute. My daughter also understands the sacrifices our family is making and why. We've always let her know that even if it is difficult, she is contributing to America's well-being by sharing her daddy with our country."

★ ★ ★

about their grandparents to instill a respect for the past. He told *Parade Magazine* editor Larry Smith, "As training goes on, the weight and responsibility of the Marine Corps tradition really starts to sink in. When they receive that eagle, globe, and anchor pin many recruits will cry. They know the torch has been passed to them."

Former Georgia senator Zell Miller remembers the moment when he decided to enlist in the Marine Corps. He was a college dropout who had ended up spending the night in a local drunk tank and knew he had to change his life. In his book *Corps Values: Everything You Need to Know I Learned in the Marines,* he wrote, "In the twelve weeks of hell and transformation, I learned the values of achieving a successful life that have guided and sustained me . . . ever since."

Passing Your Torch

Now, we're not asking you to run your own boot camp—though you might sometimes wish you could. But in trying to instill the love you feel for America into your children, you, too, can embrace a noble mission and help pass the torch.

Courage. Service. Commitment. Loyalty. Tradition. Obviously, kids are never too young to understand these values. Remember our enemies never hesitate to fill even the youngest minds with hate and extreme propaganda that can turn innocents into terrorists. Shouldn't we use the opportunity to teach our children core values that can help make this a better, safer, and freer world?

Through the course of this book, we learned that the men and women of the U.S. military, who represent every color and creed, every class and geographic area, really practice what they preach. No, they're not perfect, but members of the military and their families do strive to live by a higher code. An Army sergeant dies saving more than a hundred of his men and is awarded the Medal of Honor. A mother sends five sons and her husband to fight in Iraq and stands behind them and her country. A young Marine lieutenant receives the Navy Cross for his courage under fire and says, "I was just doing my job." Like Frank Schaeffer, the more we came to understand the military, the prouder we became.

Taking Lessons to Heart

We hope we have shown you that for many people who are religious, for immigrants who are grateful to be in America, and for military families willing to serve and sacrifice, love of country is a deeply embedded value.

These three groups teach us, and more important can teach our children, worthwhile lessons about being good Americans. They teach us to count our blessings, to compare our country to others and realize how lucky we are to call ourselves Americans, and, finally, to live by a code of conduct that will make us better citizens and better people. We are very grateful for these powerful lessons; but there are Bad Influencers out there who are teaching our children very different lessons about our country, and they are very powerful, too. Find out who they are, what they are doing, and what you can do about it in the next chapters.

Family Core Values

Start by having this discussion with your family. It may be one of the most important ones you will ever have because it will teach you a lot about your family and yourself. For some, faith and family are the most important values. For others, working hard, being successful, or helping others are the most important.

- What are your family core values? Can you list three or four?
- How are they reflected in your actions every day?
- Does everyone agree on the family's core values or do some see things very differently?
- Is being patriotic a core value to your family?
- Ask everyone to share his or her favorite family tradition. How do they relate to your core values? Do your family traditions help encourage patriotism?

This may take more than one discussion. But it is a really interesting way to understand what is important to you—and what the kids think is important. You may learn a lot, be pleased, or use this discussion as a catalyst for change.

60-MINUTE SOLUTIONS

Traditions Bind Families

Family traditions can help children understand and take pride in America's past. Here are some ideas to make your family traditions educational and fun.

- Where did the first American in your family come from? Together trace your own family history and compile your very own American Tale. Start with a scavenger hunt for original family documents — marriage and death certificates, military discharge papers, baptismal certificates, and family Bibles. For more ideas to help discover more about your family, check out the Patriot Project on "Family History" on page 232 in Chapter 9.
- If your family has a military tradition, there are lots of ways to learn about the role the U.S. military has played to protect freedom at home and abroad. For great websites and other resources, go to "Battle Plans" on page 222, also in Chapter 9.
- Every family has its own holiday traditions, but why not add some new ones, especially for the holidays we tend to forget like Columbus Day and Presidents' Day? A new way to celebrate Thanksgiving might be to invite an immigrant family for Thanksgiving dinner. Make all the traditional dishes but add some from the immigrants' native country. Find out about "old country" recipes in Chapter 9's Patriot Projects' "The Great American Potluck" on page 235 and make a true melting pot of a meal! Chapter 7, "All-American Year," has more ideas for all of America's special holidays.

★ ★ ★

4

DON'T KNOW MUCH ABOUT HISTORY

"If a nation expects to be ignorant and free, it expects what never was and what never will be."

—Thomas Jefferson

In a visit to a college class in 2004, Supreme Court Justice Anthony Kennedy was impressed by the students' knowledge of our Constitution. They said they had been studying the Constitution since seventh grade and asked insightful questions about constitutional history. Afterward he told his wife that he would have been impressed by their interest and understanding if they were third-year law school students. The only problem? The class he was talking to was in Warsaw, Poland. "The average Polish college freshman, first year, knows far more about our Constitution than graduates of our universities," he said. Why? He explained, "They told me they studied our Constitution because they wanted the freedom we have for themselves."

Unfortunately, just like the refrain in that old Sam Cooke song, our youngsters, even those who attend our best colleges and universities, "Don't know much about history," especially, the history of their own country. In 2005, the Intercollegiate Studies Institute tested the "history I.Q" of 14,000 randomly selected college freshmen and seniors at fifty universities and colleges, including some of our most prestigious.

Here's an example of some of the questions they were asked:

1. What battle brought the American Revolution to an end?
   a. Saratoga
   b. Gettysburg
   c. The Alamo
   d. Yorktown
   e. New Orleans
2. Abraham Lincoln was elected president during which period?
   a. 1800–1825
   b. 1826–1850
   c. 1851–1875
   d. 1876–1900
   e. 1900–1925
3. The line "We hold these truths to be self-evident, that all men are created equal" is from:
   a. The Federalist
   b. The preamble to the Constitution
   c. The Communist Manifesto
   d. The Declaration of Independence
   e. An inscription on the Statue of Liberty
4. The major powers at odds with each other in the Cold War were the United States and:
   a. Germany
   b. Iran
   c. Vietnam
   d. The Soviet Union
   e. Poland

(The answers to the above questions are: 1. d, 2. c, 3. d, 4. d.)

How did you do? More important, how would your kids do? Not so hot? Well, don't feel too bad if they didn't get them right. Overall, the average score for college seniors in the new study was 54.2 percent, while freshmen scored an average 50.4 percent, which means both groups would have received an F if the survey had been a pop quiz. Not one college surveyed could boast that its seniors scored, on average, even a C in American civic knowledge. "Virtually every institution of higher learning claims some form of citizenship, leadership, or national service in their mission statement," declared Josiah Bunting III, ISI's chairman. "However, the evidence from our ongoing research shows that colleges are failing to advance students' knowledge of America's history [and] government . . . and consequently not preparing their students to be informed and engaged citizens." Czech novelist Milan Kundera once said that if you want to destroy a country, destroy its memory. If a hostile power or a terrorist group wanted to erase America's civic heritage, it could hardly do a better job than America's elite schools are doing right now other than simply prohibiting the study of American history altogether.

What They Don't Know Now

It wasn't always that way. Free public education in America was started primarily to teach youngsters our history and how our government functions. Though reading and writing were always important—during the time of the Revolution, there was almost 90 percent literacy in this country—the emphasis from the earliest days of public education was primarily on raising good effective citizens. Our wise Founding Fathers and our first devoted public educators were convinced that only those who knew their history and understood the ideals and principles on which our country was based could effectively govern themselves and preserve our democracy.

In June of 2005, Senator Lamar Alexander, a Tennessee Republican, and Senator Ted Kennedy, a Massachusetts Democrat, who may not agree on much, jointly convened a Senate hearing on one really big mutual concern. They called their hearing: "U.S. History: Our Worst Subject." Senator Alexander declared at the hearing, "According to the

National Assessment of Educational Progress (NAEP), commonly referred to as 'the nation's report card,' fewer students have a basic understanding of American history than have a basic understanding of any other subject which we test—including math, science and reading."

So, how bad is it? In 2006, the last time a national history test was administered by the Department of Education, only 18 percent of fourth graders, 17 percent of eighth graders, and 13 percent of twelfth graders scored at a proficient level. Yes, the older they got, the less they seemed to know about America. (If you're interested, you can read about the NAEP study and student responses to American history questions at **www.nces.ed.gov/nationsreportcard/ushistory**.)

It's clear that no matter how badly kids may be doing when it comes to reading, and no matter how weak we are in science or math compared to kids in Hong Kong or New Delhi, for too many of our children, American history, as the NAEP test shows, is truly their "worst subject"—something you might think would be their best, understanding their own past.

During the hearings Senator Kennedy pointed out that nine states have no standards for teaching American history and twenty-two others have standards that are generally regarded as weak. Senator Alexander said, "Our children don't know American history because they are not being taught it," adding that the Florida legislature had recently passed a bill permitting students to graduate from high school without taking a single U.S. history course. Obviously, the high schools of Florida will soon be following in the questionable footsteps of top colleges when it comes to valuing history.

What Do You Know?

We've all had a good laugh over some of the ridiculous answers Jay Leno gets when he conducts his famous man-on-the-street interviews on *The Tonight Show.* He once asked someone, "How was Mount Rushmore formed?" The man answered, "By erosion." Another time, Leno

History Bloopers You Won't Believe

Kids do say the darnedest things about American history! A couple of professors, Richard Lederer and Anders Henriksson, have been collecting student mistakes and malapropisms for years. Believe it or not, and you won't believe it, this batch is all from college students, maybe some from those fifty-five "elite" colleges and universities, who thought that Martha Stewart sewed the first American flag ("It was a good thing") and that westward expansion ended at Custard's Last Stand. Yes, you will laugh—until you cry:

- "Christopher Columbus sailed on the *Nina,* the *Pinta,* and the *Santa Fe.*"
- "Washington was the only president to be elected anonymously by the Electrical College."
- "Thomas Jefferson was the author of the Decoration of Independence."
- "The major cause of the Civil War was when slavery spread its ugly testicles across the West."
- "The civil rights movement in America turned around the corner with Martin Luther King Junior's 'If I had a hammer' speech."
- "The Carter administration had to deal with the Iran Hostess Crisis."
- "There would be no problem at all in the Middle East today if the West Bank would lend more money to the Arabs and if the Palace Indians were not so troublesome!"

★ ★ ★

asked a woman, "What American war was fought in 1812?" Clearly clueless in California, she responded, "World War I?"

Funny as those bits might be, they reflect a real problem. National polls have revealed that Americans lack even the most basic knowledge of our history. A survey taken in 2005 by Harris Interactive for the American Bar Association found that 55 percent of Americans could not correctly define the concept of the separation of powers. A Columbia Law School poll found nearly half of Americans thought

Karl Marx's favorite political slogan, "From each according to his abilities, to each according to his needs," the core of Communist philosophy, was part of our Constitution. A 2006 Zogby poll reported that more Americans knew the names of two of Snow White's dwarfs than the names of two justices of the Supreme Court. And no matter how often we watch *Law and Order*, more than half of us can't explain the role of the judiciary in the federal government.

So, how much do you know? Here's a chance to find out. Take our pop quiz version of the Citizenship Test, the new test that immigrants must take before becoming American citizens, and see how well you

The Citizenship Test!

Now, we are not going to give you the real easy ones, like who is the president? Or when do we celebrate Independence Day? But here are five questions from the test that help new citizens learn about our system of government:

1. What is the supreme law of the land?
2. What stops one branch of government from becoming too powerful?
3. What is *one* right or freedom from the First Amendment?
4. Who is the commander-in-chief of the military?
5. If both the president and the vice president can no longer serve, who becomes president?

Here are some factoids that every new citizen has to master:

6. The idea of self-government is in the first three words of the Constitution. What are these words?
7. We elect a U.S. Senator for how many years?
8. There were thirteen original states. Name *three*.
9. Name one of the two longest rivers in the United States.
10. How many amendments are there to the Constitution?

score. We've listed only fifteen questions—there are actually 100 altogether. You'll find the full test on the Web at **www.uscis.gov/newtest.** Ask your kids to take this pop quiz along with you. And good luck!

You'll see our newest citizens have to learn a lot about our country, which might be part of the reason why they value being Americans so much and have such pride in their new homeland. Be warned! The government recently revised the test.

But what about our kids? The state of history education in America's classrooms today is rapidly becoming a national tragedy, and all of us ought to care. Our future depends on it. Their future depends on it.

And finally here are some stumpers that even people who thought they would ace this test had to look up!

11. How many voting members are there in the House of Representatives?
12. Who was president during World War I?
13. In what year was the Constitution written?
14. Name *one* U.S. territory
15. The *Federalist Papers* supported the passage of the U.S. Constitution. Name one of the writers.

★ ★ ★

Answers: **1.** The Constitution **2.** Checks and balances, separation of powers **3.** Speech, religion, assembly, press, petition the government **4.** The president **5.** The Speaker of the House **6.** We the People **7.** Six years **8.** New Hampshire, Massachusetts, Rhode Island, Connecticut, New York, New Jersey, Pennsylvania, Delaware, Maryland, Virginia, North Carolina, South Carolina, Georgia **9.** Missouri, Mississippi **10.** 27 **11.** 435 **12.** Woodrow Wilson **13.** 1787 **14.** Puerto Rico, U.S. Virgin Islands, American Samoa, Northern Mariana Islands, Guam **15.** Madison, Hamilton, Jay

Why Our Kids Hate History

> "We were attacked for being American. We should at least know what being American means."
>
> —THE SHANKER INSTITUTE'S REPORT, *EDUCATION FOR DEMOCRACY*

We all have memories of teachers who have had a lasting impact on us. Here's one teacher we wish we were lucky enough to have had.

When it comes to learning history, West Morris Central High in Chester, New Jersey, is the place to be. On October 14, 2005, Roseanne Lichatin, who has taught American history there for more than twenty years, was named the national American History Teacher of the Year, receiving the prestigious Preserve America Award from another teacher, First Lady Laura Bush.

Myrna Tells a Story: My Husband, the New American

I've become a real expert on the Citizenship Test not because I'm a history whiz kid but because I have gone over (and over) the 100 questions with my husband, who, after years of living in this country, finally became a citizen a short while ago. He is a British journalist who decided, for reasons both practical and patriotic, that he wanted to become a citizen of the country he has so long considered his home.

A few weeks before his interview with the U.S. Citizenship and Immigration Service, he started boning up on the Citizenship Test. At first, he (and I) were amazed at how badly he did. (And how badly so many of our friends did when we asked them some of the tougher questions just for fun.)

Finally, after some hours of practice, my husband did pass the U.S. Citizenship Test with red, white, and blue flying colors. A week later, the big day arrived—the swearing-in.

Being British, Jeffrey said he didn't want anyone to make a fuss. But my older son and his bride drove up from Washington, D.C., during the night, arriving at 2 A.M. to be on hand for the ceremony. And my younger son joined the party, too.

In her remarks to the Gilder Lehrman Institute in New York, which makes the awards, Mrs. Bush quoted the parent of one of Roseanne's students who wrote, "Mrs. Lichatin's enthusiasm for history is infectious." (That's the kind of virus we wish would spread!) Roseanne teaches history with an emphasis on using visuals, primary sources, and documents. For instance, her students read the Declaration of Independence, presidential inaugural speeches, and even Washington's Farewell Address so they can appreciate the mind-set of our Founding Fathers and other leaders in context.

On Valentine's Day, her classes read love letters written home by Civil War soldiers; and they've also read slave narratives to better understand the war that was our nation's most costly. She goes beyond the borders of her school, getting her classes out into the field to see

On the dot of 9 A.M., the pack of us arrived at the federal courthouse on Pearl Street in downtown Manhattan ready for the main event. It took all morning for the paperwork for the hundreds of new citizens to be completed.

As we waited (and waited) for the judge to appear to administer the oath, Marshal Carara, a former New York cop who was helping out, told us that at least 250 citizens are sworn in every Friday in Manhattan. There are more than 450,000 new citizens sworn in each year.

Finally, the judge arrived and, after saying a few words about citizenship, administered the oath. My husband joined in, right hand raised proudly. Everyone was instructed to congratulate the new citizen next to him or her. And then a rousing hand-on-heart Pledge of Allegiance.

We took family pictures on the courthouse steps and my daughter-in-law went to buy a red, white, and blueberry dessert for dinner that evening. Jeffrey—still claiming he wanted no fuss—did one unexpected thing when we got home. Without saying a word, he went outside and raised the American flag.

★ ★ ★

history firsthand. She once conducted her own walking tour across the Brooklyn Bridge just so her students could see New York's architectural history up close and personal.

Roseanne cofounded a History Club at Central High School that boasts more than fifty members—an idea every school should consider. The school also has a Veterans' Club that pairs military veterans with students who record their stories of war and sacrifice. Not long ago, a World War II vet was invited to speak to students during a special lunch assembly. More than eighty kids showed up to listen to the discussion, which went more than two hours. This school is clearly doing something right when it comes to getting students interested in their country's past.

Roseanne explains her approach to teaching by saying, "Each year I return to school . . . to put a human face on history and treat the students as historians." This is an outstanding, dedicated educator whose love for her subject sparks enthusiasm and curiosity in her students.

This Is Progress?

Unfortunately, Roseanne Lichatin is more the exception than the rule. In too many schools in America today, the teaching of U.S. history has become a second-class subject taught with second-rate textbooks. It's no wonder history has become our kids' worst subject.

At one time, most high schools offered four years of history plus a course in civics. Elementary schools from the first grade on also gave children a rich mix of historical materials, teaching the lessons of America's past through wonderfully positive stories, legends, and biographies, mostly about our national heroes.

But about a hundred years ago, education "reformers" decided to create a new subject called social studies, which combined history with geography, economics, political science, psychology, and sociology. At first, history was considered the first among equals in this mishmash of subjects, but over time, history has slipped behind the others in the politically correct eyes of today's education establishment.

Instead of learning about America's noble causes and heroes, children are often taught the darker side of American history. There has also been a new emphasis in education not on lessons learned but on the importance of developing a child's self-esteem and encouraging "personalized learning" tailored to each child's interest and abilities. That notion has led to concepts like "individual study plans" and the development of "critical thinking" instead of learning basic facts. After years of so-called educational reform, rote memorization of dates, facts, and historical figures is now considered unimportant and passé. But test scores over the past twenty years have shown that educational "progressivism" has not had the outcome intended. It has not led to better educated, more engaged students but rather to the continual "dumbing down" of academic standards and a lack of basic knowledge. And when it comes to history, if this trend continues, it could have grave consequences for the future of our country.

No Time for the Past

The way history is being taught, however, is only one explanation for our children's growing history illiteracy. There's another culprit, and that's the amount of time devoted to the study of American history in our schools, which is disappearing faster than a rabbit in a magic act. While every state and school district is different, most students get a smattering of history in the lower grades, possibly one year of American history in middle school along with a little state history, and perhaps another year in high school. That's it.

In the 1960s, Sputnik shocked America into increased emphasis on science and math in our schools, but with only so many hours in the school day, it was social studies that paid the price. In 2001, the No Child Left Behind Act (NCLB) dealt a second blow to social studies. Don't get us wrong. We're all for the NCLB with its focus on testing, accountability, and parental involvement. Most important, it seems to be working. But there is an educational truism that only what is tested

Grade Your Child's History Program

Wondering if your school's social studies program would get a passing grade? Here are some warning signs to help you decide whether your kids are getting a strong education in American history.

Start worrying if your school:

- Places little emphasis on learning about important events, individuals, places, or dates
- Studies few original documents
- Uses nothing but the history textbook
- Has no clear year-by-year plan to make sure children graduate from elementary school with a solid chronological knowledge of history
- Focuses lessons more on shaping attitudes about the treatment of groups rather than teaching about events in the past
- Puts little emphasis on civic education
- Rarely studies America's heroes like the Founding Fathers, great inventors, brave pioneers, and military leaders

★ ★ ★

is taught. The NCLB, with all its good intentions, encourages kids' proficiency in math and reading first, leaving history relegated to second-class status.

So that's the first thing we need to change. If we're going to raise Americans who love their country, history must, once again, get equal time and equal standing in our schools.

History Textbooks: Boring, Biased, and Badly Written

Shannon Pugh, a history teacher and past president of the Dallas Council for Social Studies, points out, "There is the perception that anybody can teach history." They can't. So what happens in the classroom? Those who know little about the subject rely heavily on textbooks to prop up their teaching. But textbooks are no solution. To the contrary, they are a problem—a big problem. Have you read your kid's history book today? Maybe you should.

Philip Bigler, an award-winning history and social studies teacher in Virginia, has observed, "Textbooks are just dull right now. We need narrative histories that tell a story. Part of the problem is that they try to be all things to all people and they have to cover too much time."

He's right. Most of the history texts used in schools today are badly written and boring. Despite the heft of most books—check your kids' stuffed backpacks, and you will see what we mean—somehow they manage to have dull, weak content. It's not surprising many kids find social studies their least favorite class and are so ignorant or confused about history basics.

Most alarming of all, our kids' textbooks often present a disturbing portrait of a dark, corrupt America that is at odds with how most of us see our country. This skewed perspective arose out of a desire to remedy some of the faults of textbooks in the past. To be sure, earlier generations suffered because they did not learn of the many contributions that African Americans, women, and other groups made throughout our history. When the two of us were growing up, the achievements of African Americans were relegated to Booker T. Washington and George Washington Carver. Other than Betsy Ross, Clara Barton, the nameless pioneer woman, and a First Lady or two, the role women played in building this nation barely rated a mention.

But today's books have overcorrected. Political correctness and devotion to multiculturalism above all else has caused the wholesale deconstruction of history teaching and textbooks. Diane Ravitch, in her book *The Language Police,* says a "code of censorship" now determines how our kids' books are written: Textbooks have shifted the focus of our history so that now there is great emphasis on pre-Columbian civilizations and African kingdoms and a downplayed importance of "dead European white males" and the European influences that were the real catalysts of our own democratic institu-

Chriss Takes a Look

On a summer trek to the beach a couple of years ago, we managed one night to corral our seventeen-year-old son and his friend into a discussion of American history. Their reaction to the subject was something akin to eating Brussels sprouts. American history, as they put it, "was just about laws." Then, to my amazement, both said they actually liked world history because it was all about great battles and wars, kings and warriors, and other "cool stuff."

To think that the story of our country—from the courage and vision of the Founding Fathers to the pioneer tales of danger and deprivation to America's leadership in war that has changed the world—was boring to them! I couldn't understand their reaction, so, I decided that the first thing I ought to do was sit down and read my son's eleventh-grade American history text, a book he had found deadly dull. I discovered why.

His book was poorly written, "dumbed down," and, in fact, terribly boring. Equally troubling to me was the bias that permeated the book, some obvious and some subtle. I found that some important subjects were included but others were not or got short shrift. Still other information was misleading or just dead wrong. Here are just a handful of examples of what I mean:

- The book gave almost no credit to President Reagan for the end of the Cold War. Reading this book, one would think Mikhail Gorbachev got up one

tions. Western culture did, in fact, play a larger role in the founding of this country than other ethnic or political influences, yet textbooks are full of odd notions about who did what in American history. One of our favorites is the assertion that the U.S. Constitution was partially patterned after something called the League of Five Nations, a union formed by five Iroquois "chiefdoms" in the sixteenth century. Your children may know that as fact, but it probably would come as a big surprise to James Madison, the author of the Constitution.

Too often our history has become the story of groups as hapless vic-

morning and had a miraculous, unprompted conversion to the joys of capitalism and democracy.

• The authors acknowledge that some see the settlement of the West as a "powerful and deeply meaningful symbol of the American dream." But then they can't resist telling their young readers that other historians argue that cowboys "labored for others—often large companies—rather than for themselves and that the West is "a land shaped by technology, big business and the federal government."

• Perhaps the most disturbing aspect of the book was the disparity in emphasis lavished on some events and individuals in American history of little or no importance while some of our country's most heroic figures and achievements were all but ignored. This comparison says it all:

The Disco Generation: 214 words
Steven Spielberg: 381 words
U.S. intervention in Nicaragua and Iran Contra: 1,004 words
Neil Armstrong and the *Apollo* moon landing: 78 words

You can see why I wished, after reading *The American Nation,* that I had picked it up at the beginning of my son's junior year, not the tail end. I recommend that you read your children's textbook, too—at the beginning of the year—so you know exactly what they're learning.

★ ★ ★

tims rather than individuals as extraordinary achievers. Many books downplay the dynamism of the vast European immigration of the nineteenth century, only finding space to highlight the harsh treatment of many immigrants in the workplace. It's true that many immigrants were forced to earn a living under terrible working conditions; others faced anti-Catholic and anti-Semitic prejudice that children should learn about. But much of the story of these immigrants is one of survival and achievement against all odds. As difficult as life was for many, the vast majority of these strong, determined men and women found their American dream.

Textbooks' emphasis on cultural diversity diminishes more recent history, too. For example, in some books, critics say, World War II sometimes seems to be as much about the fight for women's rights as a struggle against fascism. America's internment of the Japanese, wrong as it was, is often described as equivalent to the Holocaust, which it wasn't. More pages are devoted to Joseph McCarthy's villainy than Joseph Stalin's.

We're not trying to minimize the dark chapters in America's story; our children need to understand that our country hasn't always lived up to its ideals. But they also need to understand the context in which these events happened; and that when America makes mistakes, it tries to make amends and better itself. Too many textbooks have traded balanced history for a blind adherence to cultural diversity and a negative view of America, and our children are subject to this barrage of political correctness and bias.

A Tale of Two Textbooks

Here's a tale of two textbooks that we hope will drive you to open up your child's book bag and grab her history book.

First we discuss *A People's History of the United States,* perhaps the most biased, anti-American history textbook on the market today. Its author, all-around America basher Howard Zinn, is one of the favorites of the education establishment and elite media. More and more top colleges are assigning the book. Even more frightening, high schools are, apparently, following suit. Former secretary of education Bill Bennett told us that he visited two high schools in one week that used the book, one a girls' high school in Manhattan and the other, a school in New Mexico.

To get a sense of Zinn's radical tone and point of view, consider this passage from an essay he wrote for *Progressive Online* in June 2005.

> Surely, we must renounce nationalism and all its symbols: its flags, its pledges of allegiance, its anthems, its insistence in song that God

> must single out America to be blessed. We need to assert our allegiance to the human race, and not to any one nation. We need to refute the idea that our nation is different from, morally superior to, the other imperial powers of world history.

What's difficult to understand is that Zinn's book, whose content very much reflects his thoughts in the *Progressive,* has grown increasingly popular.

In a new book called *A Patriot's History of the United States,* which we give a five-star rating, a pair of courageous historians—Larry Schweikart of the University of Dayton, and Michael Allen of the University of Washington—take on Zinn's accent-the-negative interpretation of American history.

Unlike many textbooks, theirs offers a thorough, balanced look at our past, written with flair and a sense of humor. In reviewing this book, the *Wall Street Journal* said, "History is in part a tale of grand passions and great ideas—of conflict, politics and war—but it can also be a quieter chronicle of particular people following their own sense of purpose or, to use an old-fashioned word, virtue. In 'A Patriot's History,' Larry Schweikart and Michael Allen remind us what a few good individuals can do in just a few short centuries."

Their website **www.patriotshistoryusa.com** not only gives information about the book, it's got great lesson plans for every age group, including many learning activities and discussion ideas, to help parents use *A Patriot's History.*

Take a look at the following side-by-side comparison of what we think are the best and worst in American history books.

Here's a comforting footnote to this tale of two textbooks. In one library copy of Zinn's book that we happened to see, a student had scribbled across the top of one of the pages, "I get it! He's a Communist!" At least that student was thinking for himself. We hope your child will be just as astute if he is assigned this book—and he very well may be. If he is, buy a copy of *The Patriot's History* and one for your child's school library, too.

Which Book Would You Want in Your Child's Bookbag?

THE FOUNDING FATHERS

"Honor counted to founding patriots like Adams, Jefferson, Washington. . . . Property was also important: no denying that because with property came liberty. But virtue came first. . . . It is not surprising, then, that so many left-wing historians miss the boat. . . . "They fail to understand what every colonial settler and every western pioneer understood: character was tied to liberty and liberty to property. All three were needed for success but character was the prerequisite because it put the law behind property agreements and it set responsibility right next to liberty."—*A Patriot's History*

"Around 1776, certain important people in the English colonies made a discovery that would prove enormously useful for the next two hundred years. They found that by creating a nation, a symbol, a legal unity called the United States, they could take over land, profits and political power from favorites of the British Empire. . . . When we look at the American Revolution this way it was a work of genius, and the Founding Fathers deserve the awed tribute they have received over the centuries. They have created the most effective system of national control devised in modern times, and showed future generations of leaders the advantage of combining paternalism with command."—*A People's History*

GEORGE WASHINGTON

The "indispensable man" of the Revolution. "His modesty and self-deprecation was refreshing." He "inspired his troops with exceptional self control, personal honor and high morals."—*A Patriot's History*

"The richest man in the colonies." "A slave holder from Virginia." "Land was bought by rich speculators including George Washington and Patrick Henry."—*A People's History*

ABRAHAM LINCOLN

"On racial issues, Lincoln led: he didn't follow. . . . Lincoln marched far ahead of most of his fellow men." "It is critical that an understanding of emancipation begin with Lincoln's perception that it, first and foremost, was a moral and legal issue not a military or political one."—*A Patriot's History*

[During the Civil War] "Lincoln was signing into law a whole series of laws to give business interests what they wanted." "The Emancipation Proclamation was 'a military move' that 'had all the moral grandeur of a bill of lading.' "—*A People's History*

THE SECOND WORLD WAR

"Democracy's Finest Hour."—*A Patriot's History*

"It was a war waged by a government whose chief beneficiary—despite volumes of reform—was a wealthy elite."—*A People's History*

THE AUTHORS' GOALS

"We remain convinced that if the story of America's past is told fairly the result cannot be anything but a deepened patriotism, a sense of awe at the obstacles overcome, the passion invested, the blood and tears spilled and the nation that was built."—*A Patriot's History*

"I think it extremely important for young people to learn a different history that will make them skeptical of what they hear from authority. I think if people knew, for instance the history of lies and violence that have accompanied American foreign policy, they would not be enticed into joining the armed forces."—*A People's History*

★ ★ ★

Promoting Tolerance or Propaganda?

What if someone offered your school supplemental materials like DVDs, books, handouts, teachers' workshops, lesson plans, and learning activities, and all of it was absolutely free? Most schools, strapped for funds, would jump at the chance to add some freebies to their shelf of teaching materials. This would be the time, however, to remember the old saying, "There's no such thing as a free lunch." It would also be a good time to investigate who's playing Santa Claus in your school, and most important, find out the content and message of these "free" materials because it isn't only dull or biased textbooks that parents have to worry about. Supplemental curricula, as these materials are usually called, can be as innocent as a lesson plan about George Washington's leadership downloaded from the Library of Congress's website, but it also can just as easily be subtle propaganda masquerading as educational content.

Much of this kind of material that appears in our schools is rarely reviewed or regulated or reported to parents. It is often provided to schools in the guise of teaching children the importance of tolerance and diversity. For parents, this means you may put in the time to check out your child's textbook, think you've done your job, and then find out that supplemental materials you didn't even know about may be giving your child a distorted and disturbing view of America and the world.

Here's a perfect example of propaganda, in this case pro-Arab, passing for a lesson in tolerance. After 9/11, the Saudi government sent thousands of schools a "we care" package containing a PBS documentary called *Islam: Empire of Faith.* If they'd stopped there, they might not have crossed the line, but they also included a very sympathetic book about Islam that is quite critical of the actions of Western nations in the Middle East. The Middle East Policy Council and AWAIR (Arab World and Islamic Resources and School Services), which holds workshops about the Arab world for teachers, also provided materials to schools after 9/11 with a definite point of view. Some of the material the MEPC distributed once promoted the far-fetched idea that Muslims were the first to sail across the Atlantic and land in the New World where they intermarried with the Iroquois and Algonquin. In colonial times, this Arab organization claims, European explorers met chiefs with names like Abdallah Ibn Malik. Pretty funny. This was removed from the material only when the Algonquins complained about "such nonsense."

Here's another example. Recently, Mexico's forty-seven consulates in the United States got into the business of helping to educate students in American schools. In 2005, the Mexican consulate in Los Angeles sent out nearly a hundred thousand textbooks to fifteen hundred schools in the Los Angeles Unified School District. The books, written in Spanish, are history textbooks that celebrate the troops who fought Americans during the Mexican-American War.

According to these textbooks, America's victory 160 years ago was "disastrous" because "Mexico was obligated to sign the treaty of Guadalupe-Hidalgo" by which the country lost half its territory to the United States. Heather MacDonald, a Fellow at the Manhattan Institute, writes about the book, "This narrative is accurate and rather tame by Mexico's usual anti-American standards. But a student in the U.S. could easily find himself confused about his allegiances. Is his country Mexico or the U.S.?" Of course, one might ask why the Los Angeles School District allows this material in their classrooms at all? Maybe some parent should.

But these materials don't have to come directly from those with an agenda. One supplemental curriculum, approved by the California State Department of Education and purchased with state funds, supposedly gives high school students an insight into the Arab-Israeli conflict. One learning activity that was part of the study program divided students into two groups, the "Jeds" and the "Pads." No, this is not *West Side Story* run amok—or maybe it is. During the activity, the classroom's furniture is rearranged so that the Pads are in a very small space, an area which the Jeds keep trying to enter. The teacher plays the role of the "Great Power" who only favors the Jeds and ignores the Pads' "reasonable" complaints. It doesn't take long to see the point of view being promoted as a "progressive learning activity." It is simply to make students sympathetic to the Palestinian cause and critical of Israel while not really teaching anything of factual import about the long-standing and complex Middle East conflict.

Sandra Stotsky, former head of the Center for Teaching and Learning at the Massachusetts Department of Education, is one of the few educational specialists who has reviewed a broad cross section of supplemental materials. She has said that far too often, "in the guise of providing teachers with ideas for a more engaging pedagogy and deeper understanding of a historical phenomenon, purveyors of supplemental resources and professional development workshops recruit unwitting teachers as their agents in cultivating hostility toward America as a country, toward Western culture and toward Americans of European descent."

What Teachers Sometimes Teach

By now, it is fairly widely accepted that the majority of professors at our colleges and universities tend to have left-of-center views, and some, like Howard Zinn, are often far out of the mainstream of American thought. In fact, a 2005 poll taken by S. Robert Lichter, a professor at George Mason University, reported that 72 percent of those teaching at American universities and colleges, by their own description, are liberal and 15 percent are conservative.

The poll's findings were no big surprise to many college students who realize early on that professors have political views that can be very different from their own and their families. Many students learn to handle this by simply "going along to get along," parroting back what the teacher wants to hear rather than honestly expressing their divergent point of view. Others are more active in challenging their teachers, and there are movements on various campuses demanding a students' Academic Bill of Rights to ensure that teaching is more "fair and balanced."

Once our K–12 schools were, for the most part, kind of bias-free zones. Today, however, teachers at all levels often share their biases and political views with their students. In 2004, for example, in a Delaware public school, an eight-year-old second grader wrote in a composition that he wanted to be a soldier like his grandfather had been. The teacher threatened him with a trip to the principal's office, "If you ever write anything like that [again]." Kids in a third-grade class in Madison, Wisconsin, were each asked to write twelve letters to encourage an end to the war in Iraq, including one to the president, their congressional representatives, the media, and other children. Parents were asked to send in stamps for the letters.

Similar incidents at high schools are even more common. There have been reports of students given anti-Bush vocabulary tests in English and encouraged to sing a song, written by the music teacher, critical of the president.

We all heard about the Aurora, Colorado, high school geography teacher, Jay Bennish, who delivered a twenty-minute rant in class after President Bush's 2006 State of the Union address. Among other things, the teacher compared what he called the "eerie similarities between Bush's remarks and Adolf Hitler's speeches" and called the United States "the single most violent nation on planet Earth."

This example of political correctness really tugged at our heartstrings. A young man in northern California who finished high school early and joined the Marines wanted to attend his high school graduation in his Marine uniform. Who can blame him? We'd be proud, too. But his principal objected, saying, "We are only interested in education here, not the military."

Outside speakers can also pose a problem if students hear only one side. Unfortunately, more often than not, liberals are invited to speak at high school events; conservatives rarely are. One who managed to arm-twist an invitation to speak to students at California's Pacific Palisades High School is conservative activist David Horowitz, who is leading the drive for the Academic Bill of Rights. When he squared off against an antiwar activist, he was particularly troubled by the attitude of the many teachers toward him and the atmosphere at the school.

Students told him that the school was "very political" and their teachers, who were very left wing, constantly "harangued them on controversial issues." One even volunteered that a teacher had thrown him out of class for simply stating that Saddam Hussein had used biological weapons against his own people. Apparently, the teacher simply refused to believe it or the pictures that we've all seen of hundreds of dead Kurds who were gassed by Saddam. One conservative teacher told Horowitz that he was "afraid to speak up because of inevitable reprisals from the faculty's left-wing majority." To fight against indoctrination of K–12 schools, Horowitz has started an organization called Parents and Students for Academic Freedom. Check it out at **www.psaf.org** or his own website at **www.frontpagemag.com**.

Can You Take On City Hall?

Now that you have an idea of what's going on in schools across the country and could be going on in yours, can you take on city hall, the Board of Education, or even your child's school? Realistically, the answer is no. Unless you're a miracle worker, you probably cannot change the whole school system, determine which textbooks will be bought, or hire the teachers who will be teaching your children. But you can be better informed about what and how much is going on in the classroom. To coin a phrase, "If you can't change the world, change what you can."

A Parents' Checklist

Here are some ideas to help you break down the walls of political correctness and bias that are boxing our children into a mind-set that isn't good for them or the country.

- **Check out your state's standards for U.S. history and history teachers. Are they good enough for your kids?** The Thomas B. Fordham Institute published a guide called *Effective State Standards for U.S. History: A 2003 Report Card,* written by historian Sheldon Stern, that is a fair and honest assessment. Ten states get As; more than twenty states get Fs. Get the full report available, free of charge, at the Thomas B. Fordham Institute, 1700 K Street NW, Suite 1000, Washington, DC 20006, or online at **www.edexcellence.net**. You can also get a comprehensive state-by-state report from the Organization of American Historians at **www.oah.org**. The Fordham Foundation also has a new report on all academic subjects, including U.S. history, in the *State of State Standards 2006,* by Chester E. Finn Jr., Michael J. Petrilli, and Liam Julian, also available free of charge from the Institute or available online.
- **Take a good, long look at your child's history book.** If you can, read along with him or her to get an idea of the content, tone, and attitude of the book. If it's not doing the job or overdoing the PC, use an alternative text or materials like Schweikart and Allen's *A Patriot's History of the United States,* published by Sentinel, or some of the materials we've already suggested (and there's more to come later in the book). These will help give your child a more balanced view of what he or she should be learning and help give you facts to be able to discuss and refute misinterpretations or biased views if you find them in your child's text.

Unfortunately, there are few places to go to find reviews of history textbooks, but we suggest these:

1. The Thomas B. Fordham Foundation has prepared a review of popular high school texts by Diane Ravitch called *A Consumer's Guide to High School History Textbooks,* which rates both American history and world history texts and gives a comprehensive explanation of why the books have received their ratings. It is also available through the mail and on the foundation's website, **www.edexcellence.net**.
2. Another source of reviews is The Textbook League's *Textbook Letter,* which focuses on false science and history. The website for the League is **www.textbookleague.org**.
3. Another organization that reviews textbooks is the American Textbook Council. Its mission is to improve the social studies curriculum and civic education in elementary and high schools. The Council's website is **www.historytextbooks.org**.

• **Examine, with a skeptical eye, your school's supplemental materials and the projects your child is asked to do.** You may also want to read the Fordham Foundation's guide, *The Stealth Curriculum: Manipulating America's History Teachers,* by Sandra Stotsky, to get a fuller picture of the material that is brought into the classroom. It is available free and online. According to Stotsky, we should be especially wary of some material supplied by Facing History and Ourselves, the Teachers' Curriculum Institute, the Middle East Policy Council, and AWAIR, along with some teacher training programs.

• **Courage!** Knowing what your child is reading is important, but it's also important to talk directly with your child's teacher. We're the first to admit this can get a little dicey. No teacher likes to feel her authority, dedication, or qualifications are being challenged, so step lightly. If we seem too probing or critical, it can impact negatively on how a teacher treats and grades our kids.

But there is a respectful way to show both your interest in how and what your child is learning and your concern if you do not like all that your child is being taught. A dedicated teacher's goal is to do what is best for her students. And making sure parents are enthusiastic about what is going on in the classroom is a benefit for the student, the teacher, and the school.

- **Ten questions to ask your child's teacher.** These ten questions to ask should help you assess your children's history teaching. But get off on the right foot. Don't put the teacher on the spot by asking him or her at back-to-school night. Bad idea. Instead, set up a private parent-teacher conference and offer to bring coffee and donuts or take the teacher a potted plant to get things started on a positive note.

1. *What do you want to achieve in this course?* Nowadays, it is very fashionable for a teacher to say something like "I am trying to improve my students' critical thinking skills." Or "I want to help them better understand our country." But what you really want to hear from a history or social studies teacher is, "I want to teach these kids the history of our country. I want them to learn what makes America a special place." Keep pushing for specifics if you seem to get a vague or canned response.
2. *How much history did you take in college? Why did you become a social studies teacher?* This might be best asked as an icebreaker at the beginning of your conversation. Start with a reference to your own history education. "I loved history in high school [or college]. I only wish I'd taken more. How about you?" Or "I wish I had studied harder in my history classes because I find it a lot more interesting now. Did you always like history?"
3. *How do you teach the history you cover in the course? Do students learn chronologically what happened when?* Often, social studies today is taught in thematic units, frequently leaving kids to spend weeks studying units on "tribes" or "women" without really being clear about the time in history in which events are taking place. While this has some value, it also can be very confusing because kids have no context for what they are learning.

Jane Hall, a professor at American University, is astonished at her students' lack of basic chronological knowledge. She said, "I hate to sound like a neoconservative but maybe more students should be asked to memorize (yes, even retain) more dates and facts about American history. Those timelines are instructive especially in this hopped-up, present-tense world." So, ask the teacher how many basic facts, like important dates, are part of the course's curriculum and whether your child will be tested on these basic facts.

4. *What textbook do you use and how much do you rely on it?* Of course, teachers can rarely choose which textbook they use. But it is important to know how much she relies on it and what she feels about the quality and even the accuracy of the text. You might ask her if she has ever read reviews of the textbook she is using.
5. *What do you do if you disagree with the textbook the class is using?* If the teacher does have disagreement, does she tell the students and tell them why. Does she give them other texts or materials that support a different point of view?
6. *How many books do the students have to read besides the textbook?* In some places, the only book that is used in a class is a textbook and that, we know now, can be a big mistake. Does the course's syllabus encourage the use of additional books like biographies and autobiographies or even works of fiction about the period being studied? Inquiring about this is a good (and uncritical) way to lead into asking to see the course's syllabus, which sets forth the "scope and sequence" of what the teacher plans to cover during the year and how it will be covered. On pages 279–284 in our resource section, you'll find a model curriculum that may give you some idea of what your kids should know and when they should know it to compare to the teacher's plan. But tread gently here. Some teachers may feel asking to see the syllabus is an intrusion.

7. *What supplemental materials are used in the classroom? How many primary sources are used as well?* If the teacher uses primary sources to supplement the teaching of American history, count that as a very positive sign. The National Archives, where thousands of our country's most important historical documents are kept, has extensive programs for students and teachers to encourage the use of primary sources as a key to the teaching of history. So does the Library of Congress. Find out if your child's teacher knows about this easily available material and uses it. The National Archives website, in case you have to supply this information—and we hope you don't—is **www.archives.gov**.

   And look around the room to see if copies of the Declaration of Independence, the Constitution, the Gettysburg Address, and other such documents are posted as well as portraits of outstanding Americans. Another good sign.
8. *How do you balance the positive and negatives in our history?* Nobody wants their kids to learn a sugar-coated history that doesn't acknowledge that our country and our leaders have made mistakes in the past. We want our kids to understand that debate, disagreement, and dissent are an important part of our democratic system. Senator Lamar Alexander, who has taught history, says that he always wanted his students to realize that the tension in America is always between our ideals and our reality. He believes, "Our reality has often fallen short of those ideals but we are, as a nation and a people, always trying to get closer to living our ideals more fully."
9. *How do the students learn about democracy in the class? How much do they learn about the government and their rights and responsibilities as citizens?* Remember, the Founding Fathers wanted youngsters educated in order to make them effective citizens. Civic education and instilling a sense of pride and responsibility toward our country should be part of every social

studies program. It may be teaching first graders the correct words to the Pledge of Allegiance, instilling in fourth graders the ability to correctly identify a picture of the Capitol and understand what happens there, or asking eighth graders to explain the role of the judiciary and the executive branch. For high school seniors, it may mean getting them registered to vote and ready and willing to embrace this new responsibility. So, we think it is also important to ask the teacher if part of his or her goal is to help students develop a love for our country that transforms children into citizens.

10. *What can I do to reinforce what is being taught in the classroom? And how can I help you do your job?* It is very important to make your child's teacher realize that you want to be an ally, not an adversary. Make it clear that you are not on a hunt to find "un-Americanism" in the classroom. Most teachers are patriotic, too, and filled with the desire to help the next generation of Americans understand their country's history and fulfill their potential for themselves, their families, and the nation. Be sure the teacher understands that it is your interest and concern that makes you ask questions and that you want to work together with the teacher to ensure your child gets the best possible education.

If you've got the time, offer to be a classroom aide. You can be both a big help and see firsthand what your child is learning. Time is most teachers' biggest enemy—there's just not enough of it. So, offer yourself up as the class "webmaster" and use this book to mine the Internet for the teacher. As you will see, there are so many websites packed with wonderful free materials that can be downloaded or, if your child's classroom is wired, can be used right in class. Or be first in line to volunteer to drive for history field trips, start a history club, or put on a history bee for your school. The only way to make sure your child gets the real story of America is for you to get involved in helping to tell the story.

• **Upping the ante.** But what should you do if you are unsatisfied by the answers your teachers provide or they are simply not forthcoming? Well, you may be a fussy consumer about many other things, so be a fussy consumer now when it comes to what your child is learning. But it's going to take some courage and a willingness to buck the system regardless of the cost.

You may have to talk to the school's principal to ask that changes be made or bring other parents who share your concerns and point of view into the discussion. Find out more about how textbooks are chosen for your school and see if parents can have some input in these decisions. It's probably done by the school district, but there may be some flexibility.

Ask that a list of supplemental material used in the classroom, and where the material comes from, be provided in a written form to parents at the beginning of the school year. Also, ask for a list of workshops that teachers in your school are attending, paid for by the school, to give you an idea of the school's emphasis and direction. Be prepared for a fight and the consequences.

School's Out

We hope we've taught you some lessons about what your children are learning. But, hey, school's out and the kids are going home, iPods in their ears, to chill out in front of the TV, the computer, the XBox, or all of the above. And, let's admit it, our 24/7 media can be even more influential in shaping their attitudes about our country than what they learn in school. And that isn't good.

DINNER TABLE DEBATE

Character Matters

As *A Patriot's History of America* shows, American history depends to a large extent on men and women of character—and that character truly counts. Depending on which period of history they are studying, ask your kids to discuss what would have happened:

- If there had not been a group of brilliant, well-educated men such as Washington, Jefferson, Adams, Madison, and Franklin living at the time of the Revolution?
- If Washington had wanted to be, not president, but king?
- If Abraham Lincoln had lost the presidency in 1860? Would there still be a United States of America? Or would the North and South have become two different countries?
- If Franklin Delano Roosevelt had not given aid to Great Britain when it stood alone fighting Hitler?
- If Ronald Reagan had not been determined, in the face of world opposition and even ridicule, to "win" the Cold War?

Hear what they have to say.

★ ★ ★

60-MINUTE SOLUTIONS

Play *History Jeopardy!*

Play your own version of *History Jeopardy!* at home. It will be fun for the family and help you find out exactly what the kids know and don't know.

Here, in chronological order, are some *Jeopardy!*-like answers and questions. But mix 'em up and let the winner pick where the whole family goes out to dinner on your next night out.

- Pilgrims' written agreement on how to govern themselves

What is the Mayflower Contract?

- First battles of the Revolutionary War

What are Lexington and Concord?

- Idea that the United States was meant to expand to the Pacific Ocean

What is Manifest Destiny?

- The forced removal of the Cherokees from Georgia

What is the Trail of Tears?

- Voyage of slave ships from Africa to America

What is the "Middle Passage"?

- FDR's programs to end the Great Depression

What is the New Deal?

- U.S. naval base attacked by Japanese at the beginning of World War II

What is Pearl Harbor?

- Nazi's most infamous concentration camp

What is Auschwitz?

- Allied invasion of Europe

What is D-day?

- 1954 Supreme Court decision that ended school segregation

What is *Brown v. Board of Education?*

- Neil Armstrong's first words on the surface of the moon

What is "One small step for a man, one giant step for mankind"?

- The attack on the World Trade Center and the Pentagon

What is 9/11?

★ ★ ★

5

THE MEDIA VIRUS

"Those who do not study history are forced to get it from Hollywood."

—ALLEN BARRA, SPORTS COLUMNIST FOR THE *WALL STREET JOURNAL*

It seemed like just another star-studded Oscar night when host Jon Stewart surprised everyone by taking a well-placed shot at the hand that feeds him. The sarcastic prince of political comedy tweaked the always left-wing gathering by implying that the crowd with its ultraliberal credentials, dripping in diamonds and twenty-thousand-dollar dresses, and gifted with $100,000 goody bags, might be just a little "out of touch" with most of America. Stewart on his own *Daily Show* usually pokes fun, and a lot more stridently, at conservative points of view. Still, George Clooney just couldn't let that little jab go unanswered as he stepped onstage to accept the award for Best Supporting Actor. Wearing his moral superiority on his expensively cut sleeve, Clooney told the audience, "We are a little bit out of touch in Hollywood every once in a while. I think it's probably a good thing. . . . I'm proud . . . to be part of this community and proud to be out of touch." The crowd roared its approval.

Proud to be out of touch with America? What does that say about Hollywood's attitude toward the rest of us?

Nothing good.

We see that out-of-touch attitude on display when Hollywood celebrities hop up on their soapboxes and spout anti-American nonsense. We also see it in the demoralizing movies and television programs that Hollywood stars and studio executives produce, which tell our children that America is a nation of intolerance, greed, aggression, drugs, sex, and violence.

But Hollywood isn't the only problem. Indeed, to place all the blame on Hollywood would let too many others off the hook. Today, the vast majority of "the media elite" in this country suffer from the same disconnect with America we saw on Oscar night. We see it as a kind of "media virus" that stems from an inability or unwillingness to see this country in a positive light.

There are the late-night comics, who now go far beyond political satire or good-natured jokes to snide personal attacks on our political leaders.

There's the music industry, which targets the youngest generation with obscenity-laden lyrics and explicit music videos, just in case the kids don't understand the words.

There are the video games that so many of our kids can't stop playing, the games that feature extreme violence and even more extreme antiestablishment messages.

And, perhaps most important, there's the news media—the print and broadcast journalists and producers who feed us and our children a steady diet of pessimism, bias, and bad news, always bad news. These men and women paint the picture of America we see every day in our newspapers and on the network news, and it's an ugly caricature of what most of us think is a great and good country.

The real problem is that this media virus can infect our children and protecting them completely from the effects of this virus is no small task. The media's influence is so widespread in our culture that asking parents to guard against the virus is a little like telling them during cold and flu season: Don't let anyone sneeze near your child. You may already recognize some of the symptoms of the virus in your own kids and their friends: cynicism, apathy, and skepticism.

But involved parents can inoculate kids against the media virus. And we'll give you plenty of tips on how to do it.

Tinseltown Versus Small Town

> "Hollywood used to try to entertain Americans; now it tries to indoctrinate them."
>
> —LINDA CHAVEZ, COLUMNIST

Have you ever walked out of a movie theater and moaned, "Why don't they make movies like they used to?" Because the people who make the movies don't think like they used to. One recent poll asked Americans whether Hollywood moviemakers shared their values. A whopping 70 percent said no; only 13 percent agreed. We are not arguing that every movie that comes out of Hollywood must have a happy face quotient somewhere between *The Sound of Music* and *The Wizard of Oz* (though kids—and lots of their parents, too—still love Dorothy and those singing von Trapps). But why do so many have to be so very harsh, painting such a bleak picture of life in America today? Or as George Clooney put it so aptly—so "out of touch."

Of course, when it comes to the question of how great an influence visual media has on our children, those in charge like to pretend it has very little influence at all. But study after study over the past decade has consistently shown that movies and TV and its reigning princes and princesses are some of the most influential factors in our children's lives. Kids spend an average of six and a half hours a day, as much time as they spend in school, interacting with media, primarily visual media. Do they spend that much time interacting with you?

There have been lots of studies specifically about how sex and violence on television and in the movies affect children. The American Academy of Pediatrics has said, "Media violence may cause aggressive and antisocial behavior, desensitize viewers to future violence and increase perceptions that they are living 'in a mean and dangerous world.' " Another expert, Dr. David Walsh, president of the National Institute on Media and the Family, says, "The real impact is not so much that violent images create violent behavior, but that they create an atmosphere of disrespect. . . . It's a subtle shift, from 'Have a nice day' to 'Make my day.' "

There is little doubt that Hollywood is negatively impacting our children when it comes to sex, violence, and, often, values, but it's becoming clear that we should also be concerned that the sex and violence that permeates our entertainment media is creating a grim picture of America for our children as well, an America without moral

Out of Touch? You Be the Judge

Here's a sampling of quotes about America that you don't want your kids repeating from some of the most privileged people on planet Earth—the Hollywood elite. What they say shouldn't matter but it does because our children watch the television shows and movies, play the video games, and listen to the music these same people produce. More than ever before, celebrities influence the way our kids, even fairly young kids these days, want to dress, behave, and, sad to say, think. And here is what some of these "influencers" are saying about our country.

Gwyneth Paltrow: "I worry about bringing up a child in America. . . . At the moment there's a weird, overly patriotic atmosphere over there, like, 'We're No. 1' and the rest of the world doesn't matter."

Alex Baldwin: "I believe that what happened in 2000 [the election] did as much damage to the pillars of democracy as terrorists did to the pillars of commerce in New York City."

Johnny Depp: "America is dumb; it's like a dumb puppy that has big teeth that can bite and hurt you, aggressive."

George Clooney: "We can't beat anyone anymore."

values, corrupted by an endless parade of stereotypical villains: evil corporations, a U.S. military out of control, and power-hungry politicians almost always of the conservative stripe. If Hollywood has made our children more promiscuous and violent with its products, is it really a stretch to believe that the subtle and not-so-subtle anti-American messages that infect so much of entertainment today are having a similar negative effect on our young people's attitudes toward their country?

Once upon a time, the motion picture industry's own code of conduct said, "If motion pictures present stories that will affect lives for

Rosie O'Donnell (voicing her 9/11 conspiracy theory): "I do believe it is the first time in history that fire has ever melted steel. I do believe that it defies physics for the World Trade Center Tower Seven . . . which collapsed in on itself, it is impossible for a building to fall the way it fell without explosives being involved . . . I have no idea [who was responsible]. But it apparently wasn't the terrorists."

Michael Moore: "[Americans] are possibly the dumbest people on the planet. . . . Our stupidity is embarrassing."

Oliver Stone: "We should look to [Castro] as one of the Earth's wisest people, one of the people we should consult."

Woody Harrelson: "We've killed a million Iraqis since the start of the Gulf War—mostly by blocking humanitarian aid."

Donald Sutherland: "We're back to burning books in Germany."

Bill Maher: "We have been cowards lobbing cruise missiles from 2,000 miles away. Staying in the airplane when it hits the building. . . . it's not cowardly."

Martina Navratilova: "The most absurd part of my escape from the unjust system is that I have exchanged one system that suppresses free opinion for another."

★ ★ ★

the better, they can become the most powerful force for the improvement of mankind." Yet, too often today, Hollywood's elite equates "improving mankind" only with criticizing ourselves. Clearly, the pendulum has swung too far from the values and mores of most Americans who see their country as a great nation and a force for good in the world. And although Hollywood's relentless criticism of America is troubling to most adults, it appears to be very damaging to our children.

Where's John Wayne When You Really Need Him?

Take a look at Hollywood's choices for Best Picture in 2005:

- *Brokeback Mountain,* a story of gay love
- *Crash,* a story of racism alive and well in L.A.
- *Munich,* a story that brings moral relativism to terrorism
- *Good Night and Good Luck,* a story of America not at its best
- *Capote,* a story about serial killers and a conniving gay writer

Our history books, as we've told you, no longer focus on America's heroes to bring history to life for our children. Neither does Hollywood or at least, not often enough. Most of our greatest Americans are of interest to Hollywood today only to showcase their faults. And it is a rare film that tells the story of ordinary American men and women just trying to do good, be brave, exhibit moral courage, who our kids could admire and from whom they could learn. It's as if Hollywood is so "out of touch" that it doesn't seem to realize Americans like that still exist and their stories still deserve to be told.

In the past, many heroic films about ordinary Americans have been military stories, but the creative elite's disaffection with the U.S. military has made movies like *Saving Private Ryan* the exception not the rule. Film critic Michael Medved says that today, more often than not, U.S. troops are portrayed as sick, demented, or excessively violent, and our military's role in the world is rarely shown in a positive light. Rarely are both sides of a conflict given equal time so our children can see a balanced or thoughtful portrayal of the complex questions that war raises.

The truth is our children have always needed and wanted heroes in their lives, and still do. Kids love and are inspired by movies that depict ordinary men and women of courage fighting for good causes or striving to achieve against overwhelming odds. Movies in which good and evil, right and wrong are clearly defined.

When Hollywood clashes with America's values, American families register their unhappiness by staying home. It's no surprise, then, that in 2005 box office receipts dropped by a whopping 9 percent.

Some movies did bring in huge audiences—just not Hollywood's idea of the best movies. For example, in 2005, the total box office for the five films nominated for best picture ($240.25 million) didn't equal the box office for the number one grossing film that year—*Star Wars Episode III* ($380.27 million), the ultimate story of good and evil, full of heroes and villains. The top box office hits along with *Star Wars* were *Harry Potter, The Chronicles of Narnia, War of the Worlds,* and *King Kong.* At their core, all these movies are old-fashioned morality tales complete with noble heroes and heroines, who stand up to evil in the world, even if one was a giant ape.

Jonah Goldberg, of *National Review Online,* nailed it when he said Hollywood's real problem isn't violence per se but rather the "trendy moral relativism that characterizes so many movies and TV shows." What is missing in too much entertainment today is "a well-defined sense of moral right."

So What's a Parent to Do?

How can a parent effectively discourage kids from watching movies and television programs that will warp their understanding of America and leave them adrift in the moral relativism that afflicts so much of what Hollywood puts out today? How can you help them see a better, and still entertaining, portrait of our country and its past? Here are what we think are some helpful—and workable—suggestions:

- **Exercise your parental rights.** Turn off the tube, at least a good part of the time. Yes, there are some good things on some channels like the History Channel, Discovery, the Learning Channel, Hallmark Channel, National Geographic, Disney, Nickelodeon, and PBS, but always check out the programming even on these channels. And schedule "appointment TV" with your kids. Go over the TV listings together as a family and decide in advance what you are going to watch. Talk together about what you see and rate what you see. Was it worth watching?
- **Instill basic television rules.** Don't use the TV as a babysitter with young kids, and as a way to keep older kids from giving you a hard time. Don't watch TV during the dinner hour unless you are doing it for a very specific purpose. And don't keep the TV on as background noise when you are doing other chores. Even if you are not watching, the kids will be.
- **Know what's on TV.** Keep track of the values that are being promoted in television programs and ask your child to do the same. Are they the core values in which your family believes? Are positive or negative values being promoted? Make your children aware of the way they could be influenced by the attitudes in the programs they watch.
- **Talk about the movies you see together.** Ask the kids to review them. Is the picture of America in the older movies they watch very different from the America of today? Are American values still the same?
- **Watch what you believe in.** In Chapters 7 and 9 we give you recommendations for movies and documentaries that you can watch on special occasions or when you are working on projects with the kids. Search your own memory and make sure the kids see the movies that impressed you when you were young and made you feel good about America. On pages 99 and 100 we've listed some of our favorites.

100 All-American Movies

Who says television, or at least your DVD, can't be good for your kids? Here is a list of our favorite "All-American" movies. While not all are suitable for all ages, they are tales of heroes and heroic deeds and illustrate the kind of American values that have made this country strong and free. We hope they will leave your family feeling good about America.

So throw the popcorn in the microwave, find a spot on the sofa, and enjoy!

1. *Abe Lincoln in Illinois*
2. *The Alamo*
3. *Alex Haley's Queen*
4. *American Graffiti*
5. *Apollo 13*
6. *The Autobiography of Miss Jane Pittman*
7. *Band of Brothers*
8. *Battle of the Bulge*
9. *Big Red One*
10. *Blackhawk Down*
11. *Boys Town*
12. *Breaking Away*
13. *The Bridge at Remagen*
14. *The Buccaneer*
15. *Buffalo Soldiers*
16. *Centennial*
17. *A Christmas Story*
18. *Cinderella Man*
19. *Coal Miner's Daughter*
20. *The Crossing*
21. *Driving Miss Daisy*
22. *Fame*
23. *Felicity: An American Girl*
24. *Field of Dreams*
25. *The Fighting Sullivans*
26. *Flags of Our Fathers*
27. *Friendly Persuasion*
28. *From the Earth to the Moon*
29. *Gettysburg*
30. *Glory*
31. *Grapes of Wrath*
32. *The Great Escape*
33. *Halls of Montezuma*
34. *Having Our Say*
35. *High Noon*
36. *Hoosiers*
37. *How the West Was Won*
38. *The Hunt for Red October*
39. *Into the West*
40. *I Remember Mama*
41. *It's a Wonderful Life*
42. *The Jackie Robinson Story*
43. *Jim Thorpe: All American*
44. *Knute Rockne: All American*
45. *Last of the Mohicans*
46. *A League of Their Own*
47. *Lean on Me*

48. *Little House on the Prairie*
49. *Little Women*
50. *The Longest Day*
51. *Meet Me in St. Louis*
52. *Midway*
53. *Miracle*
54. *The Miracle Worker*
55. *Mr. Smith Goes to Washington*
56. *My Family, Mi Familia*
57. *My Dog Skip*
58. *The Natural*
59. *Norma Rae*
60. *October Sky*
61. *On the Waterfront*
62. *Our Vines Have Tender Grapes*
63. *The Patriot*
64. *Patton*
65. *Pearl Harbor*
66. *The Pride of the Yankees*
67. *PT 109*
68. *Real Women Have Curves*
69. *Remember the Titans*
70. *The Right Stuff*
71. *Rudy*
72. *Rocky*
73. *Roots*
74. *The Rosa Parks Story*
75. *Rosewood*
76. *Sands of Iwo Jima*
77. *Sarah Plain and Tall*
78. *Saving Private Ryan*
79. *Seabiscuit*
80. *The Searchers*
81. *Sergeant York*
82. *Since You Went Away*
83. *So Proudly We Hail*
84. *Sounder*
85. *Spirit of St. Louis*
86. *Stand and Deliver*
87. *Stars and Stripes Forever*
88. *Sunrise at Campobello*
89. *To Hell and Back*
90. *To Kill a Mockingbird*
91. *Top Gun*
92. *Tora! Tora! Tora!*
93. *The Tuskegee Airmen*
94. *United 93*
95. *We Were Soldiers*
96. *World Trade Center*
97. *Yankee Doodle Dandy*
98. *Young Mr. Lincoln*
99. *Young Tom Edison*
100. *1776*

If you want more information about these movies, when they were made, the cast, and a short summary of the plot, reviews, and trivia, you'll find it at one of the Internet's best movie sites, **www.imdb.com**.

★ ★ ★

• **Know what's in the theater.** Check out the movies that your child may want to see on a website called "MediaWise," which includes movie ratings and reviews of current movies and a movie review archive as well. Find it at **www.mediafamily.org** on the Web. Another helpful site you might try is called "Kids in Mind," which gives you three numerical scores for the movie's "ingredients"—how much sex and nudity, violence and gore, and profanity. They count; you decide. Find it at **www.kids-in-mind.com**.

Facing the Music

"That's the way the game goes, gotta keep it strictly pimpin
Gotta have my hustle tight, makin change off these women, yeah
You know it's hard out here for a pimp."

—Djay f/ Shug
2006 Oscar for Best Song

It was just a week after Hurricane Katrina turned New Orleans and the Gulf Coast into what looked like a war zone. The pictures on television were devastating to see; and, as Americans always do, they reached into their pockets to help neighbors in need, donating millions of dollars to relief efforts in those first weeks after the disaster.

Celebrities and entertainers of every political stripe put aside their usual political sniping for one night to join the crusade to help Katrina's victims—well, almost. NBC hurriedly put together a network musical special that featured performers from Faith Hill to Randy Newman to raise money for the relief effort. Hollywood celebrities pled the cause of Katrina in between acts and about halfway through the show actor Mike Myers was paired with rapper Kanye West to pitch the folks.

Myers followed the script, dutifully delivering his lines about the devastation in New Orleans. Then, he turns to West, the self-described "Savior" of hip-hop, who immediately dove into an angry political rant. After suggesting that the media was racist in its coverage of the looting in New Orleans, West charged that America "is set up to help the poor, the black people . . . as slow as possible," "they've given them permission to go down and shoot us," and "George Bush doesn't care about black people." It was the rap heard round the world. But what about here at home? What was a fourteen-year-old fan in Denver or a young African American girl in Detroit watching that wretched performance supposed to think about their government?

West is only the latest in a parade of rap stars to tell our kids America is a bad place, just before they get into their $50,000 SUVs. Sadly, West has plenty of company in the rest of the music industry, from Springsteen to Pearl Jam. Rapper KRS-1 actually said "America has to commit suicide if the world is to be a better place," while rocker Chrissie Hynde griped, "[Americans] deserve to get bombed. . . . I hope the Muslims win."

Turn on the radio to anything but an "oldies" station and try to think of the last song you heard (except country music, of course) that had anything nice to say about America? Maybe the Beach Boys. Certainly not most of the rap, hip-hop, and heavy metal songs that saturate many of our kids' favorite stations. And it has an effect. Every parent of a teenager knows the importance of music in their children's often crowded and confused lives. If we had a dollar for every time we said, "Turn off the music and do your homework," we'd have retired long ago. For most preteens and teenagers, music creates a separate world in which to exist, a world with a big neon sign flashing twenty-four hours a day, "No parents allowed."

No matter how much children resist, parents need to be involved because studies have shown that preteens and teenagers listen to music somewhere between three and four hours a day. No wonder they don't know much about history. Research also shows that teens see musicians as heroes even more so than athletes and rate their influence higher than either religion or books. That's a sobering finding.

And what are these musical heroes telling them about America? Look no further than our most famous expatriate, Madonna, for a clue. Her CD *American Life*, released in 2003, initially featured a video filled with militaristic images. As Madonna belted out the lyrics, dressed in a military uniform reminiscent of Nazi couture, pictures of mushroom clouds, bombs dropping, and Middle Eastern–looking child "refugees" popped up on screens behind her. The video ends with the singer throwing a fake "grenade" to a George Bush look-alike.

Madonna, who has managed to market limited talent into millionaire status, goofed on this one, however. With American troops fighting in Afghanistan and Iraq, the video quickly became a public relations nightmare; and she yanked it, as she put it, "out of respect to the armed forces who I support and pray for, I do not want to risk offending anyone who might misinterpret the meaning of this video." No need to worry there. No one could possibly miss her meaning. It was antimilitary, antiwar, anti-American, and anti-Bush—plain and simple. And, at the time, any self-respecting teenager with a working knowledge of the Internet could find it online then and probably still can today.

We're not suggesting that music must be without message—or one so bland and innocuous that it ends up with the intellectual heft of "The Macarena." After all, music has long been a source of protest and change. From slave spirituals in the nineteenth century to jazz and rock in the twentieth, music has played an appropriate and often positive role as a catalyst for social and political change in this country. But much of today's music sends a destructive message, not one of social protest, but one of anger, violence, sex, degradation, and drugs.

Studying the Problem

There have been few studies to assess the impact of this raw new music on children. One of the first, the Journal of Public Health, which in 2003 looked at African American girls, ages fourteen to eighteen, found that the girls from urban, lower-socioeconomic neighborhoods who listened to gangsta rap were three times more likely to hit a teacher, over two and a half times more likely to get arrested, twice as likely to have multiple sexual partners, and one and a half times more likely to get a sexually transmitted disease, use drugs, or drink alcohol.

If this music leads them to destructive behavior, is it such a stretch to think these same girls might also believe that their government tried to kill black people in Africa with AIDS-laced polio vaccine because Kanye West said so onstage at a Live Aid concert? We don't need a study to know that some kids will buy even the most lunatic statements if marketed properly.

Walton Muyumba, a Dallas professor and hip-hop fan, wondered about the impact of West's lyrics and statements in a column for the *Dallas Morning News:* "... do black and brown kids understand what's at stake for them? The perpetuation of hip-hop's most debilitating images, the pimp and thug mentality, impedes their access to everything from the economic mainstream to real political power."

For other kids, listening and buying into the negative messages of some of the most popular performers can lead to cynicism and more than just the usual case of teenage rebellion. Bill O'Reilly, of Fox News, who has led the charge against some of the most outrageous entertainers, warns, "Every American should be condemning rappers and rock stars who sell children subversive values."

We couldn't agree more; but for many parents, it's difficult to even understand the lyrics. What we do know is that, according to the American Association of Pediatrics, 75 percent of music videos involve sexual imagery and more than half involve violence against women. So, as Dr. Susan Buttross, chief of child development and behavioral pediatrics at the University of Mississippi Medical Center, says, "You cannot stick your head in the sand and expect your child will only look at good stuff. Parents need to know what their children are being exposed to."

Turning Down the Music

You may not win every battle with your teenager, but here are a few suggestions that we hope will help you ultimately win the war against the negative influences of some of the music you may find on your child's iPod.

- **Check the ratings.** First check out the rating on the CDs you'll probably find under the bed, at the bottom of the book bag, or at the back of the dresser drawer. What you're looking for is a little label called the "Parental Advisory," part of a program, overseen by the Recording Industry Association of America, to help parents set limits. If you see this label, warning bells should go off. It doesn't mean your child shouldn't listen to it but that listening to it ought to be a joint decision. Be forewarned that individual record companies, working with their artists, decide which of their releases should be labeled. It's a self-policing system, so don't assume no label means no problem.
- **Listen and learn.** Listen to the CDs or read the lyrics. Reading the lyrics, however, you may often feel like you need a rap or heavy metal "dictionary" to truly understand what the artists are trying to say. For a little help with the words, go to **www.ohhla.com** for rap lyrics. For other music lyrics, try out **www.lyrics.com** or **www.azlyrics.com**.
- **Start early.** We've said before that by the time kids get to college, it's too late to start building an American backbone. The same holds true for music. Younger children's musical tastes run the gamut from kids' songs to popular music to the patriotic songs we all grew up with. Along with being knowledgeable about the lyrics of your children's music, the National Institute on Media and the Family recommends that you "expose children to a broad range of music from an early age."

The All-American Songbook

Whether it's singing in the car on the way to the grocery store or on the family's summer vacation, at birthday parties, or on the Fourth of July, younger kids love patriotic songs, and America is blessed with enough anthems, marches, and scores to satisfy the musical tastes of every type of American.

- **"The Star-Spangled Banner":** On September 13, 1812, Francis Scott Key was visiting the British fleet anchored just outside the Baltimore harbor, trying to secure the release of a friend, Dr. William Beanes, who had been captured when British troops burned Washington, D.C. Key succeeded but was detained onboard overnight as the British continued their shelling of Fort McHenry, one of the forts defending Baltimore. In the morning, Key was so amazed to see the American flag still flying over the fort after the twenty-five-hour-long bombardment that he wrote a poem to commemorate the occasion.

- **"God Bless America":** Irving Berlin originally wrote our country's "unofficial national anthem" in 1918 for a Broadway show that he was working on at the time but never used it. Twenty years later, with war on the horizon, Berlin remembered the song he had penned nearly two decades earlier. The song was an immediate hit, but the proceeds didn't go to Berlin. Instead, this grateful American immigrant established the "God Bless America Fund" with all the royalties going to the Boy and Girl Scouts of America.

- **"America the Beautiful":** The words were written in 1893 by Katharine Lee Bates, a Wellesley professor, who wrote it after being awed by the view from Pike's Peak in Colorado. The music came several years later from a New Jersey church organist, Samuel Ward, whose inspiration came to him after an outing on Coney Island. ABC News reporter Lynn Sherr tells the story of the song and its author in a book called *America the Beautiful: The Stirring True Story Behind Our Nation's Favorite Song.* It's a good read for teenagers, especially for girls interested in the role of independent women in American society at the turn of the century.

• **"Stars and Stripes Forever":** John Philip Sousa, nicknamed America's "March King," said, "March music is for the feet, not the head." He composed his most famous march, "Stars and Stripes Forever," on Christmas Day 1896, after "writing" the march, as he put it, in his "brain-band" on a steamer coming back from Europe. One hundred and one years later, in 1987, Congress officially designated Sousa's "brain child" as America's "national march."

• ***America's "Star-Spangled Songbook":*** This is a rich collection that ranges from the classical to country. It includes Aaron Copland's hauntingly beautiful "Appalachian Spring," Lee Greenwood's "God Bless the U.S.A.," Neil Diamond's "America," Waylon Jennings's "America," and "The Eagle," Elvis's rendition of "An American Trilogy" a medley of "Dixie," "The Battle Hymn of the Republic," and the spiritual "All My Trials Soon Be Over." Others you might know include: Toby Keith's "Courtesy of the Red, White and Blue," Paul McCartney's "Freedom," the Beach Boys' "California Girls," and John Denver's "Country Roads."

• **Real Golden Oldies.** If your younger kids are like ours used to be, they'll get a kick out of America's patriotic "Golden Oldies" like "Yankee Doodle," "You're a Grand Old Flag," "When Johnny Comes Marching Home," "My Country 'Tis of Thee," and "This Land Is Your Land." Put them on the boom box next Fourth of July or how about a little patriotic karoke with the kids?

★ ★ ★

It's Not News to Us

> "We [Americans] like to think that we're the good guys, but we're not."
>
> —CNN's Bruce Morton

It's the day our children will never forget. Just like past generations who remembered the attack on Pearl Harbor or the day President Kennedy was assassinated, our children, even if they were only five or six at the time, will always remember 9/11. They will remember the images they saw on television of the planes hitting the skyscrapers and the horrifying collapse of the Twin Towers. They will remember the flames of the Pentagon and the terrified ash-covered crowds in the streets of Manhattan. They will remember their parents' and teachers' reactions—their tears, their fears, and their love and prayers for our country on that terrible day.

And, yes, there was a tremendous surge of patriotism across our country after 9/11 and a feeling of rage at these terrorist attacks. Yet, just weeks later when David Westin, the president of ABC News, was asked by a questioner in the audience at a Columbia School of Journalism event whether he thought the Pentagon was a legitimate military target, Westin's response was surprising, even shocking. "I actually don't have an opinion on that," he said, ". . . as a journalist, I feel strongly that's something that I should not be taking a position on."

Apparently, Westin, like Madonna, knows a public relations disaster when he sees one. After a week of bad press, Westin apologized saying, "Under any interpretation, the attack on the Pentagon was criminal and entirely without justification." But you have to wonder, if the American head of one of the great American television networks can't summon the moral backbone to say that an unprovoked attack against the Pentagon that killed 125 people is wrong, what's wrong with American journalism?

Media Relativism

Like many of the history books in your kids' backpacks, most of the traditional news media today, both print and broadcast, seem to have caught a bad case of the "equivalencies" when it comes to covering their own country. Whether it's out of a misguided sense of "journalistic objectivity," left-of-center politics, political correctness, or more likely a combination of all three, traditional media reporters and editors today—print and broadcast—shovel out a steady supply of critical coverage.

They very often paint a picture for us and for our children of America and its government as warmongering, unethical, and/or incompetent, if not downright criminal. And they do this, they claim, because it's the right way to do their job as objective journalists.

But how objective? Studies have shown journalists are, by large margins, Democrats—89 percent of Washington-based reporters, in one survey, said they voted for Bill Clinton in 1992, while twelve years later in 2004 only 19 percent of reporters in another survey said they voted for George W. Bush. And negative coverage of domestic issues like health care, the homeless, race, and the economy do seem to ebb and flow depending on who sits in the Oval Office. If this were just pure partisanship, the motivations of the news media's focus on negative news might be more understandable. But the media's distrust of and antagonism toward their own government's handling of foreign affairs isn't only because they vote Democratic. The roots can be traced back to the Vietnam conflict where so many of today's media powers cut their journalistic teeth or were in high school or college watching critical news reports of American military action in that war.

But it wasn't always this way. Once upon a time, journalists including the best of their time considered themselves Americans first and journalists second. Christopher Daly, a journalism professor at Boston University and, at the time, a *Washington Post* reporter, put it best in the *Columbia Journalism Review* when he wrote wistfully of the reporters who covered World War II. He noted that back then, most journalists used the first-person plural ("we took the hill" or the "Germans gave us heavy fire") in obvious solidarity with the troops they were covering. Then, like a good mainstream journalist today bent on "objectivity at all costs," he went on to admit he had never used the first-person plural because the "journalistic stance" has changed since World War II. "There is no single national purpose to identify with, and if there were, there's a good chance that journalists would stand aside."

And they did, even after 9/11. For example, ABC prohibited its anchors and reporters from wearing American flag pins in their lapels. ABC News president David Westin—yes *him* again—explained to *New York Times* reporter Jim Rutenberg, "It was important for . . . journalists to maintain their neutrality in times of war." ABC's *Nightline* anchor, Ted Koppel, agreed: "I don't believe that I'm being a particularly patriotic American by slapping a little flag in my lapel and then saying anything that is said by . . . the U.S. government is going to get on without comment and anything that is said by 'the enemy' [as he makes the quotation sign] is immediately going to be put through a meat grinder of analysis." Not all the networks saw an expression of support for America as a violation of journalistic neutrality. Brit Hume, lead anchor for Fox News, defended Fox's decision to allow the pins, telling *USA Today,* "Our flag is not the symbol of the Bush administration, and Fox News is not located in Switzerland."

But overt patriotism, which was once part of both journalism and entertainment, just doesn't cut it anymore. In 2001 country singer Charlie Daniels was scheduled to perform on the PBS Fourth of July special, "A Capital Fourth." Producers for the government-funded network didn't like his choice of songs, a tribute to those who perished on 9/11 called the "The Last Fallen Hero." According to Daniels, PBS objected to the patriotic anthem saying the lyrics were "too angry."

Daniels decided he wasn't going to go quietly, and in a letter he made public he told PBS, "The song in question is not an angry song. It is my feeling that our country is engaged in a battle for our very survival and that we should be constantly reminded that our enemy will do the most inhuman and dastardly things imaginable if we are to have future Independence Days to celebrate."

Some of the lyrics that struck PBS as objectionable declared: *"This is a righteous cause / So without doubt or pause I will do what my country asks of me / Make any sacrifice / We'll pay whatever price / So the children of tomorrow can be free."* Sentiments with which the vast majority of Americans on that Fourth of July would have agreed.

So Just Who Are the Bad Guys?

In the coverage of the war in Iraq, journalistic "objectivity" has more than ever become the excuse for a daily barrage of criticism of our government and the actions of our military. Day in and day out, Saddam's past cruelties and even the barbarism of terror groups seem worth little mention, but what we have done wrong is always the day's biggest story. For example, NBC aired fifty-eight stories on Iraqi prison abuse in the first few weeks after the story broke but only five reports over a sixteen-month period on the discovery by American troops of Saddam's mass graves. Abu Ghraib housed fifteen hundred prisoners, the graves held more than three hundred thousand bodies.

None of the networks treated the inhuman beheading of Nicholas Berg as anything more than a two-day story. It was all Abu Ghraib all the time, even though a CBS poll at the time found that 49 percent of people felt that the media had spent too much time on the story; only 6 percent thought it had been undercovered. So much for the argument that these negative stories are in response to the public's right and desire to "know."

But it is the members of the U.S. military who always get the shortest end of the stick when it comes to getting credit from the American media. Bing West, a former Marine and assistant secretary of defense, bitterly complained in a *Washington Post* opinion piece about the news coverage of fighting in Iraq, especially the battle for Fallujah in November 2004. In some of the most ferocious urban fighting in thirty-five years, U.S. Marines battled against suicidal jihadists as "hundreds of gripping stories of valor emerged that would have been publicized in World War II," Bing wrote. But what made the news? Not stories about America's hard-fought victory against a brutal enemy. No, once again it was allegations that American soldiers had beaten prisoners there *two years* before.

Once, appearing on the *Today Show* to promote her new children's book about George Washington crossing the Delaware, Lynne Cheney was asked by host Matt Lauer to compare America's Revolutionary soldiers to today's insurgents in Iraq. He said, "Let me ask you to think about what is going on in Iraq today, where the insurgents—not well-equipped, smaller in numbers—the greatest army in the world is their opposition. What's the lesson here?" She replied, "Well, the difference, of course, is who's fighting on the side of freedom."

How the News Affects Our Kids

Now we know that young children, of course, don't sit glued to the network evening news or the cable news channels. They aren't wrestling their dad for first dibs on the daily paper. But they do catch frequent glances of what their parents and the parents of their friends are watching and hear their parents talking about the news. All of us, kids included, get a daily dose of criticism toward our country—sometimes subtle, sometimes not—if the set is on for the network news, the morning talk shows, *Law and Order, Boston Legal,* or *The View,* or twenty other programs we could name. Media is an enormously powerful influence on the thinking of adults about current events; so why shouldn't children, even more gullible, be affected? Similarly, TV news, whether it's coverage of the war or just the daily "crisis in America" story, can shape what they believe.

According to the American Academy of Child and Adolescent Psychiatry, there have been a number of changes in the media that can be especially harmful to our children. They include the increasing critical focus on the private lives of public figures and role models and the emphasis on stories about frightening events. For example, although statistics show that crime in America is down, media reports about crime in the last few years have increased 240 percent. What do our children think when they hear crime stories night after night followed by *CSI*? Probably that America might be a scary, crime-ridden dangerous place, when in fact, it's not.

Some "news junkie" teens do tune into the news and give it their full attention or even read a newspaper once in a while. But most get their updates from the Internet or from Jon Stewart on *The Daily Show.* Stewart may be funny once in a while. But that drip, drip, drip of sarcasm and cynicism about America and our leaders from comedians such as Stewart, Stephen Colbert, and Bill Maher certainly takes a toll on the respect that kids feel about our country. If our president, our lawmakers, and even the justices of the Supreme Court are constantly being mocked, how can it not erode the respect our kids have for the institutions of our government? Researchers at East Carolina University, who did a study of college students who watched *The Daily Show,* actually coined a name for this negativism and suspicion toward government and politics—the "Daily Effect."

So, again, what's a parent to do?

- **Put news media reports in proper context.** Give your kids some perspective for what they're hearing from the news media, especially when the topic is frightening or puts America in a bad light. Start by watching the news together and talking about what they have seen and heard. Yes, media is very influential but nothing is more influential with your children than your views on the news.
- **Play "Let's Grade the News."** To be more interactive while you watch the news, give everyone a scorecard to write down the topic of each story. Then, give each report a grade from A to C for accuracy, objectivity, and negativity. Ask your kids to explain why a story was good or bad in their eyes, and be ready to give them on-the-spot analysis of what you think.
- **Turn your kids into reporters.** Have them choose a story idea. For younger children, give them a list. Older children can find subjects

that interest them on their own. If you have a video camera, have your child write a sixty-second "news report" and give it on camera. The replay is always fun. You can also have them write a newspaper article as well. The exercise will give them insight into how a reporter's own views can influence the content and tone of the story.

- **Play photo editor.** Another way to inject some fun into learning about the media is through photographs. Cut out photos from the daily newspaper or one of the newsweeklies for a discussion about the story they tell. Ask the kids to make a list of words that describe the picture and what it means to them, and, finally, ask them to write captions for the photos. Then, check it with the caption that was in the paper or magazine.

An American Tale: Who Really Protects Freedom of the Press?

Journalist Matt Pottinger spent seven years covering China for the *Wall Street Journal.* During his years there, he saw protesters beaten in Tiananmen Square, had to flush his notes down a toilet to keep them away from the police, and was roughed up by a government "goon." Living abroad made him realize that in much of the world, the liberties Americans take for granted are as rare as a Marine on the San Francisco Board of Supervisors.

But when Matt would come home to America for visits, he was surprised and disturbed by what he saw and heard. "I would come home and you didn't feel we were a country at war," he said. He was also enraged by a video he saw of the beheading of an American contractor in Iraq. "At first, I admit I felt a touch of the terror [the terrorists] wanted me to feel, but then I felt anger." Soon after, he met a Marine colonel who had just come back from Iraq and was impressed by his experience in war. The next morning he toured the USS *Intrepid,* the World War II aircraft carrier that was a museum in New York Harbor at the time and found himself drawn to the Marine Corps recruiting center on board.

Matt was thirty-two years old and out of shape, the kind of guy who, he says, could sit at his desk twelve hours straight, "Fourteen if I have a bag of

• **Step back in time.** If you are visiting Washington, D.C., visit the new "Newseum," scheduled to reopen in a new headquarters near the Mall in early 2007. This is one of America's most fun museums, teaching children the history and importance of a free press along with plenty of hands-on activities, too. You can touch an actual section of the Berlin Wall, watch breaking news from a forty-foot video wall, see a live television broadcast, or go to the movies for a thrilling ride back in time to some of history's biggest news events. Or you can be part of the exhibit. Kids can be a news anchor or reporter complete with teleprompter and a background of the White House or a global hot spot. Check out this great interactive family-friendly museum at **www.newseum.org**.

• **Use the Web.** Many news websites are designed especially for

Reese's Pieces." The recruiting officer wasn't impressed by that or his press credentials. To become a Marine, Matt would have to pass a physical fitness test that consisted of twenty pull-ups, a hundred crunches in two minutes, and a three-mile run in eighteen minutes. Matt took the application form and went back to filing stories in China.

Then came the Asian tsunami. Inspired by the work the Marines were doing in Thailand to spearhead the relief effort, he started training to pass the physical. Five months later, Matt made a quick trip back to New York. He managed to pass the test on the *Intrepid,* though at the end of his run, he says, he threw up all over the tarmac. The recruitment officer "liked that a lot," Matt says. "That's when we both knew I was going for it."

He was accepted as an officer candidate and, after basic training, was sworn in as a second lieutenant. At the swearing-in ceremony, an officer congratulated him and joked, "It's an honor to have somebody from the dark side come over to our side"—somebody who understands that it's soldiers not journalists who truly protect our freedom of the press.

★ ★ ★

kids and can help inform them about this country and the world at large. These sites include games, quizzes, lesson plans, lots of photos, links, and sections for parents, too. Check out the *New York Times*'s "Learning Network" at **www.nytimes.com/learning**, the *Washington Post*'s "KidsPost" at **www.washingtonpost.com/kidspost**, and the Nickelodeon Channel website, **www.nick.com** (click on All Nick and then Nick News). Our favorite website for kids' news is the Scholastic website at **www.scholastic.com**; to go directly to the News section, visit **www.teacher.scholastic.com/scholasticnews**.

We Must Do Better

The teenage son of a friend of ours saw a screening of *Syriana*, a caustic anti-American film that blames a conspiracy of global oil companies and the U.S. government for the death of a "moderate" Arab prince bent on reform, and, afterward, asked his parents, "Why are we always the bad guy?" That's a tough question to answer. Why, indeed, do Hollywood, the music industry, and the news media paint such a bleak and condemning portrait of a nation most of us think our children should be proud to call home?

There is no easy answer to the question, but there are ways to combat the problem. Recognize the impact "Bad Influencers" are having on your children, step in and make sure that your influence—and it's more powerful than you may think—gets equal time.

Winston Churchill, in the darkest days of World War II, just after Pearl Harbor, crossed the Atlantic at the end of that bleak December 1941 and made a great speech. To stiffen resolve, he said, "We have not journeyed across the oceans, across the mountains, across the prairies because we are made of sugar candy."

We all would agree that this is certainly not the time, with a future full of challenges and dangers, to be raising a couple of generations of sugar candy kids. They have to be better than that. And we have to do better than that for their sake and for the sake of our country.

DINNER TABLE DEBATE

Free Speech Isn't Always Free

If the media always makes us the "bad guys," is there anything we can do about it? That is a great question to kick off a dinner table discussion that gives you the opportunity to talk to your children about the strengths and the costs of our important First Amendment. Unlike many countries, America's guarantee of freedom of speech protects the media—entertainment and news—from nearly all government censorship or interference. But what happens when the media uses its power irresponsibly—for example, when it constantly portrays America in a negative light or puts "getting the scoop" ahead of national security? Get your children ready for the debate by asking them to keep a media journal for twenty-four hours, listing examples of media negativity, bias, or irresponsibility they see or hear on television, in the newspaper or newsmagazines, on a CD, or in a film. Begin the discussion by reading the First Amendment and then going over their examples, asking them to explain why they chose them. Then get to the heart of the matter with some tough questions.

- What do you think the Founding Fathers had in mind when they wrote the First Amendment? Did they believe there should never be any censorship of the press under any circumstances?
- Do you think the government has a right to place limits on free speech? And if so, when? What about crying fire in a theater or exposing top secret national security programs that fight our enemies?
- Does free speech mean you can say anything you want in music, like profanity, for example? Does it mean a movie can show any kind of violence or sexual behavior without restrictions?
- How would they ensure that media is free but responsible in its actions?

★ ★ ★

Fighting the Virus

• To get your children's toes tapping to America's most patriotic songs at a young age, you can find all the patriotic songs you need, music and lyrics, online at the National Institute of Health Service kids' page at **www.niehs.nih.gov/kids/musicpatriot.htm**.

• For ideas on how to help your children understand the sacrifices made for freedom by our military they won't read about in the newspapers, check out "Memorial Day" on page 157 in Chapter 7.

• To help kids learn about the heroes they won't see at the movies, let your child pick a favorite hero's birthday to celebrate. There are plenty of ideas and resources in the section "What Happened When," page 214 in Chapter 9, "Patriot Projects."

★ ★ ★

6

THE PATRIOT PLEDGE

"I am only one, but still I am one. I cannot do everything, but still I can do something. And because I cannot do everything, I will not refuse to do the something that I can do."

—EDWARD EVERETT HALE

Here's a tale of real parent power about a woman named Rose Chavez who lives in Albuquerque. When Rose, one of ten children, was growing up, her family lived in a house with no electricity or running water. By working hard and saving they managed to move to a better house—or so they thought until the city built a sewage plant virtually in their backyard. "When the plant would start up there was a lot of noise," she recalled. "The house would shake and you could smell the sewage. I hated it."

Years later, the sewage plant loomed over her sons' and daughters' childhood much as it had hers. Her oldest son, Marty, remembers, "We heard the story over and over when we were growing up." And the story's lessons were clear. You come from poor circumstances and have no power. You live in a world where little is expected of Hispanics. But you can overcome it. You *will* overcome it.

Rose Chavez never went to college, but she had a dream—a very big dream. One of the family legends is that Rose, when growing up, once said she either wanted to be a nun or have a family with ten children who all went to Harvard. And, even though she ended up only having five children, she was determined to make it happen.

Rose worked for the Air Force at the Sandia National Laboratory as a secretary but quit her job after her first three children were born. To help make ends meet, she typed court transcripts at home until 4 A.M. every night, got a couple hours of sleep, and then would get up to take care of her family. The kids went to school, did homework, and practiced the piano. Money was tight. There was no second car, no second television set. Son Tom says, "I remember complaining about all the beans we were eating. There was a lot of money out the door for schools and not a lot of money for different flavors of lasagna."

Marty was the first in the family to go to Harvard, followed by Rick, Tom, Andrea, and, finally, Elena. Financial aid helped, and they all had part-time and summer jobs. But even with that, affording Harvard was "barely possible," said Marty. Still, Rose was determined, and the family home purchased for $25,000 in 1968 was mortgaged over and over again. Rose and her husband, Ray, scrimped and scrimped as their children went on to succeed. "She was the chief operating officer," said Raymond Chavez about his wife. "When I look back, I think—'How did we do it?' My wife is just an amazing worker. I think they got it from her." Marty and Tom went on to earn doctorates at Stanford. Andrea finished law school and a master's at Stanford, while Elena received a master's at the Kennedy School at Harvard. All have successful careers.

In 2001, when the last of Rose's brood graduated, Harvard hosted a reception for the family. Former dean Harry Lewis said: "There are families who have a lot of kids who go to Harvard, though I don't know too many who have five who have gone. What was unusual was that it was a family with not only a 'no Harvard tradition,' but there was 'no college tradition' in the family." But there was Rose. And something else. He said he considered the Chavezes' achievement a compelling story not only about five smart kids with a very special mother or about Harvard, "but about America."

This American Tale reaffirms that our country remains a place of great opportunity, but it also reminds us how extraordinarily effective determined and dedicated parents can be. In the previous pages, we've given you the facts on why it is, indeed, hard to raise an American today. If what you read in these first chapters about our schools and the media surprised and disturbed you, or maybe even made you angry, congratulations, you're halfway to producing a patriot—understanding the problem. Now, we're asking you to do something really important: Make a personal commitment to teach your children about the greatness of this country, to teach them to love it, honor it, and accept responsibility for keeping it great.

We've already shared with you practical suggestions on how to effectively handle some of the negative influences that impact our children. But there is so much more you can do. To be honest, the question you have to ask yourself is: What more do I want to do? How much time and energy can I commit to between Little League, Sunday school, and car pool duty to make sure my children have the right grounding in American history, American ideals, and American values?

We know this is tough. We've been part of the chauffeur brigade, too. But we want you to realize that there is a lot you can do just as part of your family life that both you and the kids would benefit from and really enjoy.

Historian David McCullough, who wrote *1776* and *John Adams*, is very clear about the problems we face in raising kids today who understand and honor America's past. He has often complained that our kids and many of our teachers don't know enough about history, and that our history textbooks can be "so deadly dull that they were designed to kill one's interest." But he has also said, "The example . . . has to be set at home. That may be the most important thing. We've got to start talking about history with our children and in front of our children. We've got to encourage them to read good books about history, books that a person would want to read. We have to take children to historic sites, presidential homes or battlefields or whatever. And we can all do that. We can also talk about that part of American history that has interested us most and who our personal heroes of the past are in front of our children." We couldn't agree more.

Test Yourself

In the mid-1980s, the mayor of New York, Ed Koch, used to wander around his city asking the folks, "How'm I doin'?" Good question, we thought. So, how are you doing at "raising an American"? Are you already following any of McCullough's suggestions? Here's a way to find out. Take the following little quiz and give yourself a grade. It's not a statistical survey, but it may give you a sense of how much more you may want to do to help your children become the knowledgeable and patriotic Americans you want them to be.

1. Did you vote in the last election? ____Yes ____No
2. Did you take your kids with you when you voted? ____Yes ____No
3. Besides a barbecue on the Fourth of July, did you attend an Independence Day parade or local fireworks display? ____Yes ____No
4. Have you, as David McCullough suggests, taken your children to a historic site in the last year? ____Yes ____No
5. Does your family own an American flag and do you fly the flag on important dates? ____Yes ____No
6. Did you do anything special with your kids on Veterans Day, Martin Luther King's Birthday, Constitution Day, or Presidents' Day? ____Yes ____No
7. Have you bought a biography of an American you admire for your kids or encouraged them to check one out of the library? ____Yes ____No
8. Have you and your kids explored a website in the last year that focuses on an aspect of your state's or America's history? ____Yes ____No
9. Have you watched a movie with them that tells part of the story of America? ____Yes ____No
10. Have you encouraged your kids to join a club or church group that includes as an activity some type of volunteerism in the community? ____Yes ____No

★ ★ ★

If you answered yes to most of these questions, then give yourself an A for making the right effort and a pat on the back from us. You are doing great—and in the next pages, we think you will find lots of new ideas and resources to help you build on the foundation of pride in our country that you are already creating in your children.

If you answered half or more of the questions with a yes, your kids certainly know that you think patriotism and love of country is important. So, don't let up now. Keep reading for more tips and ideas.

Less than half? We know you are busy, but you wouldn't be reading this book if you weren't worried about your kids and whether they are growing up to become good Americans. Your heart is in the right place. You know that promoting patriotism is part of your responsibilities as a parent. So, now, channel your concerns by making patriot-building activities an important part of your family life, and we're here to help you.

Taking the Pledge

We think the best way to start putting your beliefs into practice is by pledging that you will. In fact, we believe all American parents would benefit from signing what we call "the Patriot Pledge."

A good way to commit fully to any goal is by taking a pledge. Girl Scouts do it. So do Boy Scouts. Brides and grooms, too. Many schools today insist that the parents of athletes sign a pledge to promote fair play and good sportsmanship on the athletic field. Students often have to sign an honor pledge at the beginning of each academic year, a declaration that they will uphold standards of integrity and honesty. All our federal government officials including the president are sworn in with a pledge to uphold the Constitution, an oath that goes back to Washington's day. Making a public promise always seems to have more staying power than a private commitment. Taking it seriously can be an important, sometimes even a life-changing event. We hope it will be for you and your children. Besides, you'll be in good company.

Every recruit in our armed services also swears an oath of

President for a Day

If you're in Philadelphia, stop by the Constitution Center, a wonderful museum dedicated to teaching children about the history and importance of the Constitution and the Bill of Rights. One of the hands-on exhibits lets your child be "sworn in" as president of the United States. Kids stand in front of a wall-sized photo of the Capitol's West Front just as it looks for a real presidential inauguration. Each reads the presidential oath from a teleprompter as the "swearing-in" ceremony is captured on tape to take home for posterity. It's lots of fun, and who knows? It might just inspire a presidential run.

★ ★ ★

enlistment when inducted. Marine Corps officers have told us one of the first steps in "making a Marine" is to ensure a recruit understands the significance of his or her enlistment oath, the responsibilities and the personal commitment it entails. In much the same way, the Patriot Pledge is about engendering the appropriate amount of respect we should all feel for our country and its traditions. So before you sign, there are some important things to do as well. Read it aloud with your children. Let them know of your resolution and commitment and why you think adding some family time to read, think, and talk about America is important. Ask them how they feel about this and discuss with them ways you all would want this Pledge to impact your time together.

Then, sign the Pledge in front of your children and sign with a big flourish. This is a perfect time to tell them the story behind John Hancock's supersized signature on the Declaration of Independence. He said he wanted it large so that George III could read it without his spectacles! Then, make a copy and post it in a prominent place. We're all for you laminating the Pledge or framing it. Hang it up and be proud to show off your concern and your commitment. Most important, make it an important family document.

One of the best things you can do with the Pledge is share it with the parents of your children's friends as well as other members of your family, your neighbors, and your friends. We hope that they will want to sign the Pledge as well.

Also, tell your children's teachers about your family's Pledge. Ask for ideas for group activities that would benefit all the kids in the neighborhood or in your child's class.

Finally, commit your family to celebrating all patriotic holidays, to visiting some of our country's most historic sites, and to spending at least one hour each week in a way that can help your children become proud and patriotic Americans.

Writing this book has certainly been an adventure for us. It began as what we thought would be an interesting and constructive project, but it has become our passion. We do know that asking you to add other responsibilities to an already crowded schedule means sacrifice. But we're asking anyway because we're worried about the future of this country if parents don't get more involved in the serious business of raising patriots—young people of hope, duty, courage, and compassion. The truth is America needs them as much today as it did in 1776. And America needs you, too—and thousands of parents like you—to fulfill the Pledge by celebrating national holidays and devoting time each week to teaching your children to love their country.

As we've said before, your children, with your encouragement, spend more than an hour a week on activities like soccer or skating or piano lessons. They also, without any encouragement, spend hours and hours more playing video games, instant messaging, or glued to their iPods. All this may be very important to them right now, but spending time trying to better understand their country and their responsibilities as citizens will impact their future far more. Teachers often talk about "the teachable moment." Well, as a parent you have lots of teachable moments. Use them.

So, put your hand over your heart, and take the Pledge you will find on the next page.

The Patriot Pledge

- ★ I recognize that parents are the most important role model for their children; and I will, through my actions, demonstrate the importance of patriotism.
- ★ I believe by encouraging a love of country in my children, I will help them become the kind of informed and loyal citizens that America needs for our country's future.
- ★ I will teach them about America's unique history and the deeply held beliefs on which this nation was founded.
- ★ I will encourage their interest in the heroes of our past.
- ★ I will strive to develop in them American characteristics such as idealism, tolerance, individualism, and courage.
- ★ I will ask them to respect the symbols of our republic such as the flag, the national anthem, the Pledge of Allegiance, and the holidays that honor our past.
- ★ And I will make patriotism an enriching, inspiring part of their lives.

This is my pledge.

____

PART TWO

STAR-SPANGLED IDEAS

Now, for the "Back of the Book," as Bill O'Reilly likes to say. You'll find more than 1,776 ideas and resources scattered throughout the pages of this book to help put the important Patriot Pledge into action and to add a little American spirit to your family's life. We want to give real-world ideas that you can use to raise the next "Greatest Generation." From here on, you'll find a grab bag of red, white, and blue suggestions—ideas, projects, and activities for your family.

1. First you'll find our suggestions for an All-American Year—lots of ways to make the holidays we celebrate a lot more important and fun for your family.
2. Next are ideas for great summer vacations and family field trips that will teach the kids more about the places where history was made and our country's great natural beauty.
3. Finally, there are special "Patriot Projects," which will give you ideas to help the kids learn more about their country, their heritage, and even more about you and the history you've lived through.

But to quote one of our favorite organizations, the Boy Scouts, you've got to "Be Prepared" with a few basics to get off to a rousing start.

• **Make sure your library card is up-to-date and ready for action.** Or build a home library of books about our country that the kids will want to read, keep, and cherish. They make great birthday and Christmas gifts. By the way, children's books are designated for different ages or grade levels, although not all booksellers agree. So, remember, you are the best judge of your own children's reading skills. Pick books with them that they will enjoy reading and books that younger kids will want to hear you read to them.

• **Get connected.** Most of you probably already are connected, but access to the Internet (go to your library if you don't have a computer) is essential along with a big dose of curiosity to search the Web, which is jam-packed with ideas, information, and activities to help you raise patriots.

• **Plug in your DVD or video player.** Be ready to watch the many movies and documentaries that the whole family will find interesting. We've already given you a list of one hundred movies that we think can help combat the media virus that so easily infects the kids. Throughout the following pages, you'll find even more suggestions for interesting films and documentaries you can watch together. Along with commercial video stores like Blockbuster or Netflix online, your local public library often has many of these movies on hand or can get them.

• **Put a good-sized map of the USA on the fridge or a wall.** In many of your discussions and activities, you'll want your child to not only know what happened in American history but where it happened. They'll have fun finding historic sites, tracing the routes of explorers, pioneers, and Native Americans, and seeing where battles took place.

• **Have a boom box ready with extra batteries.** You'll find plenty of uses for it from Fourth of July picnics to that patriotic karoke we talked about or even to listen to audiobooks together as a family.

• **Stock up on craft supplies especially for younger kids.** There is nothing like a fun family craft project to bring everybody together. Maybe your first project could be decorating a "patriots' supply box" in red, white, and blue.

7

ALL-AMERICAN YEAR

"Celebrate good times, come on."

—Kool and the Gang

Years ago, Art Linkletter once asked a little girl, "What's Armistice Day?" "They have Armistice Day so boys and girls can go home from school and have a day at rest," she answered confidently.

Kids do say the darnedest things. But here's the kicker. Do *you* know when Armistice Day is? If you're like most folks, these days, you may not. The answer is November 11, now called Veterans Day, which honors those who serve our country but barely registers with many people today.

The truth is, other than major holidays like the Fourth of July or Thanksgiving, too many Americans have trouble remembering why our nation's holidays were created in the first place or, for that matter, even remembering the holidays at all. We tend to treat them as just some extra time off to shop, to finally do those projects around the house we've been avoiding, or to simply put our feet up and relax. That attitude lessens the meaning of these holidays and—worst of all—takes the fun out of them. To raise Americans, we believe our national holidays should be fun *and* inspirational. These special days help create a shared heritage that unites us as one people, a heritage every child must learn.

We've cooked up some ideas (literally and figuratively speaking) to help you make family memories that will stay with your children and, in turn, be passed on by them to their children. We're going to give you some ways to make this an "All-American Year"—and our national holidays a lot more important once again in the life of your family.

Here are a few tips to get you started on your All-American Year:

- **Begin by creating a family calendar.** Highlight all the holidays you plan to celebrate. If you've got a calendar handy—great. If not, you can make one using downloads from the Internet at **www.printfree.com**. Then, a couple of weeks before each holiday, start counting down to the big day and planning exactly how the family will celebrate.
- **Read books together in advance about the holiday.** Help kids understand why the holiday is worth celebrating. There are plenty of recommendations for great reads in this and many other chapters. Also, get the material you may need if you are planning a craft project.
- **Have a festive dinner.** When it's appropriate (and it almost always is appropriate), serve special food or snacks associated with the holiday.

Our All-American year kicks off with Election Day. With a compressed primary schedule and a 24/7 cable news cycle, the campaign season does seem to start earlier and earlier, and it can wear you out long before the first Tuesday after the first Monday in November. And elections, we admit, can get pretty ugly. Still, all we have to do is think of the millions of Iraqis with their ink-stained fingers, proud that they could, at last, vote in a legitimate election for their government to be inspired by the great gift of democracy. Our children need to understand that voting is the very bedrock of our democratic system and nothing is more important for every American citizen than to get out there and vote!

In fact, if this book inspires you to do just one thing with your kids, it should be to vote and to take them along when you go to the polls. We believe that this is so important for your family and for our country that we have created a very special initiative called the Take Your Kids 2 Vote Campaign. You can find out more about it on page 135.

So, check out some facts about Election Day, and take your children with you to the polls this year. It's an all-American thing to do!

Election Day

First Tuesday After First Monday in November

A Bit of History

Why is Election Day always the first Tuesday after the first Monday in November? That day was picked by Congress in 1845 because most Americans were farmers at the time; and by November, most of the crops were in.

Why Tuesday? That's because most residents of rural America had to travel quite a way to the county seat in order to vote. Monday was not considered a good day since many people would need to begin travel on Sunday, and that would have conflicted with church services.

Why the first Tuesday after the first Monday? Lawmakers wanted to prevent Election Day from falling on the first of November for two reasons: first, because November 1, the day after Halloween, is All Saints Day, which is a Holy Day for Roman Catholics; second, since most merchants were in the habit of doing their books on the first day of the month, Congress chose a day that wouldn't interfere with the business community.

Winning Ways to Make Election Day Special

• Volunteer in a political campaign and give your kids a firsthand look at how their democracy works by getting them involved, too. Start by giving them a candidate's T-shirt, cap, or button. Plant a campaign sign together in the front yard. They'll have lots of fun going door-to-door with you, handing out flyers, or working in campaign headquarters.

• Watch the candidates' debate on TV and ask the kids who they thought won. For older kids, you might even consider attending the debate, if open to the public. If you've got a houseful, consider organizing your own "political debate." For once, the kids can actually argue with your blessing.

• Watch campaign ads on television as a family and ask for opinions. Remember almost all American children know their stuff when it comes to assessing someone's TV performance or the effectiveness of TV advertising. As the election nears, there will be plenty of candidate and other political websites that will stream the ads. Use a search engine with the candidate's name or just the phrase "candidate or political ads."

• Suggest to your child's teacher that the class have a mock election at school. Kids Voting USA offers special age-appropriate Election Day activities. Classes from kindergarten through high school can exercise their "right" to vote through this hands-on learning experience. Find out if there is a Kids Voting USA (**www.kidsvotingusa.org**) affiliate near you and if such a program can be established at your children's school. It's nonpartisan—and fun.

• Kids can cast a vote in lots of other ways, too. Here are three. The *Weekly Reader, Time (Magazine) for Kids,* and the Nickelodeon Poll conduct their own presidential "election" asking kids to vote during the run-up to the national elections. And kids are savvy voters. From 1956 to 2004, the *Weekly Reader* poll has accurately predicted the outcome of every presidential race.

• On Election Day, involve your kids in get-out-the-vote activities, and then throw your own election night party at your home for friends, neighbors, and the kids. Or, if you are working for a candidate, let your kids join the party at campaign headquarters to watch the returns come in.

• Got a kid with political ambitions? Encourage him or her to run for school office (even if you have to handle the tears that might go with the agony of defeat). In order to run a campaign, they will need a campaign manager, a snappy campaign slogan, and a platform. Make the campaign a family affair with everyone pitching in to make posters and buttons as well as being resident guinea pigs for the candidate's speech practices. Running for office is a great way to understand viscerally the challenge and excitement of the democratic process. It will give your child new respect for candidates who put themselves on the line this way.

The Take Your Kids 2 Vote Campaign! Make Democracy a Family Affair

"A government is like everything else: to preserve it we must love it . . . the surest way of instilling [such love] into children is for parents to set them an example."

—Thomas Jefferson

While interviewing parents for this book, many of them told us that, as children, the thing that made them feel the most patriotic was going to the polls with their parents on Election Day. They shared vivid memories of watching Mom and Dad pull the lever or put the ballot in the box and receiving their "I voted" sticker to wear proudly all day. It was a special moment they never forgot.

Sadly, many parents also acknowledged that they don't always take their own children with them on Election Day. The Citizenship Test asks those who want to become Americans: "What is the responsibility of a U.S. citizen?" The answer, of course, is to cast your ballot and vote. That's why parents, by taking their children along when they vote, can, in one easy step, both create a lasting family memory and teach an important lesson every young citizen should learn. It is the simplest and most effective way to demonstrate to our children the greatest gift of American citizenship.

That's why we have created the Take Your Kids 2 Vote Campaign to help you teach your children why voting matters and how democracy works. We want to make Election Day 2008 a true lesson in democracy for our children, make them proud to be Americans, and make our country stronger in the process.

You can find out about Take Your Kids 2 Vote and the many activities involved in this campaign on our website, **www.takeyourkids2vote.org.** You will learn how you and your family, friends, and neighbors can become involved and join in the fun. At a time when our politics can be divisive and elections can be so negative, Take Your Kids 2 Vote is a unique, positive experience and a great opportunity to teach our children about the enduring values of American democracy. It is a very important lesson for them—and critically important for our nation's future.

Please "Take Your Kids 2 Vote" and make democracy a family affair!

★ ★ ★

DINNER TABLE DEBATE

At What Age Should Kids Vote?

Ask the kids their opinion. There are some who believe that youngsters should be allowed to vote before they are eighteen, maybe even at sixteen. Supporters of the notion argue that teens often work and pay taxes on their earnings and so should not be subject to "taxation without representation." (Americans fought a war about that, now didn't we?) Some argue that if teens went to the voting booth at younger ages, they would grow accustomed to casting ballots and be more likely to become habitual adult voters—a good thing. Supporters of youth voting rights also say this might even boost the voter turnout of their parents—also a good thing.

Here's the other side. Legally, kids are not adults with adult rights until they reach the age of eighteen. Voting is a serious responsibility and requires a certain maturity most teens simply don't have. One could also argue that considering how well versed most young people are in current affairs and history these days, they are simply not prepared. Whatever side you're on, conclude the debate with a family vote on the issue!

★ ★ ★

Veterans Day
November 11

A Bit of History

What's the difference between Veterans Day and Memorial Day in May? Veterans Day is to thank all men and women who have served in the military during times of war and peace. Memorial Day honors those who died while serving our country. Yes, Veterans Day used to be called Armistice Day and celebrated the signing of a truce between Germany and the Allied forces on the eleventh hour of the eleventh day of the eleventh month in 1918 that ended the First World War. President Wilson declared the first Armistice Day in 1919 to honor those who had participated in the war.

In 1954, President Eisenhower signed legislation to change the name to Veterans Day to also honor all who had served in America's subsequent wars. Over the next nearly fifty years, the holiday gradually lost much of its meaning. For too many Americans, it was just another day off. After the September 11 attacks and the wars in Afghanistan and Iraq that followed, Veterans Day has taken on renewed meaning for many and a better understanding of the sacrifice, the "courage, duty, and honor" of the U.S. military. Today, we see special programs and activities in most schools and communities across the country and rightly so.

"I Didn't Know That"

- There are almost 25 million veterans in the United States, 1.4 million of whom are women.
- Over 48 million Americans have served in the military since 1776.

Chriss Tells a Story: A Veteran's Tale

Not too long after John F. Kennedy became the thirty-fifth president of the United States, my family was sitting around the dinner table one night in Sioux City, Iowa, where I was born and raised. Before dinner, we'd all seen a story on the local evening news about a soldier who had been awarded a medal for bravery. I was thirteen at the time; but my younger sister, Sue, was only ten and piped up, "Hey, Dad. How come you don't have any medals?" My father, a World War II veteran, saw more action than most during his five-year stint as an Army engineer—North Africa, Sicily, Utah Beach, the Battle of the Bulge.

Dad, who never spoke of the war, sighed and told my sister that he was, in fact, owed some medals, but he hadn't bothered to pick them up at the time. That would have been the end of the story except that my sister sat down the next day and ripped off a letter to the new president telling him, "My father won all these medals in World War II, and he never got any of them. Could you find them and send them to him?"

My brother and I thought this was pretty funny, but she got the last laugh. About six weeks later, a small cardboard box arrived in the mail

- The biggest battle that Americans ever fought was the Battle of the Bulge in World War II. More than six hundred thousand American troops took part, more American soldiers than had even fought at Gettysburg.

They Deserve to Be Honored

No one group of Americans is more deserving of a day honoring their service to our country than the members of the U.S. military. Make sure your children, first of all, understand that important truth. Then, find out what activities your children's schools have planned for this holiday. You might let the teachers know that the federal government

addressed to my sister with a very official-looking label—United States Department of Defense. When she opened it, she found a raft of medals including a Bronze Star and a Purple Heart. Of course, we bombarded Dad with questions about how he won the Bronze Star, but characteristically, he refused to talk about it, saying only, "It wasn't anything. I was just doing what I was supposed to do."

Thirty-five years later, in August of 1997, my husband and I took our son, then just eleven, to Normandy. There, we rented a car and followed exactly the path my father's platoon had taken, fighting all the way, from Utah Beach to Cherbourg in the D-day invasion. We did it because we wanted Ian to understand the great sacrifice his grandfather and so many others had made for him. We brought back pictures and mementos for Dad and planned on sharing them at Christmas. My father died unexpectedly a month after we returned.

The local American Legion provided a three-gun salute for Dad's funeral, and as his casket was lowered, Ian took the sand from Utah Beach he'd carefully saved in a small plastic bag for his grandfather and sprinkled it into the black Iowa earth.

★ ★ ★

has lots of material and resources that can help classes from K through 12 observe this day in an appropriate and interesting manner. One of the best places to go for ideas is the Department of Veterans Affairs, which offers a number of programs. Check out their "Lessons of Liberty" project and other kids' activities at **www.va.gov**.

- Ask your children to write a letter to their school principal suggesting that some local veterans of different generations speak about their experiences at an all-school assembly. Your local chapters of the American Legion or the Veterans of Foreign Wars are usually more than happy to help provide speakers for school assemblies or to talk to students in classes on that day.

• Ask your children to write letters to a veteran the family knows, thanking him or her for their service to our country. They can download patriotic stationery at **www.jetler.com/stationery_by_jo/patriotic_index.html** or for very young kids, on **www.billybear4kids.com/USA/flag.html.**

• Interview a relative who served in the armed forces or who is serving today and write up the veteran's experiences to share at the family Veterans Day dinner table.

• Older kids—from junior high up—can audiotape or videotape veterans and submit their interviews to be included in the Veterans History Project at the Library of Congress. The Library will send you a kit that explains exactly how your kids can help preserve history through this creative project. Request one at **www.loc.gov/vets/**. Again, don't forget your child's school. Other kids might also want to get involved.

• Younger children can pick one of the core values of one branch of the military and write a story or poem or do a drawing about what that value means to them.

• Or make a heroes' tree. You'll need some patriotic stickers and a poster board. Have your kids' draw a large tree on the poster board. Then ask them to find examples in history of men and women who exemplified the military's core values. Give them a patriotic sticker for each hero they find, and the tree will be blooming with everything from flags to fireworks.

• Most important of all, do something that supports a soldier on active duty right now. Send a letter or care package. Help a serviceman or -woman's family back home. Make a donation to a soldiers' fund. For a place to start, go to the website **www.Americasupportsyou.mil** where you'll find a list of over 150 organizations that support the military and their families. On the site, you can also read messages from the troops that tell you how important the support of those back home really is.

DINNER TABLE DEBATE

To Serve or Not to Serve . . .

In Israel, every young man and woman is required to provide one year of service to their country. Many here in this country argue that our young people, for whom service is strictly voluntary, ought to give a year to their country as well. What do you think? More important, what do your children think? Start the discussion by asking your children to list ways they have served others over the past week.

Next ask them how they would feel about spending their first year out of high school serving America rather than going to college or to work.

- Do they think a universal service "draft" is right or wrong, constitutional or not?
- What kind of service should be allowed? How would they choose to serve—in the military or in some other kind of service like Freedom Corps?
- Do they think a year experiencing the real world before going to college would better prepare young people for the rigors and responsibility of academic life—and help them grow up?

★ ★ ★

Thanksgiving

Fourth Thursday in November

A Bit of History

Most of us know something about Thanksgiving but not the whole story. We know about the turkey and the stuffing, the cranberry sauce and the pumpkin pie. And we know the holiday has something to do with the Pilgrims celebrating a successful harvest after a particularly difficult year and inviting the local Wampanoag Indians over to take part in the feast.

But there is more to it than that. Yes, the Pilgrims in the Plymouth Colony did have a Harvest Feast in 1621. And during colonial times, various Harvest Festivals were held in many of the colonies on different dates, usually in October. In November 1789, George Washington declared an official day of thanksgiving after the Constitution was signed but that was just one day. It was Abraham Lincoln in 1863, over seventy years later, in the midst of the Civil War, who made Thanksgiving Day a national holiday to be celebrated every year on the last Thursday of November. His official declaration establishing the holiday is interesting to read because even in the middle of that terrible war, he rightly saw that there are always reasons for Americans to be thankful and optimistic about the future. Help your children read it and learn from it at **www.historyplace.com/lincoln/thanks.htm**.

"I Didn't Know That"

- The main course for the Pilgrims at that first Harvest Feast wasn't turkey but was probably venison, supplied by their Indian guests. And the meal definitely didn't include pumpkin pie, bread rolls, or stuffing. The Pilgrims had no ovens for baking and very little sugar for sweets. Yes, it was a hard life!

• The Pilgrims didn't use forks so it was knives, spoons, and fingers only for the first Thanksgiving.

• Each year, the president pardons a turkey, and nobody knows exactly why. Some say it happens because Abraham Lincoln pardoned his son Tad's pet turkey. After President Bush pardoned a turkey in 2005, the gobbler, like a Super Bowl champion, was flown to Disneyland to serve as grand marshall in Disneyland's Thanksgiving Parade.

• In case you ever wondered, the average American consumes, on average, forty-five hundred calories at a Thanksgiving dinner, but then who really cares? Just pass the mashed potatoes.

Giving Thanks

Here are some extra "helpings" to enrich your family's celebration of this special day.

• Attend a local Thanksgiving service at your church or synagogue—often held to give thanks during the holiday week.

• Around the Turkey Day dinner table, ask everyone to "count their blessings" by sharing what they are most thankful for.

• Ask one of the younger family members to tell the story of the first Pilgrim celebration. A book that a third or fourth grader can read aloud to the family is *Pilgrim's First Thanksgiving* by Ann McGovern and Elroy Freem (Scholastic) or *The First Thanksgiving* by Linda Hayward (Random House for Young Readers).

• One of the most interesting things you can do on Thanksgiving is to invite a newly arrived family from another country to take part in your family's holiday dinner. An immigrant family may surprise your kids with their stories of hardship and happiness in coming to America. Make sure to serve at least one dish from your guests' native country, and let the kids make it.

• You can also get them involved in doing some craft projects for Thanksgiving ahead of the big day. One of the nicest, suggested by Enchanted Learning at **www.enchantedlearning.com/crafts/thanksgiving/thankfultree**, is making a "Thankful Tree." First, have the kids trace an outline of their hands on colored construction paper and cut it out. Then, they can write their names and what they are thankful for on their "hand." Finally, make a tree with plenty of branches out of brown construction paper and paste it to another sheet or a bulletin board. Tack or paste the hands on the tree.

• There are lots of other websites that also have some fun suggestions for holiday crafts of all kinds and Thanksgiving jokes (mostly groaners) that can be told at the table such as "How did the *Mayflower* show that it liked America? It hugged the shore." Well, the kids might think that they're funny! Go to **www.kinderart.com** or **www.parents.com** or **www.theholidayspot.com** for ideas.

• Everybody getting a bit restless waiting for dinner? Play the "Let's Talk Turkey" Thanksgiving History quiz on **www.familyeducation.com** (click on Quiz Central) or make your own version of *Thanksgiving Jeopardy!* The top scorer gets his or her choice of white, dark, or the drumstick.

• Commit the family to an act of community service to help those in need during the holiday season that begins after Thanksgiving—help restock a food pantry, contribute toys to a toy drive, bake cookies for a charity bazaar, work at a food bank. Make the kids understand that "giving" is part of Thanksgiving as well. You can find opportunities for serving in every community. The websites **www.idealist.org** and **www.pointsoflight.org** also list volunteering ideas for people of all ages.

Learning to Give

The important values of giving and sharing have characterized the American spirit since that first Plymouth thanksgiving feast. But, let's face it, most children aren't born generous. They have to learn the value of sharing. And while we may not have Bill Gates's billions to donate, children need to understand that everyone has something to give. Help your children learn this important lesson by talking about the "giving" part of Thanksgiving.

- Ask your kids, if they won a million dollars in the lottery, how much would they keep and how much would they give to help others? Who would they give it to and why?
- Another angle to explore: Who does more to help people—private individuals or government? Do they help in different ways?
- What are the ways they could give? Help out at a food pantry? Help deliver Meals on Wheels? Collect toys for Christmas gifts for needy kids? Could the whole family commit to giving to others during the holiday season?

★ ★ ★

Dr. Martin Luther King Jr. Birthday

January 15

A Bit of History

This holiday is observed on the third Monday in January around the time of Dr. Martin Luther King Jr.'s birthday, which is January 15. After King's death in 1968, a bill was introduced in Congress to make King's birthday a national holiday. An important supporter of the holiday was musician Stevie Wonder, who released a single called "Happy Birthday" to popularize the idea. Six million signatures were collected on a petition asking Congress to pass the bill, which was the largest petition in favor of an issue in U.S. history. In 1983, President Reagan signed legislation creating a federal holiday to honor the great civil rights leader who changed America.

"I Didn't Know That"

- He went to Morehouse College when he was only fifteen years old.
- He got a PhD from Boston University and met his wife, Coretta, in Boston.
- He was the first African American to be on the cover of *Time* magazine.
- He was the youngest man to win the Nobel Prize.
- On January 17, 2000 for the first time, Martin Luther King Day was officially observed in all fifty U.S. states.

Honoring Dr. King

Most schools will mark Dr. King's birthday with programs or projects, but here are some suggestions for other ways you can help your children understand the importance of Martin Luther King Jr.'s birthday and his importance to America.

• Have your child read a book about Martin Luther King Jr. or other leaders of the civil rights movement. Here are some we recommend:

- *Martin's Big Words: The Life of Martin Luther King Jr.* by Doreen Rappaport (Jump at the Sun), ages 4–8
- *A Picture Book of Martin Luther King Jr.* by David Adler and Robert Casilla (Holiday House), ages 4–8
- *I Have a Dream* by Margaret Davidson (Scholastic Paperback), ages 9–12
- *If You Lived at the Time of Martin Luther King* by Ellen Levine (Scholastic), ages 9–12
- *Rosa Parks: My Story* by Rosa Parks and Jem Haskins (Dial Books), ages 10 and up

• The website **www.enchantedlearning.com** has several printable books about Dr. King, including one called *I Have a Dream,* which describes his dream of equality for all. It encourages kids to write about a personal dream of theirs that would improve the world and how they would make their dream come true.

• Watch a DVD about Martin Luther King Jr. Some suggestions: *Biography: Martin Luther King Jr.: The Man and the Dream,* A&E DVD Archives or do a little time traveling in an animated adventure called *Our Friend Martin,* starring Ed Asner and Levar Burton (Twentieth Century Fox).

• On his actual birthday, take your kids on a Web tour of the most important sites of the civil rights movement. You will find a guided

An American Tale: The Little Girl in a White Starched Dress

In 1960 when she was six years old, Ruby Bridges made history by becoming the first African American child to attend an all-white elementary school, the Frantz Elementary School in New Orleans. For an entire year, she was the only child in the school as white parents kept their children home in protest.

Recalling that time to *Guidepost* magazine, Ruby remembers walking through the angry, shouting mob as someone held up a black doll in a coffin, which frightened her. But she has also said that on her first day at school, "A young white woman met us inside the building who smiled at me." It was her teacher, Mrs. Henry. "I couldn't have gotten through that year without Mrs. Henry," she said. "Sitting next to her in our classroom, just the two of us, I was able to forget the world outside. She made school fun. We did everything together. I couldn't go out in the schoolyard for recess, so right in that room we played games and for exercise we did jumping jacks to music.

"I remember her explaining integration to me and why some people were against it. 'It's not easy for people to change once they have gotten used to living a certain way,' Mrs. Henry said. 'Some of them don't know any better and they're afraid. But not everyone is like that.'

tour on the National Park Service website, "We Shall Overcome: Historic Places of the Civil Rights Movement," at **www.cr.nps.gov/nr/travel/civilrights.**

- Martin Luther King Jr.'s "I have a dream" speech is one of the most important speeches in American history. You and the kids can listen to it on the History Channel at **www.historychannel.com** as well as Robert Kennedy's sad announcement of Dr. King's death. Ask your children why they think the speech is so powerful and had such an impact on America?

"Even though I was only six, I knew what she meant. The people I passed every morning as I walked up the school's steps were full of hate. They were white, but so was my teacher, who couldn't have been more different from them. She was one of the most loving people I had ever known. The greatest lesson I learned that year in Mrs. Henry's class was the lesson Dr. Martin Luther King Jr. tried to teach us all. Never judge people by the color of their skin. God makes each of us unique in ways that go much deeper."

In 1964, Norman Rockwell, America's most well-known illustrator of the time, did a painting of a little girl in a starched white dress holding a book and marching bravely off to school escorted by four federal marshals. Ruby Bridges is probably the little girl in that now-famous painting, though no one knows for sure because the artist left no notes. The painting, which appeared in *Look* magazine and was called *The Problem We All Live With,* touched a nerve and became a symbol of the civil rights movement's struggle for justice and equality, opportunity and respect. You can show your children the painting on the website at **www.guggenheim.org/exhibitions/past_exhibitions/rockwell/problem.html** and read *The Story of Ruby Bridges* by Robert Coles, ages 4–8, or *Through My Eyes* by Ruby Bridges, ages 9–12, both published by Scholastic.

★ ★ ★

- Dr. King's life was one of service to others. Make his birthday a day of service for your family by volunteering at a local organization. Many areas also have special events around Dr. King's birthday that emphasize tolerance, diversity, and understanding. Check your local newspapers.

DINNER TABLE DEBATE

I Have a Dream

Dr. Martin Luther King's "I have a dream" speech, given on the steps of the Lincoln Memorial, is one of the most powerful and moving moments in American history. There is no better time than his birthday to talk with your children about the ability of one individual with a dream to change the world.

- Ask your kids how Dr. King, just one man, was able to make such a difference in American life and then ask them to name other great men and women with a dream who changed their world.
- What characteristics do they share: courage, determination, fortitude, a belief in right and wrong, the power to persuade, leadership?
- Why have dreams been important to America? What role have they played in our history?
- Then, get to the heart of the matter. Ask your children to share their dreams, what they hope to achieve in their lives. Find out how big they can dream.

★ ★ ★

Presidents' Day

Third Monday in February

A Bit of History

Presidents' Day started out as George Washington's Birthday, who, according to the calendar that has been used since at least the mid-eighteenth century, was born on February 22. At the beginning of the nineteenth century, it had become a big-deal national holiday celebrated with speeches and festive dinners, usually given by prominent people, in honor of the "Father of Our Country." Then, along came Abraham Lincoln, whose birthday was on February 12. The first official observance of his birthday occurred in 1866, the year after his assassination. Lincoln's birthday, unlike Washington's, wasn't a federal holiday and was never celebrated in the states that had been part of the Confederacy. For over a hundred years, however, both holidays were celebrated in many states as schools, banks, and most government offices closed in honor of our two greatest presidents.

Then, in 1968, Congress designated the third Monday in February as a day to honor all presidents, the great and the not-so-hot. This, in our humble opinion, wasn't the best idea ever concocted in those hallowed halls. Given their extraordinary lives and their unmatched service to this country, we believe Washington and Lincoln ought to have their own celebrations as they once did. If for no other reason than that our children need heroes, Congress ought to reconsider Presidents' Day and give our two greatest presidents their due.

"I Didn't Know That"

Some Facts About the "Father of Our Country"

- Washington left school at fifteen to become a surveyor. His mother couldn't afford to send him to college.

• At six feet tall and two hundred pounds, he was one of our tallest presidents and considered unusually tall for a man of his time.

• He survived smallpox; and, yes, he suffered from toothaches for years. He had all his teeth pulled when he was fifty-seven and wore false teeth made of ivory.

• Maybe that's why the six white horses in his stables had their teeth brushed every morning on his orders.

• He also bred hound dogs that he treated like members of the family. He gave some of them unusual names such as True Love and Sweet Lips.

• He had two ice cream freezers installed at Mount Vernon.

• But he had to borrow money to attend his inauguration.

• He was our only president elected unanimously.

Some Facts About "Honest Abe"

• Before becoming a lawyer and a politician, he worked as a rail splitter, store clerk, surveyor, postmaster and, briefly, as a soldier.

• At six feet, four inches he was the tallest president in U.S. history, and his favorite sport was wrestling.

• He was the only president to receive a patent, for lifting boats over shoals.

• He grew a beard at the suggestion of an eleven-year-old girl who thought it would improve his looks.

• He was not the featured speaker at the dedication of the Soldier's National Cemetery in Gettysburg. The featured speaker spoke for two hours. Lincoln spoke for two minutes and thought his speech was a failure. So did the *New York Times* in its review. You can read the Gettysburg Address—in fact, you can see Lincoln's drafts and the only known photograph of Lincoln at Gettysburg—at the Library of Congress website, **www.loc.gov/exhibits/gadd/gadrft.html**.

• He is the president most frequently portrayed in movies and written about by historians.

- About ten days before he was assassinated, he dreamt that he would die.

Let's Be Proud of Our Presidents

As a young boy, Abraham Lincoln was inspired by reading stories about one of his heroes, George Washington. It worked. So, we believe, it can work again for our children if we make our children proud of our presidents.

Sadly, for much of the school year, our presidents—including our greatest—can get short shrift in social studies classes. Once upon a time, Americans learned to read by reading tales of our presidents. Children, like young Abe Lincoln, knew the story of George Washington and the cherry tree. Later generations learned that Abraham Lincoln was so honest he walked miles to return a few pennies a customer had mistakenly given him when he was a clerk.

Your kids, however, may have been taught to have a slightly different view. They may know that Washington was a slaveholder, that he was vain and not very intellectual. They may have also learned that Lincoln suffered from depression, was fiercely ambitious, and did not have the enlightened beliefs about race that we now hold. So on Presidents' Day, help your children understand that both of these men were genuine heroes, who saved our country at critical times. Emphasize the achievements of these two great past leaders who contributed so much to our and their heritage and here are some ways to do it.

- Read a book about Washington. Some good choices are:

  ✻ *A Picture Book of George Washington* by David Adler (Holiday House), ages 4–8

  ✻ *George Washington and the General's Dog* by Frank Murphy (Random House Books for Young Readers), ages 4–8

- *When Washington Crossed the Delaware* by Lynne Cheney (Simon and Schuster), ages 6–10
- *His Excellency George Washington* by Joseph Ellis (Knopf) or *1776* by David McCullough (Simon and Schuster), for older readers or for the whole family to listen to on audiobooks

• DVDs or videos to watch: *The Crossing,* A&E Home Video; *George Washington, Founding Father,* A&E Biography; *George Washington: The Man Who Wouldn't Be King,* WGBH Boston; *Founding Brothers* and *Founding Fathers,* A&E Home Videos.

• Take a virtual tour of Mount Vernon, the home Washington loved, preserved as it was in Washington's day. It's a wonderful site to learn how people lived in colonial America with photos and information about everything from how Washington's food was cooked to how his garden grew. Kids can even send an online "postcard" of George Washington to a buddy or Grandma and Grandpa. The website is at **www.mountvernon.org**.

• Silhouettes were very popular in Washington's Day. There is a silhouette of George Washington at the website **www.apples4theteacher.com/coloring-pages/presidents-day** that can be colored online. Then, print it out and create a masking-tape frame.

• And, sure it is corny, but who would refuse some cherry pie, cherry cookies, or a cherry parfait for dessert in honor of our first president?

• Good books about Lincoln include:

- *Abraham Lincoln's Hat* by Martha Brenner (Random House), ages 4–8
- *Meet Abraham Lincoln* by Barbara Cary (Random House), ages 9–12
- *Abraham Lincoln: The Great Emancipator* by Augusta Stevenson (Aladdin), ages 9–12
- *Abraham Lincoln Grows Up* by Carl Sandburg (Voyager Books), young adults

- *Commander in Chief: Abraham Lincoln and the Civil War* by Albert Marrin (Dutton Young Adult), 12 and up
- *The Gettysburg Address* by Abraham Lincoln (Houghton Mifflin). Can be looked at by the whole family because of its powerful illustrations

• DVDs and videos to watch: *Biography: Abraham Lincoln*, A&E; *American Experience: Abraham and Mary Lincoln—A House Divided*, PBS; *Abe Lincoln in Illinois* starring Raymond Massey, Turner Home Entertainment; *Young Abe Lincoln* starring Henry Fonda, Criterion.

• A little girl might want to make a Lincoln penny pendant to wear on Presidents' Day. Cut out three stars, red, white, and blue, each a little larger than the other. Paste one on top of another and glue the penny in the middle of the top star. Punch a hole in the largest star and wear on a red, white, or blue ribbon.

• We love the Lincoln rap on **www.childfun.com** that includes this verse: *"Abraham Lincoln, I've been thinking / How you bravely led the land. / Once divided, now united / You made sure our house would stand."* Could your kids or their friends come up with their own rap for George or Abe? Maybe they can call it, "It's Hard Out Here for a President."

DINNER TABLE DEBATE

Want to Be President?

Most parents, at one time or another, wonder whether their child might one day be president, or at least they used to. We told you in our first chapter that the vast majority of youngsters today say they wouldn't want to be president. That's a sad commentary on what our kids are being taught about past presidents. It's also a reflection of what they see and hear from the media today about our political leaders. What about your child? Has he or she succumbed to this onslaught of negative messages about the value of public service? Why not ask them around the dinner table? Would they want to be president of the United States; why or why not?

For those who still might want to serve, discuss what they would want to accomplish for America. What would their top priorities be? And find out who they think were our best and worst presidents and why. It will tell you a lot about what they learn in school.

★ ★ ★

Memorial Day

LAST MONDAY IN MAY

A Bit of History

Memorial Day is much more than the three-day weekend when the pools open. To many people, especially the nation's thousands of combat veterans, this day, which has a history stretching back all the way to the Civil War, is an important reminder of the brave men and women who have made the ultimate sacrifice for their country.

The holiday was originally known as Decoration Day, when flowers were lain on the graves of the Civil War dead, both Union and Confederate. After World War I, observances began to honor all who had died in any of America's wars. Today, amidst family picnics, the end of school, and, yes, the opening of pools, there are still many observances of the solemn nature of the day. Flags are lowered to half-mast from dawn until noon local time and many communities observe a moment of remembrance in ceremonies throughout the nation.

The president or vice president lays a wreath on the tomb of the Unknown Soldier at Arlington National Cemetery where an American flag is placed on each grave. Many people in the Washington area, not just presidents, visit Arlington National Cemetery where over 240,000 servicemen and women are buried. There are many touching stories about those buried there. One is about Lieutenant Colonel William Joseph Potter Jr. who had been an Honor Guard, for a time, at the Tomb of the Unknown Soldier. During the Vietnam War, he went missing over Laos in December 1967. His remains, along with his crewmates, were returned almost thirty years later in August 1996, and he was finally lain to rest in the cemetery where he had once stood guard over so many others who had given their lives for their country.

Observing the Day

How can you and your family observe Memorial Day in meaningful ways? Here are some ideas.

- One friend of ours, who lives in Washington, D.C., takes his young children to the Vietnam Memorial each year at dawn on Memorial Day. It has become a family tradition and every year as his children grow, so does their understanding of the meaning behind this holiday. But you don't have to be in Washington to honor those who have served our country so honorably and with such courage. Almost every community has a war memorial or veterans' cemetery where you could take your children, too.
- There are also many observances at military bases, in churches, and put on by veterans' organizations throughout the country. Your best bet to find out what's happening in your area is to check your local American Legion or Veterans of Foreign Wars posts.
- Remember those who fought and lived to tell about it. Have your children take some flowers, books, and cookies to a nearby veterans' hospital.
- Watch a TV show about our fighting men and the most famous battles of the past. Or watch a video or DVD documentary about conflicts in which our soldiers fought and died such as *Iwo Jima* or *The Iraq War: One Year Later.* The History Channel and the Military Channel have many such DVDs available.
- There are also many movies or television series that your family can watch this weekend. One of the best miniseries about D-day made for cable is HBO's *Band of Brothers,* which Steven Spielberg and Tom Hanks produced and can now be bought or rented. But there are many good war movies, depending on the age of the children watching. Here are 10 American favorites to get the ball rolling:

1. *Saving Private Ryan*
2. *To Hell and Back*

3. *The Great Escape*
4. *Midway*
5. *The Longest Day*
6. *Patton*
7. *The Patriot*
8. *Gettysburg*
9. *Blackhawk Down*
10. *The Battle of the Bulge*

• For younger kids, try some craft activities. Have them design a poster to mark the day or a postage stamp to honor our soldiers. They can print out and color the flags of the Army, Air Force, Marines, and Navy, which can be found on **www.enchantedlearning.com/usa/flags**. And on the website **www.billybear4kids.com**, they can print out God Bless America bookmarks, stationery, and a symbol for their webpage if they would like to design one honoring our soldiers for the day. You can also print out a Medal of Honor Coloring Book from the Web at **www.homeofheroes.com/coloringbook.**

• In case they want to make a medal of their own, they can do that, too. Click on **www.va.gov/kids/k-5/medal.asp** and kids can create their own version of a Silver or Bronze Star. Ask them what act of bravery they think would deserve such a medal.

• As on Veterans Day, it is really important that you and your kids do something special to support our troops and especially those wounded in battle. One of our favorite organizations is Soldier's Angels (**www.soldiersangels.org**) and its goal: "Helping to bring home healthy soldiers." Their "Adopt a Soldier" program asks people to write a letter or a card to a soldier and send him or her packages a couple of times a month. Soldier's Angels also sends phone cards to the troops, asks for donations of air miles, and sends homemade "blankets of hope" to the wounded. It serves as an umbrella organization for many other smaller groups that support and help our soldiers and their families. You've probably asked your kids more than once to "be an angel." Now, you can give them real wings.

DINNER TABLE DEBATE

The Most Difficult Question of All

If your children ask—and they surely might on the day we honor fallen soldiers—"Is America worth dying for?"—we believe the answer is yes. But explaining this is never easy. Certainly, we have to acknowledge that we all feel tremendous pain when we hear of a soldier dying.

When eleven Marines were killed by a roadside bomb in Fallujah in 2005, a Navy corpsman who helped treat the wounded sent this e-mail home: "It's been tough on me & the other corpsmen because that group was some of our guys. So close to coming home, then this happens. I'm just so devastated, but I have got to pull myself together for my Marines. These guys became my family, my joy away from home and I'm grateful. I will give my life at any cost to protect them."

But ask your kids how they feel. And don't be startled or dismayed if they find this a very hard, very frightening question to answer. Who doesn't?

At the end of the movie *Saving Private Ryan,* young Private Ryan comes to the realization that many soldiers have died to save him, and he is confused by their sacrifice. As Captain Miller, the platoon leader, lies dying, he challenges Ryan to, "Earn it." On Memorial Day it is important to tell our children that we honor the fallen of the past by living responsibly and being grateful that there are men and women willing to make the greatest sacrifice to protect us and our freedoms.

★ ★ ★

Flag Day

June 14

Even though humorist Mark Twain once declared that "Old Glory" was the "gaudiest symbol the world has ever seen," the flag is very special to most Americans even if the day honoring it is usually ignored by most Americans. Flag Day, the holiday, which doesn't get anyone off from school or work, was first celebrated in 1877, exactly one hundred years after the Continental Congress adopted the Stars and Stripes as the official flag of the United States.

"I Didn't Know That"

What's the best way to celebrate Flag Day? By displaying the flag properly, of course. Here's what you should know about how to handle the flag with care.

- The flag is normally flown from sunrise to sunset. In the morning, raise the flag briskly. At sunset, lower it slowly. Always, raise and lower it ceremoniously.
- The flag should not be flown at night without a light on or in the rain.
- After a national tragedy or death of a national leader, the flag is flown at half-staff for a period of time only on orders of the president. It's called "half-staff" on land and "half-mast" on a ship. A governor can do the same for a state figure.
- Never let your flag touch the ground, never ever . . . period.
- Fold your flag when storing it. Don't just stuff it in a drawer or box. You can see exactly how to fold it on **www.usflag.org/foldflag**.
- When your flag is old and has seen better days, it is time to retire it. Old flags should be burned or buried according to the "flag code." Your local Boy Scout troop will know the proper ceremony and

An American Tale: Showing the Flag

To help your children understand the special meaning of our flag, tell them this story about Senator John McCain's time as a prisoner of war in Vietnam. One of his fellow prisoners was a young man named Mike Christian, who came from a small town near Selma, Alabama. At seventeen, Mike enlisted in the U.S. Navy. He later earned a commission by going to Officer Training School. Then he became a naval flight officer and was shot down and captured in 1967.

The Vietnamese allowed prisoners to receive packages from home. In some of these packages were handkerchiefs, scarves, and other items of clothing. Mike made himself a bamboo needle. And then, over a couple of months, he created an American flag, using what he had been sent, and sewed it on the inside of his shirt.

McCain told it this way: "Every afternoon, before we had a bowl of soup, we would hang Mike's shirt on the wall of the cell and say the Pledge of Allegiance. I know the Pledge of Allegiance may not seem the most important part of our day now, but I can assure you that in that stark cell it was indeed the most important and meaningful event."

One day, the Vietnamese guards searched the cell and discovered Mike's shirt with the flag sewn inside and confiscated this symbol of America's freedom and one American's courage. That evening, they returned and beat Mike Christian severely for more than two hours.

"The cell in which we lived had a concrete slab in the middle on which we slept," McCain recalled. "Four naked lightbulbs hung in each corner of the room. That night, I looked in the corner of the room, and sitting there beneath a dim lightbulb with a piece of red cloth, another shirt, and his bamboo needle was Mike Christian. He was sitting there with his eyes almost shut from the beating he had received, making another American flag.

"He was not making the flag because it made Mike Christian feel better. He was making that flag because he knew how important it was to us to be able to pledge allegiance to our flag and our country."

Every American child should hear Senator McCain's story. Ask your children to think about it the next time they say the Pledge of Allegiance to our flag.

★ ★ ★

probably performs it on a regular basis. If you have an old flag, give it to them; and take your kids to the ceremony. If you want even more information about flag etiquette, check out the American Legion website at **www.legion.org**, which is full of information, not just on the flag, but on all things patriotic. They also have a very informative DVD, *For Which It Stands*, that includes even more flag facts.

Saluting Flag Day

Although Flag Day, in many respects, has become one of those forgotten holidays, you can help your children remember why our flag is important as a symbol of our heritage and our values. Here are some ideas to let your children "salute" their flag in some fun and interesting ways.

- How about starting with a look at the original flag that inspired Francis Scott Key? Go online to "America's Attic," the Smithsonian Institution at **www.americanhistory.si.edu/ssb**, where you and your family can roll your mouse over the flag and find out lots more about it.
- Read a book about the flag; here are two good ones:
    - *The Flag We Love* by Pam Munoz Ryan (Charlesbridge Publishing), ages 4–8
    - *I Pledge Allegiance* by Bill Martin Jr. and Michael Sampson (Candlewick), ages 6–9

- When it comes to the flag, there are lots and lots of arts and crafts activities for young children on the Internet. There are coloring pages, downloadable songs, poems, and stories, and even instructions on how to cut a five-pointed star with just one snip (**www.surfnetkids.com/flag**). Here's our list of some great sites to help salute the flag:

www.apples4theteacher.com
www.enchantedlearning.com
www.annieshomepage.com
www.theholidayspot.com
www.childfun.com
www.kidsdomain.com
www.surfnetkids.com

- One of our favorite craft projects, considering the season, is making a patriotic plant pot. All you need is a terra-cotta pot, your child's imagination, and red, white, and blue acrylic paints. Decorate the pot with stars or stripes. Then fill with red and white impatiens and blue petunias and enjoy all summer long. Also, we love the idea of the whole family tacking up some paper on the wall and working together on a patriotic mural about the flag and what it stands for.
- Check out the website **www.pencilflag.com/remember** where you can download lots of different American flags and a very special pencil flag in honor of 9/11.
- Best of all, order a flag for the family that has flown over the Capitol. Anyone can do this by writing his or her senator or congressman and making the request. You can even ask that you receive a flag that has flown on a special day such as one of your children's birthdays. Enclosed with your flag will be a Certificate from the Architect of the Capitol certifying that your flag was flown as requested. If you mention in your letter that this flag is for a specific occasion, that information will be included on the certificate. You can get the information about cost on your senator's or congressman's website, usually under constituent services. It may take a while to receive, but wouldn't that be a great flag to fly on the Fourth of July!

DINNER TABLE DEBATE

"How Proudly We Hail"

Old Glory is more than just a flag for most Americans. It is a symbol of our nation's character and spirit. But should the reverence and respect we feel for the flag give it special protections? What do we tell our kids about those who want to burn and trample on our flag? Those are difficult questions because most Americans also value the right to free expression as well. So ask your kids:

- What does the flag mean to them? What comes to their mind when the flag goes by or when "The Star-Spangled Banner" is sung?
- Some are proposing an amendment to the Constitution to protect the flag. Is that a good or bad idea and why?
- Which is more important—respecting the flag or freedom of speech?
- If we place restrictions on attacking the flag, do we effectively ban protest? Protests kicked off our own Revolution. Remember the Boston Tea Party?

★ ★ ★

Independence Day

JULY 4

The Best of Holidays

We're sure you already make a big deal out of the Fourth of July, at least in the barbecue department. (Sales of barbecue sauce surge all over the country the week before the holiday.) But even before that grill was a gleam in Mr. Weber's eye, Americans have, right from the start, made a big deal out of our Independence Day.

A Bit of History

Just a day after signing the Declaration, John Adams wrote his beloved wife Abigail his instructions on how to celebrate America's birthday party. He knew it was going to be big, really big. He wrote, "I am apt to believe that it will be celebrated by succeeding Generations as the great anniversary Festival. It ought to be commemorated, as the Day of Deliverance by Solemn Acts of Devotion to God Almighty. It ought to be solemnized with Pomp and Parade, with Shews, Games, Sports, Guns, Bells, Bonfires and Illuminations from one End of this Continent to the other from this Time forward forever more."

"I Didn't Know That"

- How many changes did Thomas Jefferson make to the Declaration of Independence? The Continental Congress asked him to make eighty-six. And he did it—gritting his teeth.
- What's on the back of the Declaration of Independence? People who have seen the movie *National Treasure* want to know. Well, on the back, at the bottom, upside down is simply written: "Original Declaration of Independence dated 4th July 1776." According to the Na-

tional Archives, "While no one knows for certain who wrote it, it is known that early in its life, the large parchment document was rolled up for storage. So, it is likely that the notation was added simply as a label." Sorry, there are no hidden messages.

- Who besides America was born on the Fourth of July? Well, Louis Armstrong, the greatest of all jazz musicians, always said he had a Fourth of July birthday. Broadway song and dance man, George M. Cohan, who wrote "Yankee Doodle Boy" and, during World War I, "Over There," also said he was born on Independence Day. Others include songwriter Stephen Foster, who wrote "Dixie," President Calvin Coolidge, playwright Neil Simon, Yankees owner George Steinbrenner, and advice givers Ann Landers and her twin sister, Abigail Van Buren.
- Both Thomas Jefferson and John Adams, onetime rivals, ultimately friends, died on the Fourth of July, 1826, fifty years after they had signed the Declaration. Adams's last words, allegedly, were, "Jefferson still lives." But he was wrong; Jefferson had died two hours earlier.

The John Adams July 4 Celebration Plan

- Read all about it! So they will absolutely understand what they're celebrating, ask the kids to read a book about the Fourth or about a youngster living during Revolutionary times. Some good ones are:

  - *The Story of America's Birthday* by Patricia A. Pingry (Candy Cane Press), Preschool
  - *The 4th of July Story* by Alice Dalgliesh (Aladdin), ages 4–8
  - *Happy 4th of July, Jenny Sweeney* by Leslie Kimmelman (Albert Whitman and Company), ages 4–8
  - *Felicity: An American Girl* by Valerie Tripp (The American Girl Collection), ages 7–12
  - *Johnny Tremaine* by Esther Forbes (Yearling), ages 9–12

Myrna's Fourth of July Memories

For years, Macy's fireworks displays were over the Hudson River. Since our apartment windows look out over that river, we always hosted parties to watch the fireworks. One of the best Independence Days ever was in 1976—the Bicentennial. That year, hundreds of tall ships from around the world, mostly sailing ships from the nineteenth century, converged in New York Harbor to take part in the celebration. We had an all-day party to watch them as they made their stately voyage up to the George Washington Bridge. I remember my sons, who were very small at the time, helped me make a flag birthday cake. It is easy to do on any Fourth of July. Just bake or buy a sheet cake and decorate it to look like Old Glory with strawberries or raspberries and blueberries, all in season, and lots of whipped cream.

My son, the one who had his nose pressed against the glass watching the ships that day, is now an officer in the Navy Reserve who works and lives in Washington, D.C., in a condo overlooking the Potomac River with a great view of the Capitol and the Washington and Lincoln Memorials. Following family tradition, Jonathan, too, always hosts a Fourth of July party to watch the D.C. fireworks. A couple of years ago, a friend brought a wonderful young woman to the party who loved the fireworks, the view—and, not long after, my son. They were married recently and now host their own Fourth of July celebration every year.

★ ★ ★

- Make reading even more fun by making it a yearlong contest ending on July 4. Have the kids each make an American flag with stripes but no stars. Buy some gold stars—the old-fashioned "lick 'em and stick 'em" kind—and as your child finishes a book, give him or her a star. First one to get to fifty stars and fill in the flag wins a special treat. You decide the treat.
- Go to a parade. Many small towns have one and, kids, even today's kids no matter how many computer games they have, still

think it is fun to hear the bands playing, see the fire trucks with lights and sirens, and wave to their friends and neighbors who are marching or, if possible, take part themselves with their Boy or Girl Scout troop.

• No parade in your area? Make your own. Round up the neighborhood kids for an old-fashioned bike parade and let them decorate their bikes with red, white, and blue crepe paper and streamers. Judge the best decorations, but make sure that everyone gets a prize. Follow up with a neighborhood barbecue if you've still got the energy.

• As for "shews" or shows, most small towns and cities have concerts, too, and one of the best ways for the family to end a hot and busy day is sitting down and listening to a medley of patriotic tunes. The most well known—and televised—concerts are on the Mall in Washington, D.C., and the Boston Pops celebration on the banks of the Charles River.

• The Fourth of July without fireworks would be like Thanksgiving without the turkey. The first official Independence Day fireworks we know of took place in 1777 when the city fathers of Philadelphia shot off thirteen rockets—one for each of the states in the new union. If you want to have that once-in-a-lifetime experience of seeing an extraordinary fireworks display, then plan a Fourth of July in New York, or in Boston or Washington. Other spectacular shows are in State College, Pennsylvania, the largest all-volunteer firework display in the nation, and on the West Coast in San Francisco, Los Angeles, and Seattle.

• But if you want to have a New York– or Boston-sized fireworks display over the skyline of your own hometown or even in your backyard, you can, sort of, at least on your computer. Check out Phantom Fireworks at **www.fireworks.com** where you can upload a picture of your town or home and then set off your choice of Fourth of July fireworks on the screen. The kids can also download a fireworks screen saver! It will blow them away!

• For all the historical information on the Fourth of July you could ever want, go to **www.american.edu/heintze/fourth.htm**. You'll find an amazing Independence Day database, compiled by Jim Heintze at American University.

The Boy Who Created Our Flag

No debate tonight but how about a really patriotic story to tell the kids on the way to the fireworks?

Our current fifty-star flag was designed, believe it or not, in 1958 by a shy seventeen-year-old named Robert G. Heft for a school project in Lancaster, Ohio. Heft's class assignment was to create a new design that incorporated two new stars for Alaska and Hawaii, which were about to become our forty-ninth and fiftieth states. Heft spent his weekend arranging and sewing a new combination—five rows of six stars alternating with four rows of five stars.

But despite his hard work, his teacher gave him a B minus on the project. As Heft tells the story, the teacher said it lacked "originality" but promised the disappointed Heft that he would give him a higher grade if he could get Congress to accept the design.

No quitter, Heft took up the challenge and sent his flag to his congressman, who submitted the design to the appropriate committee in Washington. When Alaska and Hawaii were admitted to the union, it was Bob Heft's design that beat out the competition. On July 4, 1960, he stood next to President Eisenhower as his handmade flag was raised over the Capitol's dome.

Heft has said, just in case we need it, that he has also designed a flag with fifty-one stars!

★ ★ ★

Labor Day

First Monday in September

A Bit of History

Nobody knows exactly whose idea it was to celebrate the contributions of working men and women with a special day off from work. Two union officials, one named McGuire and one named Maguire, just to confuse things, both have some claim to creating the day. The first Labor Day parade was held in New York City in 1882 when the organized labor union movement was growing in strength. The workers' unions chose the first Monday in September for the celebration because it was halfway between Independence Day and Thanksgiving. The idea of honoring workers with a special day—and a vacation day—spread across the country, and some states designated Labor Day as a holiday before the feds did the same. Nowadays, Labor Day is also the kickoff for the campaign season in election years.

When it comes to Labor Day, it's important for youngsters to understand not only the contribution of workers but also how well protected, by law, workers are in this country, unlike so many nations around the world. Probably the best way to make children realize how lucky we are is to help them understand that, at one time, even young children in the United States worked long hours on farms, in factories, and in mines—the way many children still do in many parts of the world.

Also, Labor Day is a perfect opportunity to put some emphasis on that most American of values—hard work. This holiday can help kids understand that jobs give people dignity and hope and that there is honor in every kind of work.

Labor Day Activities That Make Work Fun

- For an interesting and educational end-of-summer read, try some of these books that can help your children learn about the history of labor in America as well as the importance of work.

  - *Curious George Takes a Job* by H. A. Rey (Houghton Mifflin), ages 4–8
  - *I Want to Be* series, published by Firefly, ages 4–8
  - *Fire! The Beginning of the Labor Movement* by Barbara Diamond Goldin (Puffin Books), ages 9–12
  - *Growing Up in Coal Country* by Susan Campbell Bartoletti (Houghton Mifflin), ages 9–12
  - *The Bobbin Girl* by Emily Arnold McCully (Dial), ages 6–9

- To give your children a vivid and powerful look at how things used to be for children in America, check out labor reformer Lewis Hine's photographs of the grueling lives of child workers in the early twentieth century. You can find these remarkable photographs and read the stories about hardworking children in 1908 at **www.historyplace.com/unitedstates/childlabor**.
- If school has already started, suggest a Jobs Day to precede the holiday. Parents can come to class and discuss their jobs and how they got to where they are today. Make it really fun by letting younger kids come dressed for the job they'd like.
- For fun Labor Day weekend activities, create worksheets with a line for each letter of the alphabet. Then ask your smaller children to think of a job for each letter or have them make their own minibook describing and illustrating their parents' workday.
- A good movie for teens to watch after the Labor Day picnic is *Norma Rae* (Twentieth Century Fox) in which Sally Field gives an Oscar-winning performance as a factory worker trying to unionize a company.

DINNER TABLE DEBATE

To Work or Not to Work

On the day when no one ought to be working, here are some questions the family just might want to consider about work. Ask everyone, "What do you think life would be like if no one ever had to work?" Or "Is all work of equal value to society?" Why or why not? Ask the kids how they would feel if they had to go to work.

The older members of the family might want to say something about the biggest changes they have seen since their first jobs and whether or not hardworking Americans work more or less than they used to. Also, ask them about those first jobs—and what they earned. Grandparents, especially, love to talk about how little they earned, and kids can't believe it. They might also want to think about one question that is especially important as they return to school, "So what do you want to do when you grow up?"

★ ★ ★

Constitution Day
September 17

A Bit of History

It's America's newest patriotic holiday and commemorates the day the Constitution was signed, September 17, 1787, in Philadelphia's Independence Hall. It used to be called Citizenship Day, but no one paid much attention to it. Then, in 2004, Congress passed a new law establishing Constitution Day, and now every school that receives any federal funding—even a beauty academy—must have some type of educational programming about the Constitution on that day.

In 2005, the first Constitution Day was celebrated on Friday, September 16, since the seventeenth fell on a Saturday, and schools across America celebrated in different kinds of creative ways. One awarded an iPod to the student who did best on a quiz about the Constitution. Others had debates about the Constitution, including one that asked whether establishing Constitution Day was even constitutional! In a fairly typical celebration, students in an elementary school in the Chicago area read the Constitution's Preamble together, dressed in red, white, and blue, and sang patriotic songs during assembly. Each student also received a small flag.

"I Didn't Know That"

- At the time, the Constitution was "penned" or written out by a clerk for a fee of $30 or about $325 today.
- Alexander Hamilton actually pushed the idea that state legislatures should be the natural home of farmers and merchants but that the national legislature (what would become the Congress) should be dominated by lawyers!

• At eighty-one, Benjamin Franklin was the oldest person to sign the Constitution. He was also the only person to sign both the Declaration of Independence and the Constitution. He needed help to sign the Constitution and cried as he penned his name.

• Only one amendment to the Constitution has ever been repealed. You guessed it. The Eighteenth—Prohibition.

• The entire document is displayed at the National Archives only on September 17 each year. During the rest of the year, visitors see only pages one and four through a bulletproof case in the Archives's rotunda.

Constitution Day, at School and at Home

Find out how your school is observing Constitution Day. Because it is new, some schools may not know about all the resources that are available to help them celebrate. Why not pass on this list of great websites to help your school celebrate Constitution Day with some fun programs and activities:

• To find out everything you ever wanted to ask about the Constitution but didn't know where to ask, check out the information on the websites of the National Constitution Center at **www.constitutioncenter.org** or the National Archives at **www.archives.gov**. Both are treasure troves of information about the document on which our country is based.

• Kids from all fifty states can be "Constitutional Convention delegates" at a unique two-day conference sponsored by the Constitution Center. This modern-day Constitutional Convention is held during the week surrounding the anniversary of the signing of the original. See if representatives from your children's school will be taking part in the event. If not, encourage them to apply for the next Constitutional Convention.

• There are also dozens of interesting programs about the day for educators and students as well as for parents and homeschoolers on the websites of a variety of organizations that include:

The American Bar Association	**www.abanet.org**
Court TV	**www.courttv.com**
The Bill of Rights Institute	**www.billofrightsinstitute.org**
C-Span	**www.c-span.org**
The Constitution Project	**www.constitutionproject.org**
Justice Learning	**www.justicelearning.org**
The Council for Excellence in Government	**www.excelgov.org**
Scholastic Magazine	**www.scholastic.com**
Campaign for the Civic Mission of Schools	**www.civicmissionofschools.org**

• Learning about the Constitution should be fun, too. Offer to bring in a red, white, and blue sheet cake or flag-topped cupcakes for the kids to have at the end of their Constitution Day activities. This is a birthday party, after all.

• And at home that night at dinner, read the Preamble aloud. It only takes forty seconds, and then ask the kids what they learned about the Constitution that day.

Does the Constitution Need Work?

This is one of those discussions for teenagers with no right or wrong answers. Adults, including constitutional scholars, differ on this one and have differed for more than a hundred years. And perhaps, it is one discussion to have with kids who have a real interest in the subject.

The question is whether they think that the Constitution is a "living document" and its meaning should be reinterpreted as times change. Or do they believe we should always try to interpret issues to reflect what the original Framers of the Constitution intended? For example, Article II created the Electoral College to provide protections for smaller states in the selection of our presidents. Today, some argue that the Electoral College is outdated and presidents should be elected directly by the people. Others say that would put larger states at a big advantage by almost guaranteeing that candidates will ignore the wishes and needs of states with small populations. See what your kids think.

★ ★ ★

Columbus Day

Second Monday in October

A Bit of History

Columbus Day was once a day filled with pride for Italian Americans throughout the country, a day for schoolchildren to honor a great explorer, and a reason for another really big parade. For years, Columbus was portrayed in our history books heroically, as a great visionary and adventurer. In 1892, the four hundredth anniversary of Columbus's voyage of discovery was such a big deal that there were festivities in every state of the Union organized years in advance. But in 1992, the five hundredth anniversary was practically ignored, and Columbus and the other early explorers received far more condemnation for their actions than praise for their achievements.

One thing we didn't know—and you probably don't, either—is that the Pledge of Allegiance was originally written for schoolchildren to recite as part of the 1892 Columbus Day celebration. That first time, 12 million children put their hands on their hearts and spoke the words of that first Pledge of Allegiance, and schoolchildren have been reciting it ever since with a slight modification.

Columbus Deserves Some Attention

If you want to downplay the debate that Columbus Day now often ignites but celebrate the holiday as something more than another sales day, there are plenty of activities, especially for younger children, that can make the day both educational and fun.

- Read a book about Columbus:

  - *Follow the Dream* by Peter Sis (Knopf Books for Young Readers), ages 4–8

❋ *Meet Christopher Columbus* by James T. Dekay (Random House Books for Young Readers), ages 9–12
❋ *Pedro's Journal* by Pam Conrad (Scholastic), ages 9–12

• Kids might also want to try some crafts projects related to maps and ships. The website **www.enchantedlearning.com** has directions for drawing a simple map that illustrates Columbus's voyages as well as making tiny replicas of his ships. Also, look for **www.kidsdomain.com/holiday/columbusday.html**, where you'll find one of the best sites for activities, books, information, quizzes, and games for Columbus Day and practically every holiday you can think of. Or take a look at the craft projects on the website **www.dltk-kids.com**, which has coloring pages that can be printed out and directions for constructing an easy-to-do but elegant Spanish galleon.

• An interesting website for older kids is the Columbus Navigation home page, which explores the history, navigation, and landfall of Columbus (**www.columbusnavigation.com**).

• Best of all, find out about the Christopher Columbus Fellowship Foundation (**www.columbusfdn.org**), an independent agency of the federal government that seeks to nurture and recognize pioneering individuals and programs that reflect the visionary spirit and pioneering heritage of Christopher Columbus. One way they do this is by giving Christopher Columbus Awards for sixth through eighth graders who work in teams with an adult coach. The team must identify a problem in its community and devise a solution that requires hands-on experience with the scientific process. Finalists get an all-expense paid trip to Walt Disney World and a week at the Christopher Columbus Academy. Each member of the winning team takes home a $2,000 saving bond, and they also have the opportunity to win a $25,000 community grant. Maybe the best way to celebrate Columbus Day is to make sure your kids' school knows about this program and makes plans to compete.

• And, of course, Columbus Day is the perfect excuse to order in pizza. You can find the history of pizza at **www.foodmuseum.com/pizzahistory/pizza**. Spaghetti's a great Columbus Day dinner, too.

The Case for Columbus

Whether it's pizza or spaghetti, asking whether Columbus is a good guy or a bad guy is a great dinner table discussion. If you have a teenager who has read Howard Zinn's dissection of Columbus or has heard in his or her social studies class that "Columbus makes Hitler look like a juvenile delinquent" and is half-convinced that Columbus Day should be changed to "Indigenous People's Day," this is a perfect time to debate the current case against Columbus. Is it really all that fair?

Yes, Europeans like Columbus brought diseases to the New World, but no one understood the causes of diseases at the time nor did they know that the native populations would have no resistance. Yes, the actions of the early explorers were cruel at times, but so were some of the practices of the native populations. Perhaps most important, shouldn't we ask—is there a right and wrong when cultures collide? It's important to learn about the positive qualities and culture of Native Americans, but isn't it also important that children learn that many explorers were daring, ambitious, and devout? Remember, we may need our own generation of "explorers" to one day take us far into space. That's worth some discussion, too.

★ ★ ★

8

LET'S TAKE A TRIP

"Tell me and I'll forget, show me and I may remember, involve me and I'll understand."

—Chinese Proverb

When we talked to parents in focus groups about their favorite childhood memories that were associated with patriotism, many recalled going on trips with their parents to historic sites. One woman told us that every one of her family's summer vacations was based on going to Civil War battlefields. Another said her father was determined to visit as many presidential libraries as possible, and that's what they did at least once a year.

Both of us have memories of visiting historic sites as well, and both of us have taken our kids on such excursions, which were usually big hits as long as a trip to the historic site included a visit to the gift shop.

Just as our children have, your children will remember family trips to see America's wonders—man-made and Mother Nature's—for the rest of their lives. So, get out a map, gas up the car, and get going!

We thought we'd give you a head start with what are our favorite places for family visits. Some are cities that have so many historic sites they can fill a whole vacation. Others are places that can be the historic highlight of a vacation that may pack in lots of other fun activities beyond studying America's past, like seeing the country's natural wonders by foot or bike or even burro. Many of our suggested spots are in some of the country's most beautiful areas.

Our Top 10 "Top Spots"

1. **Washington, D.C.** The mother lode of historic sites. Start with a tour of the Capitol and go from there. You can walk to the Washington Monument and then to the major memorials: the Jefferson, Lincoln, Vietnam War, Korean War, and World War II. Don't forget the National Archives, the Smithsonian, especially the Air and Space Museum, the Library of Congress, the White House, and the Mint. Kids also love the Spy Museum, Ford's Theater, and the Newseum. And nearby is Arlington Cemetery and George Washington's Mount Vernon. Kids usually end their visit to this city by asking, "When are we coming back?"
2. **Philadelphia Freedom.** If Washington is the "mother lode," then Philadelphia is the "father lode." Begin with Independence Hall National Park, where the Liberty Bell is displayed, and you can tour that small, hot, cramped hall where the Founding Fathers started it all. You'll also find the Constitution Center there, a remarkable interactive museum that clearly and exuberantly brings the Constitution to life. Nearby are various places associated with the framing of the Declaration of Independence and the Constitution. Also in Philadelphia is Betsy Ross's house and the Franklin Institute, and nearby is Valley Forge.
3. **The Grand Canyon (Grand Canyon National Park, Arizona).** Our pick as the grandest of our many national wonders. Make it part of a Best in the West trip to the region that could also include visits to the Lake Powell and Lake Mead recreational areas, Bryce Canyon and Zion National Parks, and the mighty wonder of Hoover Dam.
4. **New York City.** Start with the Statue of Liberty, the symbol of America; Ellis Island, the disembarkation point for so many new

Myrna's Family's Trip

Some of our vacations included visits to Colonial Williamsburg and to the nearby sites of Jamestown. Although my young sons fell asleep and snored through a New Year's Eve concert at the Governor's Palace in Williamsburg, they enjoyed the "18th Century" town itself and, of course, Yorktown, where the last battle of the Revolution was fought. I think both of them wrote reports about the visit that impressed their teachers, who gave them an "A" in history that term.

We also went to Washington, D.C. One of my sons, at age thirteen, insisted on having his picture taken in front of the White House. He's the one, naturally, who ended up, ten years later, working in Washington in Congress and then for the State Department.

On another great family vacation, we took our New York city slickers out west on a covered wagon ride through the Grand Teton National Park, helping them experience, for just a little while and in a lot more comfort, what the pioneers went through on the trek west. We also visited Indian pueblos near Santa Fe and Taos and went down the coast of California from Muir Woods to Alcatraz to Hearst's Castle, ending up on the beaches of Santa Monica. And, sure, in the backseat there were occasional sulks and squabbles, but we all look back on those family vacations as great times when we all were together and they learned about the many interesting and beautiful places in our country.

★ ★ ★

Americans; and 9/11's Ground Zero, the place we will never forget. Make sure to add a trip to the top of the Empire State Building and a tour of Wall Street. And there is a lot more to see as well in this "heckuva town."

5. **The Battlefield of Gettysburg (Gettysburg National Military Park, Gettysburg, Pennsylvania).** The "hallowed ground" where the battle that was the turning point in the Civil War was fought.

If you plan to visit only one Civil War battlefield, this is the one. Also nearby, find the Eisenhower home and Harpers Ferry. It's also a beautiful area tailor-made for the family who likes the outdoors.

6. **The Golden Gate Bridge (Golden Gate National Recreation Area, San Francisco, California).** An art deco masterpiece that they thought couldn't be built. It was—and under budget. Not to be missed with kids: the Exploratorium, a fire engine tour of the city, plus, of course, Alcatraz and the obligatory ride on a cable car.
7. **Boston's Freedom Trail.** A three-mile walking tour that begins with the Boston Commons and ends at the Bunker Hill Monument. Visit sixteen sites and structures of historic importance, including Old South Meeting House and Old North Church. See where John and Samuel Adams and Paul Revere, when he wasn't in the saddle, walked the walk.
8. **Mt. Rushmore (Mt. Rushmore National Monument, Rapid City, South Dakota).** Portraits in stone of Washington, Jefferson, Lincoln, and Theodore Roosevelt make up the world's largest sculpture, most impressive when illuminated at nightfall. An American site like none other—and another area perfect for the family who likes learning about Native American heritage and vacationing in the great outdoors.
9. **John F. Kennedy Space Center (Cape Canaveral, Florida).** On the way to Disney World, take a tour of the nation's space center, and your kids may even have the chance to have lunch with an astronaut and touch a real piece of Mars. Get a close up look at the Space Shuttle Launch pad and tour the Apollo/Saturn V Center. If you time it right, you can even view a shuttle or rocket launch.
10. **Colonial Williamsburg (Williamsburg, Virginia).** Walk the tree-lined streets of Virginia's "Revolutionary City" or listen to George Washington, Patrick Henry, and Thomas Jefferson expound on the times (colonial times, that is); tour historic buildings or learn how the colonials cooked their food, repaired their shoes,

and made music. It's all there and so much more in Colonial Williamsburg, Virginia's first capital, preserved as it was when it was the political and cultural center of one of America's most influential colonies.

Law and Order—Family Style

Traveling with kids can seem sometimes like herding cats. So, in the interests of finding peace—in the backseat, that is—we offer some tips, learned the hard way from our own experiences on the road, to make your family trips as fun and enjoyable as possible.

Tips for Visiting Sites Close to Home

- **Make it part of your schedule.** At the beginning of the year, sit down and plan your family history trips together—maybe every couple of months or, possibly, once a season. Put them on the family calendar at least two months in advance so that everyone knows—including teenagers—they have a family commitment they cannot break. No excuses.
- **Get exact directions.** Sometimes small museums or historic homes, for example, can be tucked away in obscure neighborhoods, and a lot of time can be wasted just trying to find where you want to be. If a spot has a website (and most do), check for directions. There's always Mapquest and other Internet map sites.
- **Call ahead.** Find out if there are any special exhibits, movies, or lectures ongoing or coming up and whether the site has helpful guides on hand to show your family around.
- **Check with the school.** Find out if your child's teacher is interested in him or her writing a report on the visit or discussing it with the class.
- **Read a book.** Use the visit to further spark your child's interest by reading a book in advance about the events associated with the

place you visit and the time when it was important. There are plenty of suggestions in this book to help.

• **Bring a friend.** Since you will be traveling probably quite nearby, let the kids bring a friend or two to share the day, lunch, and a souvenir for each.

Tips for Vacation Visits

• **Start with a winner.** On your first trip, go somewhere you know the kids will enjoy. There are many family vacation guides that can help you make your decision and plan the details, including *Family Fun Vacation Guides* for each region published by Disney Publishing or the ZagatSurvey *U.S. Family Travel Guide.*

• **Let them help you plan.** Let your kids plot the route, help you decide where you'll stay, and when you will splurge or save on kid-friendly hotels and restaurants. After your first vacation, let them pick your next. Give them two or three choices. If they squabble, let the whole family vote.

• **Don't try to do too much.** When including stops at historic sites as an important part of a family vacation, visit no more than a couple sites a day. More than that can be confusing and tiring for most kids. Intersperse visits to museums, especially, with some fun activities like swimming in the pool at the hotel or motel where you are staying or some time playing in a park.

• **Be a history detective.** Ask the kids to read at least one book, again, in advance about the history of the destination to which you are traveling. Let them fill you in about what they've found out before you leave; and on the way, ask them to surprise you with at least a couple of offbeat facts.

• **Take the camera.** Whether it is a video camera or a digital one, take plenty of pictures and let your kids take a lot of them, too. Then, ask media-savvy youngsters to put together a visual diary or even a minidocumentary of your vacation. You'll be amazed how creative they can be.

Chriss's Family Trip

Living near Washington, D.C., our son was lucky to have some of the country's most historic sites practically in his backyard. Over the years, he's tromped through the Smithsonian, seen the monuments on the Mall, and watched Congress in session at the Capitol. He had his ninth birthday at the Air and Space Museum, and as a toddler, he used to ride his "train" down the halls of the historic Old Executive Office Building in the White House complex when I worked there as the president's head speechwriter.

We've taken lots of trips, but I think any family would be hard-pressed to find a more interesting, educational, or inspiring historical stop than the USS *Yorktown* and Patriots Point Museum in Charleston, South Carolina. Ian was fourteen when we visited the big ship, and I don't know who was more amazed — me at the conditions of the engine room, where young sailors fighting in the Battle of Iwo Jima would have suffered terrible heat and a stifling lack of air or my son who loved seeing the planes on the flight deck, slouching in the flyers' chairs in the briefing room, and sitting behind the anti-aircraft guns up top.

More than twenty thousand kids stay overnight on the ship every year, usually on trips arranged by school, service organizations, or church groups, eating in the mess and sleeping in the "racks" just like the generations of sailors who manned "The Fighting Lady," as she was called, for almost thirty years. The *Yorktown* also serves as the headquarters for the Congressional Medal of Honor Society and the Congressional Medal of Honor Museum. It is a great family stop made even better by the fact that the Charleston area is jam-packed with history from America's earliest years right through the Civil War.

★ ★ ★

Top Spots—State by State

To give you some ideas of where to visit across the country on family vacations, we asked state historical societies and other "locals" to pick their favorite places, checked state tourism sites on the Web, and then added a dash or two of our own experience and came up with five "Top Spots" in every state you can consider for a family field trip or a well-deserved summer break.

We've also included national and state parks on our list because we believe part of being a good American is having an appreciation of our country's natural beauty as well as its gloried past. We couldn't include every local or state historical museum even though almost every state and many communities have great ones worth checking out. Instead, we recommend them all for a family visit.

We hope we didn't leave your favorites out, but there are really so many great places to visit in our wonderful country that listing only five spots per state was a tough call. Here are our recommendations for every state in the Union.

For specific information on sites, go to a search engine like Google and type in the "spot." All have websites that will give you plenty of details to help you plan your visit.

250 Top Spots Your Kids Will Love

Alabama

Civil Rights, the Civil War, and historic homes

- Birmingham Civil Rights Institute, Birmingham
- Huntsville Space and Rocket Center, Huntsville
- Tuskegee Institute National Historic Site, Tuskegee
- Fort Morgan Historic Site, Gulf Shores
- Ivy Green, Birthplace of Helen Keller, Tuscumbia

Alaska

Great natural beauty, the Gold Rush, and Native American heritage

- Denali State Park
- Glacier Bay National Park
- Alaska State Museum, Juneau
- Alaska Native Heritage Center, Anchorage
- White Pass and Yukon Route Railway, Skagway

Arkansas

A presidential library, historic towns, and the folk traditions of a region

- William J. Clinton Presidential Center, Little Rock
- Bathhouse Row, Hot Springs
- Prairie Grove Battlefield State Park, Prairie Grove
- Ozark Folkways Heritage Center, Winslow
- Eureka Springs Historic District, Eureka Springs

Arizona

Besides the Grand Canyon, other great sites of natural beauty plus our Wild West heritage

- Saguaro National Park, Tucson
- Heard Museum, Phoenix
- Town of Tombstone
- Petrified Forest National Park and the Painted Desert, Holbrook
- Wupatki National Monument, Flagstaff

California

So much to see—two presidential libraries, great national parks, and our preteens were absolutely awed by Hearst Castle

- Ronald Reagan Presidential Library, Simi Valley
- Richard M. Nixon Presidential Library and Birthplace, Yorba Linda
- Yosemite National Park
- Redwood National Park, Crescent City
- Hearst Castle, San Simeon

Colorado

America's favorite peak, western history, and great cliff dwellings

- Dinosaur National Monument, Dinosaur
- U.S. Air Force Academy, Colorado Springs
- Pike's Peak, Colorado Springs
- Colorado History Museum, Denver
- Town of Durango

Connecticut

A historic seacoast and the homes of great Americans

- Mystic Seaport, The Museum of America and the Sea, Mystic
- Mark Twain House and Museum, Hartford
- Mashantucket Pequot Museum and Research Center, Mashantucket
- Noah Webster House, West Hartford
- U.S. Navy Submarine Force Base Museum, Groton

Delaware

Lots of Revolutionary history in the first state that ratified the Constitution

- John Dickinson Plantation, Dover
- Winterthur Estate, Winterthur
- New Castle Court House Museum, New Castle

- Delaware History Museum, Wilmington
- Hagley Museum, Wilmington

Florida

So much to see and swimming, too

- Everglades National Park, Flamingo, Everglades City, and Homestead
- Historic St. Augustine
- National Museum of Naval Aviation, Pensacola
- Ringling Museum of Art, Sarasota
- Key West Lighthouse Museum, Key West, Florida

Georgia

Rich with the history of the Civil War, the advent of civil rights, and the library of a former president

- Jimmy Carter Presidential Library and Museum, Atlanta
- Martin Luther King Historic Site, Atlanta
- Chickamauga and Chattanooga National Military Park, Fort Oglethorpe
- Historic District, Savannah
- Andersonville National Historic Site, Andersonville

Hawaii

Besides the memorial to the USS *Arizona* at Pearl Harbor, interesting sites of Hawaii's ancient past and incomparable natural beauty

- Pu'ukohola Heiau National Historic Site, Kawaihae
- USS *Arizona* Memorial, Pearl Harbor
- 'Iolani Palace, Honolulu
- Pacific Tsunami Museum, Hilo
- Pu'uhonua o Honaunau National Historical Park, Honaunau

Idaho

Rich in pioneer history of both the good and the bad!

- Massacre Rock State Park, American Falls
- Nez Perce National Historical Park, Spalding
- Old Mission of the Sacred Heart, Coeur d'Alene
- Rock Creek Station and Stricker Homesite, Rock Creek
- Old Idaho Penitentiary, Boise

Illinois

The home of presidents—and Chicago, too

- The Abraham Lincoln Presidential Library and Museum, Springfield
- Ulysses S. Grant House, Galena
- Ronald Reagan Boyhood Home, Dixon
- Museum of Science and Industry, and The Field Museum, Chicago
- Lewis and Clark Interpretive Center, Hartford

Indiana

A station on the Underground Railroad, a famous battlefield, and Lincoln's boyhood home

- Lincoln Boyhood National Memorial, Lincoln City
- Levi Coffin House, Fountain City
- Tippecanoe Battlefield, Battle Ground
- New Harmony State Historic Site, New Harmony
- President Benjamin Harrison Home, Indianapolis

Iowa

Chriss's home state is filled with museums of local history, and Herbert Hoover's presidential library

- Herbert Hoover Presidential Library and Museum, West Branch
- Museum of Amana History, Amana
- Living History Farms, Urbandale
- National Mississippi River Museum and Aquarium, Dubuque
- Lone Star Steamer and Buffalo Bill Museum, LeClaire

Kansas

Frontier memories plus a civil rights landmark

- Fort Scott National Historic Site, Fort Scott
- Nicodemus National Historic Site, Nicodemus
- Dwight D. Eisenhower Presidential Library, Abilene
- Amelia Earhart Birthplace, Atchison
- Brown v. Board of Education National Historic Site, Topeka

Kentucky

The doorway to the West and Daniel Boone

- Fort Boonesborough State Park, Richmond
- Cumberland Gap National Historic Park, Middlesboro
- Kentucky Derby Museum, Louisville
- Mary Todd Lincoln House, Lexington
- My Old Kentucky Home State Park, Bardstown

Louisiana

Even after Katrina, New Orleans and its environs remain rich in history

- New Orleans Jazz National Historic Park, New Orleans
- Jean Lafitte National Historic Park and Preserve, six sites in south Louisiana including areas of New Orleans
- Cane River Creole National Historic Park, Natchitoches
- Fort St. Jean Baptiste Historic Site, Natchitoches
- National World War II Museum, New Orleans

Maine

Lots of "Down East" history. Go in the summertime!

- Colonial Pemaquid State Historic Site, Bristol
- Fort Knox State Historic Site, Prospect
- Wadsworth-Longfellow House, Portland
- Maine Maritime Museum, Bath
- Historic District and the Seashore Trolley Museum, Kennebunkport

Maryland

Where the Star-Spangled Banner waved, plus a stirring Civil War site

- Fort McHenry National Monument and Historic Site, Baltimore
- Antietam National Battlefield, Sharpsburg
- United States Naval Academy, Annapolis
- Historic St. Mary's City
- Clara Barton National Historic Site, Glen Echo

Massachusetts

Along with Boston's Patriot's Trail, two presidents, and the Pilgrims

- Plimouth Plantation, Plymouth
- John F. Kennedy Presidential Library and Museum, Boston
- Adams National Historic Site, Quincy
- Lowell National Historic Park, Lowell
- Salem Maritime National Historic Site, Salem

Michigan

Motown and Mackinac Island provide fun and history

- Fort Mackinac, Mackinac Island and Colonial Michilimackinac, Mackinac City

- Henry Ford Museum and Greenfield Village, Dearborn
- Cranbrook, Bloomfield Hills
- Gerald R. Ford Presidential Library, Ann Arbor, and Museum, Grand Rapids
- Great Lakes Shipwreck Museum, Paradise

Minnesota

Discover the history of the 1862 U.S.-Dakota War and the home of an aviation superstar

- Birch Coulee Battlefield and Lower Sioux Agency, Morton
- Fort Ridgely Historic Site, Fairfax
- Minnesota History Center, St. Paul
- Northwest Company Fur Post, Pine City
- Charles A. Lindbergh House, Little Falls

Mississippi

The cradle of the Civil War and the home of a civil rights leader

- Vicksburg National Military Park, Vicksburg
- Natchez National Historical Park, Natchez
- Beauvoir, Jefferson Davis's home, Biloxi
- Tupelo National Battlefield, Tupelo
- Medgar Evers House, Jackson

Missouri

Home to Harry Truman, Tom Sawyer, and the Pony Express

- Harry S. Truman Library and Museum, Independence
- Pony Express National Memorial, St. Joseph
- Mark Twain Museum, Hannibal
- Museum of Westward Expansion, St. Louis
- Laura Ingalls Wilder Home and Museum, Mansfield

Montana

Custer's last stand and where Meriwether Lewis on his way west signed his name

- Bighorn National Battlefield, Crow Agency
- Glacier National Park, West Glacier
- Museum of the Rockies, Bozeman
- Grant-Kohrs Ranch, Deer Lodge
- Lewis and Clark Trail, Pompey's Pillar, Billings

Nebraska

The home of the Homestead Act and lots of pioneer memories

- Homestead National Monument, Beatrice
- Strategic Air and Space Museum, between Omaha and Lincoln
- Museum of Nebraska History, Lincoln
- Chimney Rock National Historic Site, Bayard
- Fort Robinson, Crawford

Nevada

Great natural beauty, Hoover Dam, and towns that claim they are the best of the West

- Hoover Dam and Lake Mead, Boulder City
- Carson City Historic District, Carson City
- Virginia City Historic District, Virginia City
- Nevada Historical Society Museum, Reno
- Nevada State Museum, Las Vegas

New Hampshire

Heroes of New Hampshire's past

- American Independence Museum, Exeter
- Museum of New Hampshire History, Concord

- Christa McAuliffe Planetarium, Concord
- John Paul Jones House Museum, Portsmouth
- Daniel Webster Family Home, Franklin

New Jersey

Where Washington turned the tide

- Washington Crossing Historic Park, Titusville
- Monmouth Battlefield State Park, Manalapan
- USS *New Jersey,* Camden
- Princeton Battlefield State Park, Princeton
- Thomas Edison National Historic Site, West Orange

New Mexico

Great blend of Anglo, Hispanic, and Native American culture

- Chaco Culture National Historic Park, Nageezi
- Bandelier National Monument, Los Alamos
- Taos Pueblo, Taos
- Museum of Spanish Colonial Art, Santa Fe
- El San Miguel Mission, Santa Fe

New York

Besides the Statue of Liberty and the site of 9/11, there's the military, women's rights, and Niagara Falls, a very wet family vacation destination that Myrna's sons loved

- Franklin D. Roosevelt Home and Library, Hyde Park
- U.S. Military Academy, West Point
- Fort Ticonderoga, Ticonderoga
- Women's Rights National Historical Park, Seneca Falls
- Niagara Falls

North Carolina

The birthplace of flight and a historic lighthouse

- Wright Brothers National Memorial, Kitty Hawk (Kill Devil Hills)
- Cape Hatteras Light Station, Buxton
- Biltmore Estate, Asheville
- Fort Raleigh National Historic Site, Manteo
- Roanoke Island Festival Park, Manteo

North Dakota

The place that Theodore Roosevelt said made him the man he wanted to be

- Theodore Roosevelt National Park, Medora
- Chateau De Mores State Historic Site, Medora
- Double Ditch Indian Village State Historic Site, Bismarck
- Fort Totten State Historic Site, Fort Totten
- Former Governors' Mansion State Historic Site, Bismarck

Ohio

The history of aviation, the remains of an ancient civilization, and stop off for some music

- Dayton Aviation Heritage National Historical Park, Dayton
- John and Annie Glenn Historic Site, New Concord
- Hopewell Culture National Historic Park, Chillicothe
- Rock and Roll Hall of Fame, Cleveland
- National Underground Railroad Freedom Center, Cincinnati

Oklahoma

Yes, cowboys and Indians where the Trail of Tears ended

- Oklahoma City National Memorial
- Museum of the Great Plains, Lawton

- Tahlequah, Capital of the Cherokee Nation, Tahlequah
- Fort Gibson Historic Site, Fort Gibson
- National Cowboy Hall of Fame, Oklahoma City

Oregon

The last spot on the Oregon Trail and Lewis and Clark's final destination

- Lewis and Clark National Historic Park, Astoria
- End of the Oregon Trail Interpretive Center, Oregon City
- McLoughlin House National Historic Site, Oregon City
- John Day Fossil Beds National Monument, Kimberly
- Oregon Historical Society, Portland

Pennsylvania

Besides Independence Hall and Gettysburg, history from every era in our past

- Valley Forge National Historic Park, Valley Forge
- Brandywine Battlefield and River Museum, Chadds Ford
- Delaware and Leigh National Heritage Corridor, Bristol to Wilkes-Barre
- Eisenhower National Historic Site, Gettysburg
- Flight 93 National Site, Shanksville

Rhode Island

Newport and Providence are full of great places to see

- Newport Mansions, Newport
- Touro Synagogue National Historic Site, Newport
- South County Museum, Narragansett
- Roger Williams National Memorial, Providence
- First Baptist Church, Providence

South Carolina

A rich military history from the Revolution's "Swamp Fox," the beginning of the Civil War to the USS *Yorktown*

- Cowpens National Battlefield, Chesnee
- Fort Sumter National Historic Monument, Charleston
- Fort Moultrie National Monument, Sullivan's Island
- Patriots Point Naval and Maritime Museum, Mount Pleasant
- Historic District, Drayton Hall, Middleton Place, Charleston

South Dakota

Besides Mount Rushmore, a new memorial to Crazy Horse, plus where Wild Bill Hickock roamed

- Wounded Knee Battlefield, Pine Ridge Indian Reservation, Batesland
- Crazy Horse Memorial, near Mt. Rushmore
- Historic District, Deadwood
- Corn Palace, Mitchell
- Minuteman Missile National Historic Site, Western South Dakota

Tennessee

The home of two presidents, a Civil War battle, and a salute to icons of all-American music

- Shiloh National Military Park, Shiloh
- The Hermitage, Home of Andrew Jackson, near Nashville
- Andrew Johnson National Historic Site, Greeneville
- National Civil Rights Museum, and Graceland, Memphis
- Country Music Hall of Fame, Nashville

Texas

So much history packed into the Lone Star State

- The Alamo, San Antonio
- George H. W. Bush Presidential Library, College Station
- San Jacinto Monument and Museum, La Porte (near Houston)
- The Sixth Floor Museum at Dealey Plaza, Dallas
- Lyndon B. Johnson Library and Museum, Austin

Utah

Great natural beauty, where the railroad met and the Mormons settled

- Golden Spike National Historic Site, near Brigham City
- Temple Square, Salt Lake City
- Bryce Canyon National Park, Bryce
- Canyonland National Park, Moab
- Beehive House, Home of Brigham Young, Salt Lake City

Vermont

Remembering the Green Mountain Boys

- The Bennington Battle Monument, Bennington
- Ethan Allen Homestead, Burlington
- Mount Independence State Historic Site, Orwell
- Shelburne Museum, Shelburne
- Historic District, Montpelier

Virginia

So many places to see—the home of our first president, fabulous Colonial Williamsburg, and the cemetery that honors our bravest

- George Washington's Mt. Vernon, Mt. Vernon
- Jamestown Settlement and Yorktown Victory Center, near Williamsburg

- Appomattox Court House National Park, Appomattox
- National Air and Space Museum Udvar-Hazy Center, near Dulles Airport
- Jefferson's Monticello, Charlottesville

Washington

The place from which gold miners went north and the pioneers went south and the techies settled

- Klondike Gold Rush National Park, Seattle
- Whitman Mission National Historic Site, Walla Walla
- Fort Vancouver National Historic Site, Vancouver
- Mount Rainier National Park, Ashford
- Microsoft Visitor Center and Museum, Redmond

West Virginia

Focus on John Brown's raid, an important canal, and a stop at a historic hotel

- Harpers Ferry National Historic Park, Harpers Ferry
- Jefferson County Courthouse, Charles Town
- Kruger Street Toy and Train Museum, Wheeling
- Independence Hall, Wheeling
- The Greenbrier, White Sulphur Springs

Wisconsin

Almost every town has a museum of local history and a historic home

- Pabst House, Milwaukee
- Wingspread, Racine
- Hazelwood, Green Bay
- Richard I. Bong WWII Heritage Center, Superior
- Outagamie Museum and Houdini Historical Center, Appleton

Wyoming

Fort Laramie—the "Ellis Island" to the trail west and Buffalo Bill

- Fort Laramie National Historic Site, Fort Laramie
- Oregon Trail Ruts State Historic Site, Guernsey
- Independence Rock, Casper
- Fort Bridger State Historic Site, Fort Bridger
- Buffalo Bill Historical Center, Cody

Hit the Trails!

For families who love the outdoors, there are important and beautiful trails that run through many states that have facilities, in most cases, for either driving or hiking. So take some comfortable shoes and hit America's best trails.

- **The Appalachian Trail:** Georgia to Maine.
- **The Lewis and Clark National Trail:** Begins at Hartford, Illinois, and passes through portions of Missouri, Kansas, Iowa, Nebraska, South and North Dakota, Montana, Idaho, Oregon, and Washington.
- **Mormon Pioneer National Historic Trail:** Travels through five states—the general route is from Nauvoo, Illinois, to Salt Lake City, Utah, covering about 1,300 miles.
- **Oregon National Historic Trail:** The more than 2,000-mile-long trail passes through Missouri, Kansas, Nebraska, Wyoming, Idaho, and Oregon.
- **Nez Perce Historic Trail:** The Nez Perce (Nimiípu or Nee-Me-Poo) trail stretches from Wallowa Lake, Oregon, to the Bear Paw Battlefield near Chinook, Montana.
- **Pony Express National Trail:** More than 1,800 miles in ten days from St. Joseph, Missouri to Sacramento, California.

- **Santa Fe Historic Trail:** Was a commercial highway connecting Missouri and Santa Fe, New Mexico, and also went through Kansas, Colorado, and Oklahoma.
- **Trail of Tears:** National Historic Trail encompasses about 2,200 miles and runs though nine states—Tennessee, Georgia, Alabama, North Carolina, Arkansas, Kentucky, Illinois, Missouri, and Oklahoma.

America's Ten Most Historic Small Towns

Even America's smallest towns have their own website on the Internet called ePodunk at **www.epodunk.com**, which has put together its list of the most historic small towns in America based on the number of buildings listed on the National Registry of Historic Places and the number of Historic Districts. You can go to the site and find the most historic small town in every state and the Top 10 list of most historic small towns in the country. In case you'd like to visit, here they are:

- Shirley, Massachusetts
- Woonsocket, Rhode Island
- Wheeling, West Virginia
- Bristol, Connecticut
- Montpelier, Vermont
- Natchez, Mississippi
- Deadwood, South Dakota
- Hudson, New York
- Newport, Kentucky
- Quincy, Illinois

Still Looking?

- **National Park Service:** There are an amazing number of places to take youngsters in this country and some may be much closer to your home than you might imagine. A quick way to check for possible destinations is on the National Park Service website at **www.nps.gov** where you can check parks, recreation areas, and historic sites by zip codes and usually find a place to visit within driving distance. Your own state's official website also can be helpful because it almost inevitably lists local museums and places to go.
- **U.S. Military Bases:** The U.S. military has bases around the country; and while security has tightened since 9/11, many give tours, have open houses, or annual programs like the Andrews Air Force Base air show, which draws thousands to the Washington, D.C., area every year. Check with bases in your area to see if your kids could get a firsthand look at how our military protects them and all of us. And make sure they say, "Thanks for your service." Many bases have websites, so check them out.
- **Museums:** Of course there are great not-to-be-missed museums that kids will really enjoy in large cities, such as the Smithsonian in Washington, D.C., the Franklin Institute in Philadelphia, the Museum of Natural History in New York, and the Field Museum in Chicago as well as many children's museums in cities throughout the country. A list of children's museums, which often have a component about American history, can be found at the website of the Association of Children's Museums **www.childrensmuseums.org**. There are also hundreds of state and local historical museums that are worth a visit. Most state websites list these museums, often county by county. A good website that will lead you to every state's site is **www.govspot.com.**

Even though there may be squabbles along the way, a visit to a historic site or a vacation based on seeing several such sites will turn out to be among the happiest of your family's memories. Yes, going there is worth the trip. Trust us!

9

PATRIOT PROJECTS

"Individual commitment to a group effort—that is what makes a team work, a company work, a society work, a civilization work."

—COACH VINCE LOMBARDI

Andrea Warren, who writes history books for kids, told us that her love for history grew out of hearing stories as a child about her own family, especially her great-grandmother, Florence Abby Howe. Abby's life is a very typical American story. She was born in Vermont in 1849 and saw her brother go off to fight in the Civil War. He became very good friends with another young man in his unit; after the war, the young man, John Wesley Forest, came to visit and, there in Vermont, met Andrea's great-grandmother. He was heading west to Kansas, and a few months after he arrived, Abby got a letter from John asking her to marry him.

A proposal of marriage back then wasn't quite like tying the knot today. It meant leaving her family and traveling alone thousands of miles to a place called Kansas that might as well have been the other side of the world. It meant danger and uncertainty. But Abby Howe was like so many Americans of her day. She packed up her few belongings, said good-bye to a family she might never see again, and headed west for a new life.

Andrea tells the story: "For a long time, they lived in a one-room house, had three sons and lost them all to diphtheria, then had three more children, two daughters and a son. My great-grandfather started a bank and prospered, but lost it all in one of the financial panics of the time. When he died, he left Abby penniless, but she was very resourceful and she managed. She was very community-minded, started the town library, and when women got the vote, she ran for mayor with an entire female slate of candidates and they all won.

"They put into effect all the laws they wanted, things that the men had ignored—like fixing the roads, making sure dogs were on leashes. And when they accomplished what they wanted, they resigned and turned the town back over to the men. It was a lesson—don't ignore what is important to women!"

Abby Howe Forest followed the man she loved and made the best of a tough life. Andrea says she was a true example of America's "can-do spirit," and she wishes she could have known her great-grandmother. We'd like to have known her, too.

60-Minute Solutions

Abby's story is just the kind of inspirational American Tale that we hope will make your children want to learn about and love their country. We hope it also inspires you to want to make an even stronger commitment to put in that one hour a week to help them. We know it's tough; and, if you're like the rest of us, you're always swamped. But if Abby could cross miles of dangerous country, raise a family in very difficult times, and take on the town fathers as well, can't we find one hour a week to help raise the next generation of good Americans?

This chapter is full of ideas—a little like lesson plans—to fill that hour a week with activities that will help your kids discover America and have a lot of fun along the way. Our 60-Minute Solutions are designed primarily for elementary and middle-school students, although we've included a few suggestions for older students, including more Dinner Table Debates.

Getting Them on Board

Whatever the age, the crucial question is whether the kids will be really interested at first. Some children, already bored by school and jaded by the media, will be a challenge, but most younger kids and even middle schoolers up to seventh or eighth grade like to spend time with their parents whether they'll admit it or not. If you make it clear that this is something you are doing together for a short time each week, and that it is interesting and important, you will be halfway home. If you are enthusiastic, chances are they will also be excited about this special time together. What is important is to get your children involved in what you are doing and to create your own All-American plans that are based on their interests and their age levels.

Patriot Projects

Now, let's do it. We've put together ten easy-to-follow "Patriot Projects" that make learning about history fun, not work. These are broad "action plans" on a range of different subjects with plenty of ideas and resources to help you—whether you decide to focus on a topic for a week or many weeks. Most include suggestions for books that your children can read or interesting websites to visit and recommendations for films or documentaries to watch together as a family.

You'll find some projects may be of more interest to boys, like "Battles," and some will be more appealing, we think, to girls, like "Remember the Ladies." Don't forget, these are just examples to get you started. You and your children will come up with lots of other ideas of your own once the gang gets into the "history habit" as they explore America's past in order to help build America's future.

Here are some tips to make this special time together a hit from the get-go.

• **Start slow and don't push it.** And start by doing the things you know your kids like to do, whether it is coloring pages or reading a book together for the younger ones or watching a movie or documentary.

• **Follow your children's interests and ideas.** Encourage your kids to talk about what they might like to do or their ideas about the topic you are studying. As we all know, people can interpret history—and current events—in a lot of different ways. What's important is that you always let children know you take their interests and ideas seriously and that you value their efforts to learn. Most of the activities we are recommending will work with elementary and middle-school kids. Teens, no doubt, will be most responsive to "Dinner Table Debates" or discussing current events. If they always want to argue, that's all right, too. Movies and field trips can sometimes get their attention, so don't give up too easily.

• **Be prepared for each week's project.** Yes, you need to spend some time beforehand going over what you will be talking about. If this is a joint effort and you work with one or more parents, you can take turns preparing. Remember, you and the kids will be learning together about many things, but they will look to you, especially at the start, to be their guide.

• **Less is more.** Don't try to do too much in any one session. Sometimes an hour can be spent curled up watching a video or reading a book aloud, making a poster, writing a report, or surfing the Internet. Part of the appeal for kids is just doing something together as a family or in a group with friends and their families.

• **What if the kids give you a hard time?** What if they seem less than enthused and say, "It happened so long ago, and it is so-o-o boring." Or, "What has this got to do with me?" We acknowledge some kids may be an annoyingly hard sell at first. That's because what we know is important just may not be obvious to them. We need to clarify the reasons we ask them to learn about America's history. When a child says, "So what?" it is important to relate the event and concept to them in as personal a way as possible. Really thinking about the way to answer them when they say, "Why should I care about this?" can be the key to helping them understand what's worth knowing—and why.

• **If your child is a reluctant reader.** Look for books about the past that will be easy for him or her to read. Even if a book's grade level is lower than your child's, he or she might enjoy the book and get a sense of accomplishment simply by completing it. Also, if a book becomes a favorite, let the child read and reread it. Just make sure he reads another book in between before going back to a favorite.

• **Different ages, different tasks.** If you are working with kids of different ages, always, of course, find age-appropriate books on the same subject for each to read. Or read aloud to younger readers the book older children may be reading by themselves. There are many books for children eight and up that younger kids will enjoy as well. Also find a craft or simple game activity for younger children to keep them interested while older ones work on more complicated projects. There are plenty on the Internet, as you will see in the coming pages.

• **Most important: Always do things that you find interesting as well.** You won't get the kids on board unless you are yourself. This should be an adventure of exploration for you, as well.

Create a History Club

Whether it's Mickey Mouse, 4-H, or the Girl Scouts, kids love clubs because everything is always more fun when it's done in a group. And when it comes to your "sixty-minute" promise, a history club could be a big help to you, too. So, one way to honor your pledge is to start a history club either through your children's school or at home by inviting the kids in the neighborhood or friends of your children to join the adventure. Ask other parents to work with you as club sponsors. With busy schedules, having a group of parents involved will let you share the workload of preparing for your weekly project.

Many schools, especially middle and high schools, have club opportunities. Usually, it only takes a couple of kids and an adult adviser to get a club off the ground. Teens, the ones who have developed a genuine interest in American history and want to get more deeply involved in this subject, may be the most interested in starting a history club at school with a favorite teacher as an adviser.

Here are some ways to create your own club:

- **Pick a name.** At your first meeting, number one on the agenda ought to be a name for the club. Help the kids invest in the club by letting them vote on the name. That's the democratic way, after all.
- **Choose a set time and place for your club meetings every week.** That doesn't mean the club can't change a meeting time for a field trip, but clubs always do better with a permanent time and place that is as convenient as possible for everyone involved.
- **Begin with a promise.** One way to begin each weekly session is with an oath that will put kids in the right frame of mind—understanding that learning about America is important and especially important to you. Here is an oath your child could take; we call it "A Patriot's Promise," but you may want to create your own pledge with your kids as one of your first activities.

The Patriot Promise

★ **I promise** I will do my best to learn about my country, its history, traditions, ideals and values.

★ **I promise** that I will love my country.

★ **And I promise** that each day I will try to represent the best of America in my thoughts, my words, and my deeds.

• **Design a membership card.** For younger children, a crafts project is a good way to get them interested right from the start. Once the club name has been selected, let the kids design a membership card and maybe even a pin to go with it. The small American flag lapel pins we see so often these days, except on the network news, of course, are perfect for a club pin.

• **Find your focus.** The younger the children, the more guidance you will need to give them when it comes to choosing projects. You can select a particular time period, American heroes, American values, how our government works, U.S. military history, or American achievers or achievements to name a few. Discuss some options with the kids and, once again, let them vote on the areas that interest them the most. Choosing subjects that inspire children is half the battle, so brainstorm possible history projects with them at each meeting.

• **Change names.** Depending on the focus of your study, younger children might like to pick a "history" name for themselves—much like children in language classes often select a new name in French or Spanish just for class. Your kids could choose George, Thomas, or Benjamin or Dolley, Martha, or Abigail if studying the Revolution, for example.

• **Check out the pros.** There are a couple of states, Texas and North Carolina, with particularly effective "Junior Historians Associations," sponsored by their state historical association (Texas) or state museum (North Carolina). Both focus on state history, but their websites may give you some ideas as well. Find them at **www.tsha.utexas.edu/education/jh/** and **www.ncmuseumofhistory.org/thjha/index.html**. Another spot for ideas on the Internet is *The Concord Review,* home of the National History Club. It publishes an online newsletter twice a year that highlights activities of its many history club chapters. Find information about the *Review,* its history clubs, and its prestigious essay contests at **www.tcr.org/index.htm**.

• **Don't forget the food.** If an army travels on its stomach, well, kids' clubs don't go far without a little food, too. Make sure each child is assigned a week to bring a "snack." If it can be connected in some way with the project of the week, so much the better.

What Happened When

In Chapter 7, we gave you ideas to help celebrate our national holidays, but what about the other 354 days in the year? Here are two approaches to studying and celebrating the rest of America's not-so-famous but important days in history nonetheless.

You Say It's Your Birthday

First, you say it's your birthday—as the Beatles put it. The birthdays of famous Americans make perfect jumping-off points to study a range of topics from the achievements of the birthday boy or girl to what America was like during the times in which he or she lived. What was going on? How did people dress and what did they eat?

Your Patriot's Project could be a one-time-only birthday celebration or a monthlong birthday party, or you might even choose twelve famous Americans, one for each month, as your club or family's framework for the whole year.

Here's an example of how one birthday can expand into a number of Patriot Projects that are both fun and educational. And there is no better choice than Colonial America's original "party animal," Ben Franklin, who was born January 17, 1706, in Boston, Massachusetts.

- **First, let's eat!** Have a Ben Franklin birthday dinner. The menu? Philly cheese steaks, naturally; Boston baked beans; and French fries in honor of the United States of America's first ambassador to France. Don't forget dessert. For the man who first said "An apple a day keeps the doctor away," serve apple pie and ice cream for dessert.
- **Watch a biography of Ben.** A good one is *Ben Franklin* from A&E Home Video. You can even watch a movie about Franklin (and other American heroes) free of charge on the Internet at **www.earlyamerica.com**. A film to rent in which Franklin figures prominently is the charming musical *1776*. It portrays Franklin's skills as a

diplomat, able to convince Jefferson and Adams, who really didn't get along at the time, to work together on the Declaration of Independence.

• **Read a book about Franklin.** Have the kids share what they learn with the rest of the group. Some good ones are:

* *Meet Ben Franklin* by Maggi Scarf (Random House Books for Young Readers), ages 4–8
* *How Ben Franklin Stole the Lightning* by Rosalyn Schanzer (HarperCollins), ages 6–9
* *Ben and Me* by Robert Lawson (Little, Brown), ages 9–12
* *A Dangerous Engine: Ben Franklin from Scientist to Diplomat* by Joan Dash (Farrar, Straus & Giroux), ages 9 and up
* *Who Was Ben Franklin?* by Dennis Brindell Fradin (Grosset & Dunlap), ages 9–12

• **Check out the Franklin Institute website (www.fi.edu/learn.html).** The Franklin Institute, one of the nation's premier science and history museums, is located in Philadelphia and along with the National Constitution Center, Independence Hall, and the Liberty Bell is a "must stop" if you're touring the "City of Brotherly Love." The website is chock-full of information about Franklin and various facets of his career, especially as a scientist and an inventor. One of the most fascinating parts of the site is the Center for Innovation in Science Learning, a part of the Institute, which honors Franklin's long interest and many achievements in science. This exceptional website has games, interactive projects and programs, and plenty of information about all kinds of science to go along with lots of biographical information on Ben. You can find lots of experiments the kids can try based on Franklin's scientific studies at the Institute's website.

• **Check out what Franklin had to say.** Benjamin Franklin was never at a loss for words. Find his "notable quotables" at a website called "Quotable Franklin" at **www.ushistory.org**. See how many of his sayings the kids would agree with.

• **Take a "Franklin Field Trip."** Ben Franklin was a true Renaissance man whose accomplishments would fill a book, in fact several books; and they have. Why not take the club or the family on a Franklin Field Trip to honor some of those achievements? Here are a few suggestions:

Tour a local newspaper—Franklin was a printer and published the *Pennsylvania Gazette* and *Poor Richard's Almanack.*

Visit the local library—Franklin established the first subscription library in America.

Tour the fire station—Franklin started the Union Fire Company in 1736.

Visit the local Post Office—Franklin helped set up Philadelphia's postal system and became its postmaster.

The truth is Ben Franklin could probably keep you in Patriot Projects for the whole year but give the rest of America's heroes a chance, too.

More Birthdays

Just celebrating one birthday can be as small or big a celebration as you and the kids choose. Another way to select candidates for birthday celebrations might be to choose someone important in history who was also born on your child's own birthday or those of other children in the group. A good website at which to check out famous birthdays is **www.worldalmanacforkids.com**. Here are some other suggestions of well-known birthday boys and girls and the month in which they were born to match with your kids.

January: Paul Revere, Franklin Roosevelt
February: Ronald Reagan, Rosa Parks
March: Sandra Day O'Connor, Andrew Jackson
April: Thomas Jefferson, Colin Powell
May: Harry Truman, Sally Ride

June: Helen Keller, Lou Gehrig
July: John Glenn, Henry Ford
August: Neil Armstrong, Orville Wright
September: Jesse Owen, Samuel Adams
October: Theodore Roosevelt, Dwight Eisenhower
November: Elizabeth Cady Stanton, Abigail Adams
December: Clara Barton, Walt Disney

• **A moment in time.** On your child's next birthday, to commemorate that day in history, make a time capsule. Take a box or jar and put in some things that will be a record of that day—like the front page of the newspaper, a printout from the Web of top news stories, a photograph of the family, a video or audio recording, and most important, a copy of your child's most important primary source document, her birth certificate. Also have your child take pictures of things that are important to him—your house, his school, a favorite toy or a souvenir—and include the picture in the capsule, too. Finally, your child should write a short letter about the day for whoever opens the time capsule in the future. Seal it, date it, and put it away in the attic or even bury it in the yard so that someone in the future will know what was important to your child on his or her special day.

This Day in History

Still another way to focus Patriot Projects by date is to simply find out what happened on "This Day in History." Make a list of all the meeting dates you have planned, and have your junior historians find out what happened of importance in the past on those dates.

There are a number of websites that can give you plenty of information. Here are three good ones.

• **The History Channel** at **www.historychannel.com** is one of the most extensive. It gives you historical events by day in a variety of subject areas including the Civil War, World War II, the Vietnam War, and the Cold War. You can even check on daily historic events in other areas like the automotive industry, Wall Street, crime, the old West, the literary field, and even entertainment.

• **The Library of Congress's website** has a page called "Today in History," part of its American Memory collection, which highlights important events in American history that have occurred each day. Check it out at **http://memory.loc.gov** and click on "Today in History."

• **The History Net.com,** the largest publisher of history magazines, also has a "Today in History" section on its website, which includes a list of historical figures who share this birthday at **www.historynet.com**.

• **On-This-Day.com** And **www.on-this-day.com** has a special section on U.S. presidents along with T.V. history, music history, and famous birthdays, too.

Go to the Source

One of the complaints some historians have about the way history is now taught in school is that original sources are not used often enough and that students are not familiar with these important documents. Through your Patriot Projects, you can easily help your children get familiar with these works. Here is our Top 10 list of original documents:

- Declaration of Independence (1776)
- Constitution of the United States (1787)
- Bill of Rights (1791)
- Louisiana Purchase Treaty (1803)
- Emancipation Proclamation (1863)
- Nineteenth Amendment of the U.S. Constitution: Women's Right to Vote (1920)
- Thirteenth Amendment to the U.S. Constitution: Abolition of Slavery (1865)

- Gettysburg Address (1863)
- Civil Rights Act (1964)
- Social Security Act (1935)

Kids can find America's one hundred milestone original documents on the National Archives site at **www.ourdocuments.gov**. Here are several other very recent documents also of great importance that are each easily found on the Internet as well.

- President Nixon's resignation speech (August 8, 1974)
- President Reagan's Farewell Address (January 11, 1989)
- The articles of impeachment of President Bill Clinton (December 19, 1998)
- President Bush's speech to Congress after 9/11 (September 20, 2001)
- Congressional Resolution on Iraq (October 11, 2002)

Before you check out these documents with your kids, help them understand the real value of looking at original sources. Explain to them that most of the history we read is often written long after the original event by people telling us what they think happened and why. By using original sources, we can get closer to the event in its own time and begin to make our own judgments. That's a good lesson for every child to learn early.

Now, for some project ideas that use original sources.

- **Become a Founding Father or Mother.** Start by looking at a document on the Web. A good one to use is the Declaration of Independence. Check it out at the National Archives website at **www.archives.gov**. On that site you can look at the original, read a transcript, download a copy of the original, and the most fun of all, the kids can actually sign a copy!
- **Goosefeathers!** Yes, the Declaration is hard to read, partly because of its age and because it was written with a quill pen. Younger

kids, especially, might like to try to make such a pen, but they will definitely need your help.

- **What you'll need.** Feather, scissors, a paper clip, paper and paper towel
  For *berry ink:* ½ cup of ripe berries, ½ teaspoon salt, ½ teaspoon vinegar, food strainer, bowl, wooden spoon, small jar with tight-fitting lid
- **Make the ink.** Collect some berries for your ink. Blueberries, cherries, blackberries, strawberries, or raspberries work well. Fill the strainer with berries and hold it over the bowl. Crush the berries against the strainer with the wooden spoon so that the berry juice drips into the bowl. When all the juice is out of the berries, throw the pulp away. Add the salt and vinegar to the berry juice and stir well. If the ink is too thick, add a teaspoon or two of water, but don't add too much or you'll lose the color. Store the ink in a small jar with a tight-fitting lid. Make only as much as you think you will use at one time, because it will dry up quickly.
- **Make the pen.** Get some feathers at a craft store. Form the pen point by cutting the fat end of the quill on an angle, curving the cut slightly. A good pair of scissors is safer than a knife, and an adult should do the cutting. Clean out the inside of the quill so that the ink will flow to the point. Use the end of a paper clip if needed. You may want to cut a center slit in the point; however, if you press too hard on the pen when you write, it may split.
- **Start writing.** Dip just the tip of the pen in the ink, and keep a paper towel handy to use as an ink blotter. Experiment by drawing lines, curves, and single letters, and by holding the pen at different angles. Most people press too hard or stop too long in one spot. Have your child write a statement about something that happened that day and sign their name. They now have an original document.

• **Time travel with original documents.** The National Archives has hundreds of interesting documents from its collection on its website, including the flight plan of *Apollo* 11, Thomas Edison's patent for the lightbulb, the letter baseball great Jackie Robinson wrote to President Eisenhower about civil rights, and the letter Elvis Presley wrote to President Nixon requesting a meeting. There are lots of extra resources about each document. You can practically walk step-by-step through the unusual meeting between Elvis and President Nixon. Make sure the kids notice that while President Nixon wore a suit and tie, Elvis, in the rock-and-roll fashion of the times, was resplendent in a purple velvet cape, a gold medallion, and designer sunglasses.

• **Keep it in the family.** Find some original sources from your own family history. You and the kids should think about what they would be. Some possibilities are your marriage license, your children's birth certificates, baptismal and confirmation certificates, the family Bible, the deed to your home, your diploma. Copy or scan them, print them out, and then put them together in a family history log.

• **Recent history.** Check out more recent documents and tell your kids what you remember about that "day in history" when "you were there." Look at the website of your local newspaper on the day after and see how the event was covered, which will show them how the first draft of history is written. On the History Channel's website, you can hear the audio of President Nixon's resignation speech and President Reagan's Farewell Address, while on **www.cnn.com**, kids can watch a video of President Bush's speech to Congress after 9/11.

• **Happy Birthday again.** Have the kids track down primary source documents for their birthday. The most obvious is their birth certificate but depending on their age, they may be able to go to a major newspaper online like the *New York Times* and find out what happened on the day they were born. A trip to the local library, newspaper, or historical society may also let them actually see the front page of the newspaper on that special day if your papers are on microfiche as so many are today. It's also fun for kids to learn how to use the microfiche machines.

DINNER TABLE DEBATE

What If?

Pick one of the country's top ten original source documents and have a "What if?" Dinner Table Debate. Ask kids, "What if" the Declaration of Independence had never been written? "What if" women had not gained the right to vote? How would America be different without the Emancipation Proclamation or the Civil Rights Act of 1964? Discuss what everyone thinks would have happened and let them vote on which of the documents they think is the most important and why.

★ ★ ★

- **Get the teacher involved.** Share with your child's teacher that you have begun to examine original documents. Ask if he or she is doing the same in school. Point out the National Archives has several programs that help teachers teach with the documents that are stored at the Archives as well as training programs for teachers on how to most effectively use these documents.

Battle Plans

From the time they are little, most boys like G.I. Joe, model planes, miniature tanks and trucks, and all sorts of toys that are based on "playing soldier." Somewhere around the fifth grade, however, they can also get very interested in learning more about the many battles our country has fought over the years. Although we have included activities and suggestions to teach younger children about America's military history, it's important that this Patriot Project is geared, for the most part, toward older children.

A website such as **www.historycentral.com** has a section on America's wars that gives a comprehensive battle-by-battle overview of each of our country's conflicts from the Revolutionary War to the current war in Iraq. For a Patriot Project, kids might want to concentrate on learning about one war or a single decisive battle during a war, like Gettysburg or the Battle of the Bulge. Either way, America's famous battles provide lots of opportunities for projects.

Here are some general suggestions to start:

• Read books on the subject. There are hundreds to choose from.

• Watch a video or DVD about the war or a battle during the war.

• Make a timeline either for the course of the war itself or for one battle.

• Try to find an original document related to the conflict, including records of friends and relatives who may have served in the armed forces during the war. The citations that go with military medals are source documents that can interest and inspire children.

• If it is a more recent conflict, they could also interview a veteran about his or her experiences and listen to radio descriptions of battles or watch films and newsreels that show aspects of the conflict.

• Kids who get very interested—and lots of boys do—might want to attend reenactments of famous battles that are held all over the country. They may also want to attend war gaming conventions where battles using miniatures are staged that teach children strategy, history, and some math as well. "Historicon" (**www.historicon.org**) is held every year in Lancaster, Pennsylvania, and is one of the biggest and best. Many of the "players" are retired military, and the program usually includes lectures by preeminent historians.

• Kids love to play video, computer, board, or miniature games that are based on specific battles and that are surprisingly complex. If you can integrate playing a game into this Patriot Project, it has far greater benefits. But as always with video games, limit the amount of time they can play, and check out the ratings of the games to make sure they are age appropriate. Find game ratings on **www.mediafamily.org** and **www.commonsensemedia.org**.

• Younger children love to listen to "old" music so if you're looking for a less militaristic idea to keep the youngest occupied while older children delve into battles, try listening to music that was popular during different wars. Musical chairs can be fun with songs like "When Johnny Comes Marching Home," "Yankee Doodle Dandy," and "Boogie Woogie Bugle Boy."

• Another family-friendly Patriot Project is to put on a "Games Night" featuring board games that focus on battles or military strategy, or go to the old standbys like Stratego, Risk, and Battleship. We've listed specific games for many of America's wars on the upcoming pages. Invite the parents of club members or your child's friends and have three or four games all going at once. If you dare, you could even serve "Spam" hors d'oeuvres in honor of the troops.

Now for some specific project ideas for some of our major wars.

The Revolutionary War

• **Find a timeline.** Many websites have comprehensive timelines for the Revolutionary War period. Here are three we like: **www.historyplace.com**, **www.ushistory.org**, and the kid-friendly site **http://cybersleuth-kids.com**. Reviewing a timeline is a good way to start the project so kids have a basic understanding of what happened when.

• **Read a book.** Good ones on the Revolutionary War are:

- *The American Revolution for Kids: A History with 21 Activities* by Janis Herbert (Chicago Review Press), ages 8 and up
- *Let It Begin Here: Lexington and Concord, First Battles of the Revolution* by Dennis Brindell Fradin (Walker Books for Young Readers), ages 6–9
- *American Revolution: Battles and Leaders* (DK Publishing), ages 9–12

✻ *George Washington, Spymaster* by Thomas B. Allen (National Geographic Children's Books), ages 9–12

• **Watch a movie.** Besides *The Patriot* and *The Crossing,* movies about the Revolution, we also recommend the series *Liberty!,* produced by PBS as well as the History Channel DVDs, including *The American Revolution, Valley Forge, Benedict Arnold: A Question of Honor,* and *Spies of the Revolutionary War.* Also, check out A&E's six-disc comprehensive history *The American Revolution.*

• **Be original.** There are also a surprising number of original documents for the kids to check out about the Revolutionary War. Read firsthand accounts by participants in all the battles of the Revolution on **www.historycentral.com** and check out the maps of all the major engagements on **www.earlyamerica.com.**

• **Check the family tree.** Do you think you might have an ancestor who fought in the Revolution? It's possible. Turn the kids into history detectives on the trail of their forefathers and -mothers. Subscription websites can help, but be prepared to pay for it at **www.ancestry.com** or **www.genealogy.org**. Another option is FamilySearch.org, the largest collection of family tree history and genealogy records in the world, a free service sponsored by the Church of Latter Day Saints. Find it at **www.familysearch.org.**

• **Research a hero.** Everyone knows George Washington was a hero of the American Revolution, but many other heroes fought for our cause as well. Ask kids to each research a different person. Some suggestions of people to learn more about include: Ethan Allen, Crispus Attucks, George Rogers Clark, Francis Marion, and Deborah Samson, who were all brave patriots. Send kids to Revolutionary War Websites for Kids at **www.kathimitchell.com/revolt.htm** for Web links to a raft of great sites. Then ask them to write a short report and read it aloud to the group.

• **Play a game.** There are few computer or video games about the Revolutionary War, but there are some board games including Tomahawk Games' "Revolutionary War Command" and Chatham Hill's

"Battle of Bunker Hill" or "The Redcoats Are Coming," as well as GMT Games's "American Revolution" series. If they have the know-how, kids can learn how to make their own board game based on Revolutionary War battles on **www.uoregon.edu/~triedman/thirdwebquest/boardgame.htm**.

• **Spy v. Spy.** Here's a fun activity for younger kids while the older ones are working on more complicated projects (although older kids would probably like this, too). Tell them the story of espionage during the Revolution when spies wrote letters in invisible ink. You can read about the spies and their sneaky tactics on **www.si.umich.edu/spies**. Then, they can write their own "spy letter" with invisible ink. Here's one way to make the ink:

4 teaspoons of water
2 tablespoons of cornstarch

Stir the water and cornstarch until smooth.
Heat and stir over a low flame for several minutes.
Dip a toothpick into the mixture and write a message on a piece of paper and let the paper dry.
Dip a sponge into a solution of 1 teaspoon of iodine and 10 teaspoons of water.
Carefully wipe the paper with the sponge. The message should turn purple and the secret information revealed!

• **"Replays."** If any of the kids get really interested, they may want to watch or even take part in a Revolutionary War reenactment. A list of such reenactments is at **www.revwar.com/reenact/**. Also, they may want to visit battle sites associated with the war, which are listed on the National Park Services site at **www.nps.org**. Colonial Williamsburg would be especially interesting, and even if they can't visit, they can watch a podcast of "The Revolutionary City" at **www.history.org**.

The Civil War

• **Read a book.** There are enough books about the Civil War to fill a good-sized library. These focus specifically on battles.

- *Bull Run* by Paul Fleischman (Harper Trophy), ages 9–12
- *Antietam: Day of Courage and Sorrow* by Sarah Elder Hale (Cobblestone), ages 9–12
- *The Long Road to Gettysburg* by Jim Murphy (Clarion Books), ages 9–12
- *Civil War Battles and Leaders* (DK Publishing), ages 9–12
- *The Civil War for Kids: A History with 21 Activities* by Janis Herbert (Chicago Review Press), ages 8 and up

• **Go to the movies.** There are also many movies and documentaries with Civil War themes; these are mainly about the battles themselves: the History Channel's *Civil War Combat, The Last Days of the Civil War,* and *Secret Missions of the Civil War.* We also recommend the movies *Gettysburg, Glory,* and, for teens, *The Red Badge of Courage.*

• **Find a timeline.** There are many timelines of this conflict available. One impressive one, with beautiful colored maps of each area where battles were fought, can be found on "The Civil War in a Glance" on the U.S. Department of Interior's website at **www.pueblo.gsa.gov/cic_text/misc/civilwar/civilwar**. Another good one with a timeline and interactive battle maps is **www.civilwar.com.**

• **Going to the source.** When it comes to the Civil War, there are thousands of original documents to check out. But probably the most touching are the letters that soldiers, both Union and Confederate, wrote home to their families and sweethearts. Ask the kids to be historians and prepare an exhibit of these letters. If you live in a state that sent soldiers to the war, try to find letters from soldiers in your state, either on the Web or in local libraries, state or local museums or historical societies. Then, make your kids history detectives and ask them to find out more about one of the soldiers who wrote the letters—what was his hometown, did he have a sweetheart, did he return home, what happened to him after the war? Can they find a picture of him or his hometown? Learn about Civil War letters on the Gettysburg National Military Park's kids' page at **www.nps.gov/archive/gett/gettkidz/kidzindex.htm**. Or to find letters from your state, enter the name of your state and the phrase "Civil War letters" on Google or one of the other search engines on the Internet.

• **Food for thought.** A great activity for younger kids is to make hardtack, the biscuits issued to Union soldiers during the war. And they were hard, indeed. Here's the recipe:

2 cups of flour
½ to ¾ cup water
1 tablespoon of Crisco or vegetable fat
6 pinches of salt

Mix the ingredients together into a stiff batter, knead several times, and spread the dough out flat to a thickness of one-half inch on a nongreased cookie sheet. Bake for 30 minutes at 400 degrees. Remove from oven, cut dough into three-inch squares, and use a fork to prick holes in the dough. Turn dough over, return to the oven and bake another 30 minutes. Turn oven off and leave the door closed until the hardtack in the oven is cool.

Confederate soldiers ate the much tastier "Johnny cakes."

2 cups of cornmeal
⅔ cup of milk
2 tablespoons vegetable oil
2 teaspoons baking soda
½ teaspoon of salt

Mix ingredients into a stiff batter and form eight "biscuits." Bake on a lightly greased sheet at 350 degrees for 20 to 25 minutes or until brown.

• **More games.** Video and computer game buffs play many games based on Civil War battles. Some are appropriate for school-age kids but most are designed for older children or teens like Sid Meier's "Civil War Collection," Battlevisions's "The Battle of Shiloh," Activision's History Channel "Bull Run," and Interactive Magic's "The American Civil War." Or they can download a free game of "Gettysburg" on **www.download-free-games.com.** There are also many Civil War board and miniature games including GMT's "American Civil War" series, Phalanx Games' "A House Divided," and Avalanche Press's "Chickamauga and Chattanooga."

• If the kids turn into real Civil War buffs, they can attend or take part in one of the reenactments that are held throughout the country. Yes, they even reenact Civil War battles in California! A state-by-state listing of battlefields and reenactments is on **www.forttyler.com/reenactmentslisting**. Can't get there for the real thing? No problem. You can take virtual tours of every single major battlefield on **www.johnsmilitaryhistory.com/cwvirtual.html.**

The Second World War

• **Talk to a vet.** What is most important is to have the kids talk to an older relative or friend who served in World War II or was growing up during the time about what they remember. If it's just a family affair, invite them over for supper and ask them lots of questions. Do they remember Pearl Harbor? D-day? Did they take part in the Battle of the Bulge or the War in the Pacific? Do they have any souvenirs or medals that they could bring along? Nothing can make this war more real to kids and help them understand it today than to talk to someone who has firsthand memories.

• **Back to the books.** These recommendations will help children become familiar with the specific battles of the war including:

- *World War II Battles and Leaders* (DK Publishing), ages 8 and up
- *Remember D Day* by Ronald J. Drez (National Geographic Children's Books), ages 9–12
- *Battle: The Story of the Bulge* by John Toland (Random House Books for Young Readers), ages 9–12
- *Flags of Our Fathers: A Young People's Edition* by James Bradley, Ron Powers, and Michael French (Laurel Leaf), ages 12 and up
- *The Good Fight: How World War II Was Won* by Stephen Ambrose (Atheneum), ages 13 and up
- *World War II for Kids: A History with 21 Activities* by Richard Panchyk (Chicago Review Press), ages 4–8

• **Pick a fight.** After getting an overview of the war at **www.thehistoryplace.com**, ask kids to pick one battle they would like to become an "expert" on. Once they pick their battle—whether it is Pearl Harbor, D-day, the Battle of the Bulge, Iwo Jima, or Midway—they can find, with your help, a website that will give them additional information and resources to create a timeline or report. The website may lead them to photos, stories from the officers who led the attacks, and descriptions of the experiences of the soldiers who were involved as well as newspaper accounts, film footage, and radio broadcasts that describe the battle and its aftermath. Ask them to collect some of this material for a report and share what they have found.

• **Off to the movies.** You won't have a problem finding good World War II movies and documentaries about battles. Some think the movies about World War II are among the best films that were ever made. They are certainly among the most patriotic. There are many documentaries as well about specific battles available to purchase or to borrow from your local library or video stores. Some battle movies we like are: *The Longest Day,* about D-day; *Ike: Countdown to D-Day; Battleground,* about the Battle of the Bulge; *Anzio,* about the Italian campaign; *The Bridge at Remagen;* and *A Bridge Too Far,* as well as *To Hell and Back,* the story of the most decorated soldier of the war. For those interested in the war in the Pacific, there is *Guadalcanal Diary, Sands of Iwo Jima, Midway,* and many others. Among our favorite documentaries is Oliver North's *War Stories.*

• **Gaming.** There are also a tremendous number of computer games with authentic video effects as well as board and miniature games about the Second World War. For the computer, check out "Combat Mission Series" by Battlefront, "Battles in Normandy" by Matrixgames, and "Hearts of Iron II" by Paradox. If it's board games you like, try the "grandfather" of all World War II board games, "Advanced Squad Leader" by Multiman Publishing. For a fun introductory-level World War II game, play "Axis and Allies" by Avalon Hill/Hasbro; or for a more sophisticated and detailed game, try "World in Flames" by the Australian Design Group.

• **Younger activities.** There are also many activities for younger kids to do while their older brothers and sisters are playing more complex games. They can build simple model airplanes, color pages, or put together jigsaw puzzles on the website of **www.homeofheroes.com,** which is dedicated to Medal of Honor recipients.

The Recent Wars

Youngsters in your family also may be interested in the battles of America's more recent wars such as Korea, Vietnam, the Persian Gulf, and the war on terror. Their interest will be keenest if their grandfather, father, a relative, or a friend served in these wars. Certainly, they should interview them about their experiences. There are fewer appropriate children's books and movies about these more recent conflicts; but, on the plus side, there are more "original sources"—newspapers, television reports, documentaries, and material on the Web available to kids. Most of the ideas we have already suggested for earlier wars can be adapted to the study of these later conflicts. Here is a good starting point site for each of these conflicts.

- **The Korean War.** For the fiftieth anniversary of the Korean War, the U.S. Department of Defense created a great website at **http://korea50.army.mil/welcome.shtml** that is filled with information about this conflict, often called "the Forgotten War." The site includes an online book for children about the war called *Peacebound Trains* by Haemi Balgassi (Clarion Books), and the fiftieth anniversary of the Korean War issue of *Cobblestone,* a children's American history magazine. At **www.korean-war.com/**, you will also find an extensive website dedicated to nearly every aspect of the Korean conflict with a detailed timeline and in-depth background information.
- **The Vietnam War.** For a comprehensive website on the Vietnam War, go to PBS's American Experience, which did a series on the war, produced by WGBH in Boston. The website can be found at **www.pbs.org/wgbh/amex/vietnam/html**. Kids benefit most from original source stories. A particularly good site for stories about Vietnam experiences written by Vietnam veterans can be found at **www.war-stories.com/warstory.htm.**
- **The Gulf War.** A good overview of the conflict including battle maps, photos, background, and links to other sites: **www.indepthinfo.com/iraq.**
- **The War on Terror.** For the latest information on the war on terror, check out the U.S. Department of Defense website at **www.defendamerica.mil/**. As of this writing, there are very few websites on the war on terror that would be applicable to Patriot Projects.

Discover Your Family History

Where did the first Americans in your family come from? Are you and your children those rare Americans descended from someone who came to settle here in colonial times? Or a Native American

DINNER TABLE DEBATE

Waging War in the Twenty-first Century

A good dinner table discussion could focus on how the battles in our recent wars are different from battles in the Revolutionary War, the Civil War, and World War II. Some good questions to ask the kids:

- What changed in each war that Americans fought—the enemy, the weapons, the medical care of the wounded, the attitudes on the home front and the outcomes?
- Will we ever fight a war again in which hundreds of thousands of men and women will be engaged in battle?
- And though weapons and strategies change, when it comes to fighting a war, what always stays the same?

★ ★ ★

whose ancestors were here for thousands of years? Were your forefathers brought here from Africa against their will? Or did you have relatives who arrived in the waves of immigration in the nineteenth and twentieth centuries or even in more recent times? Or were your great-great-great grandparents pioneers like Andrea Warren's very gutsy great-grandmother who made the trek west despite terrible hardships?

Yes, most Americans can proudly claim forebears who had the strength of character and will to cross oceans, face the unknown, live through tough times, and move ahead. Your family history of hard work, determination, and, yes, courage is just the kind of story that can inspire your children and give them pride in calling themselves Americans. And there is no better way to engender an interest in history than to be the family historian. This Patriot Project is designed to give you ideas to help your child discover his or her heritage and the histories of others at the same time.

- **Tell Your American Tale.** The first step in sorting out any family history is to figure out what you *do* know. Start by simply recounting family stories of the first in the family who arrived in America, when and why. Write down the stories in a family history journal or create a family history webpage. Try to back up the stories with "original documents" such as family Bibles, marriage and birth certificates, and immigration records. For a step-by-step guide on tracking down your family tree, including family tree downloads, go to **www.familysearch.org** and click on "Get Started with Family History."
- **Use the Web.** There are many other websites that can be of help in playing detective about your family history. In fact, there are so many sites that we suggest you look at the listings "101 Best Websites for Family History 2004" and "101 Best Websites for Family History 2005" that can be found at **www.familytreemagazine.com.** The 2004 list gives websites that are primarily free and includes many of the best known and most popular. The 2005 list gives "undiscovered" sites as well as some "hidden family history treasures."
- **Keep digging.** If your forefathers were immigrants, try to find out more about why they came here, and what the conditions were like in their home country that made them emigrate. How many miles did they travel? What was the voyage like? Not every family knows the answers to these kinds of questions. If you're in that boat, have your kids read a children's book about immigrants from the same country from which your relatives came. For example, Scholastic publishes a series of fictional books written in diary form by immigrant youngsters from a variety of countries, including Italy, Finland, and Russia, as well as stories by those brought here as slaves. There is also a series of books published by Chelsea House about the experiences of different immigrant groups such as the Germans, Czechs, Irish, and Italians. And a touching book the whole family might enjoy if read aloud is *I Was Dreaming to Come to America: Memories from the Ellis*

Island History Project, with a foreword by Rudy Giuliani. The book features fifteen youngsters who describe their many feelings about immigrating to America.

• **"Visit" Ellis Island.** To see how other people, with very different backgrounds, searched for their family's stories, kids can check out "The Ellis Island Experience" on **www.ellisisland.org**; or, if their ancestors arrived in America on Ellis Island, they can comb through passenger arrival records on the same site or see if their ancestor's name is on the Wall of Honor. If not, they can choose to have it included at **www.wallofhonor.org**. Kids can also experience, at least "virtually," what happened to their ancestors as they were processed on Ellis Island. Have them go to "The Ellis Island Experience" on **www.historychannel.com/ellisisland** where they can actually answer the Ellis Island immigrant questionnaire that decided whether immigrants would be allowed into America or sent home. Most immigrants who arrived through Ellis Island spent some time in New York. To complete the experience, have the kids visit a typical immigrant tenement apartment in the Lower East Side Tenement Museum at **www.tenement.org/**. Of course, if you're in New York, make sure you actually visit Ellis Island and see the real deal.

• **The Great American Potluck.** Families often have their favorite recipes from the "old country" handed down generation after generation, usually thanks to a long line of grandmothers and mothers who kept Old World customs alive for each new branch on the family tree. To help keep this tradition alive and well, the Library of Congress has created what it calls the "Great American Potluck," an online recipe box full of terrific food and the family stories that go with them. Go to **www.memory.loc.gov/learn/features**, and let your children look up recipes by region or by country. If your family is Jewish, check out the European categories where you'll find "Bubba's Potato Latkes" and "Babooska Kabobs." There are "Open Mouth Laugh," sesame balls usually served for New Year's in Asia; "Papa Rellenas," a potato dish from the Canary Islands; "Whoopie Pies" from Germany; "Spiced Shrimp" from Morocco; and "Chicken Mole" from Mexico. One of the most fun things about the site is that it's interactive. With a few clicks of the mouse, you and your children can add your favorites to the site along with a family story. Celebrate your family history with an entire meal of traditional Old World dishes. Some may already be in your own recipe box; but if not, the Great American Potluck has recipes to fit almost every immigrant background. Oh, and let the kids do the cooking!

- **Talk to an immigrant.** It is important for children to understand that legal immigration is still going on. Do they know someone who is a recent immigrant? For a project, have the kids "interview" them and ask why they came here. What do they like about living here and what do they dislike? How hard has it been to live in a new land? They can also read stories that new immigrants shared on **www.pbs.org/independentlens/newamericans**. Ask the kids if their families' experiences were different—and in what way?
- **Get packing.** To help children understand how difficult emigrating was for people of all ages, ask each child in the club, group, or family to come to the next meeting with his or her "traveling bag" packed and ready to go. Tell the kids to pretend they are immigrants about to go to America and that they are allowed to bring only one small bag. What would they pack? Ask them to explain to the group why they made their choices, and then let the group discuss whether their choices were good or bad. What does an immigrant really need?

If your family has a pioneer background, there are also many interesting ways to trace your family history. Here are some Patriot Projects to take you back to "pioneer days."

- **Oh, Pioneers!** First, find out when and why your family came west. Then, get a map of the period and see if you can trace their route and figure out where they stopped along the way. What was their first home when they arrived? How did they build it? If they lived on the prairie, it was probably made of sod. Ask the kids if they want to try their hand at building a sod house. They can try on the website of the Smithsonian's Museum of American History at **www.americanhistory.si.edu.** It's a game that manages to be both fun and instructive.

• **You *Can* Go Home Again.** Returning to the family roots—whether that means Grandma and Grandpa's first home across town or the original pioneer homestead of the kids' great-great-, maybe great-, grandparents—is a wonderful trip for any family. Wherever you visit, make sure you check out local museums to see the artifacts from the time when your family first arrived. Also, check the town archives and archives of the local newspaper for any mention of your family's past—births, deaths, businesses they may have owned, honors they may have received. Ask the kids to make a "photo journal" of the trip by giving each one a disposable camera to record things important to them about their ancestors.

• **Read a book.** There are many books the kids can read about the pioneer experience including:

- *Twister on Tuesday* by Mary Pope Osborne, part of The Magic Tree House historical series (Random House Books for Young Readers), ages 4–8
- *Little House on the Prairie,* the classic series by Laura Ingalls Wilder (Harper Trophy), ages 9–12
- *Sarah: Plain and Tall,* a series by Patricia MacLachlan (Harper Trophy), ages 8 and up
- *Daily Life in a Covered Wagon* by Paul Erickson (Puffin), ages 9–12
- *Orphan Train Rider* (Houghton Mifflin) and *Pioneer Girl Growing Up on the Prairie* (Morrow Books) by Andrea Warren, ages 9–12
- *Pioneer Days: Discover the Past with Fun Projects, Games, Activities, and Recipes* (American Kids in History Series) by David C. King (Jossey-Bass), ages 8 and up

• **Watch a movie.** There have been many movies and TV shows about pioneer and western life including dramatizations of the *Little House* books and *Sarah: Plain and Tall.* Other good movies that youngsters will enjoy are *True Grit* with John Wayne, *Friendly Persuasion* with Gary Cooper, *Centennial* with Richard Chamberlin, *How the West Was Won* with Debbie Reynolds, and *Oklahoma!* with Gordon MacRae. And there are old TV series like *The Best of Bonanza, Gunsmoke,* and *Davy Crockett.* Heck, just pop the popcorn or pass out some doughnuts—the pioneers' favorites—and enjoy.

• **Go west.** If your family really wants to experience the pioneer spirit, spend a family vacation reenacting a covered wagon ride. Wagon train reenactments and tours are held in various western states. There is even a book your children can read about it called *West by Covered Wagon: Retracing the Pioneer Trails* by Dorothy Patent (Walker & Company), ages 8 and up. You can search on **http://events.cowboy.com** or on the tourism websites of the states your family passed through on their way west.

• **Pack a saddlebag.** If you're going the "western route" instead of through Ellis Island, ask kids to "pack" a saddlebag instead of a traveling bag and think about what they might have taken west as a young American and why. Then, have them fill a department store shopping bag with their "essentials."

"Remember the Ladies"

That's what Abigail Adams admonished John in one of her most famous letters to her husband as he struggled to convince his fellow delegates to the Continental Congress to vote for independence. It is important for both girls and boys to "remember the ladies," too, who were so crucial to American history. But just as boys may prefer to hear about battles, girls, it seems, especially like to hear about the important women of the past, how they lived and dressed, and what they thought. There are lots of projects you can do with girls that focus on the heroines of our history and several different ways the subject can be approached.

Revolutionary Women

One good way is to look at just one period and since we certainly know a lot about the Founding Fathers, focusing in on the Founding Mothers is a good way to start. The website **www.americanrevolution.org/women.html** gives you a list of the many women who were important during those times. Probably, though, it is best to concentrate on a "star" such as Abigail Adams, Martha Washington, Phyllis Wheatley, or Margaret Corbin, a woman who fought bravely and is the only Revolutionary War veteran buried at West Point.

- **Read a book.** Some books about these memorable "revolutionary" ladies include:
  - *Martha Washington: America's First Lady* by Jean Brown Wagoner (Aladdin), ages 9–12
  - *Abigail Adams* by Jean Brown Wagoner (Aladdin), ages 9–12
  - *Betsy Ross and the Silver Thimble* by Stephanie Greene (Aladdin), ages 4–8
  - *Phyllis Wheatley* by Victoria Sherrow (Chelsea House), ages 9–12
  - *Patriots in Petticoats: Heroines of the American Revolution* by Shirley Raye Redmond (Random House Books for Young Readers), ages 9–12
  - *Outrageous Women of Colonial America* by Mary Rodd Furbee (Jossey-Bass), ages 9–12

There is also a series of books about "Outrageous Women" in various times that any feisty girl would probably find inspiring. And, as a family, listen to an audiobook of *Founding Mothers* by Cokie Roberts (William Morrow).

• **Play dress-up.** How women of the time dressed is usually an attention getter for most girls. At the National Gallery of Art's website, **www.nga.gov/collection/gallery/iadcost/iadcost-main1.html**, kids can see photos of costumes from the period with background information on the history of the dress and its material. The extensive and interesting website of Colonial Williamsburg at **www.history.org** lets younger kids learn about the fashion of the time and even dress an eighteenth-century paper doll in the proper clothing. They can also send an e-card to friends and download a picture to color and keep of an elegantly dressed young lady. If you've got a creative group, have them each design their own "costume" of the period for their Patriot Project.

• **Meet Felicity.** Felicity, who is supposed to be a girl growing up in Colonial Williamsburg, is a very popular member of the American Girl doll collection with an array of clothing and accessories as well as more than a half dozen books and a movie about her and her "family's" lives. On the website **www.americangirl.com/agcn/felicity**, girls can learn all about her and her world and play a game about her life.

• **The Way They Played.** Want to try some of the crafts girls of earlier times worked on? Make a simple cornhusk doll, which was the kind most girls played with. To find out how, check out **www.teachersfirst.com/summer/cornhusk.htm**. Or try a variety of other simple crafts projects like making an All-American sampler, learning to sew on sewing cards, or making a potholder on a simple loom. There are also lots of kits for making different kinds of simple dolls as well as the "handmade" toys children once played with. All are available at the Beeline at **www.bton.com/store**.

"First Women"

Learning about our Founding Mothers and the women of their time is a great way to help kids understand how America began. But there have been plenty of great women who have made enormous contributions to our country throughout its history. Another approach for "remembering the ladies" is to again have kids focus on a single great woman in our history who did extraordinary things in her time or was the first ever to accomplish a goal.

There are many books that describe the "best and brightest" American women of history. After reading a book, have each child pick one woman to learn more about. Three especially good books are:

- *Remember the Ladies: 100 Great American Women* by Cheryl Harness (Harper Trophy), ages 8 and up
- *A Is for Abigail* by Lynne Cheney (Simon and Schuster), ages 4–8
- *Girls Who Rocked the World* by Amelie Welden (Beyond Words Publishing), ages 9–12

The list of women who led extraordinary lives by doing something "first" is a long one, and every girl can find an American woman to inspire and interest her. For example, Elizabeth Blackwell was the first woman doctor in America; Antoinette Blackwell was the first woman to be ordained a minister. Margaret Chase Smith was the first woman elected to the U.S. Senate in her own right, and Sandra Day O'Connor, the first woman to sit on the Supreme Court. Edith Wharton was the first to win the Pulitzer Prize. Amelia Earhart was the first to fly solo across the Atlantic, while Sally Ride was the first to fly into space.

To get this Patriot Project off the ground, have your kids go to the White House Project for a comprehensive list of "first women" at **www.thewhitehouseproject.org/know_facts/women_firsts.html**. They may be surprised at how long the list is.

- **Focus on a "First Woman."** Have each child read a bio of one of these pioneering women and find out more about the times in which she lived. What barriers did she have to break down? What gave her the courage and the skills to be the first to do what she did? Have them write a news story about the woman they have chosen. If they need a little guidance, they can see an example of a step-by-step "how-to" using Amelia Earhart on the Scholastic website at **www.teacher.scholastic.com/earhart/gazette.com**. But you can use these instructions to write a news story or radio report on any historic woman.

• **Focus on a First Lady.** Another way to learn about unique women in American history is to focus on First Ladies like Martha Washington, Abigail Adams, Dolley Madison, Eleanor Roosevelt, or more recent First Ladies such as Jacqueline Kennedy, Nancy Reagan, Barbara Bush, Hillary Clinton, or Laura Bush. Information on our First Ladies is available at **www.whitehouse.gov/history/firstladies** and **www.firstladies.org**. Again, ask kids to read a biography of a First Lady and write a report describing her childhood and education, her accomplishments, how she saw her role, even what she wore to the inauguration or how she entertained at the White House.

• Some questions for a lively family discussion might include: How has the role of First Lady changed over the years? What is the most important job of a First Lady? How does one "train" for the job? What are the best qualities of a successful First Lady? If there was a woman president, would she govern differently? What should her husband's role be? And what should he be called?

Women's Rights

A third way to "remember the ladies" is to create a Patriot Project around the issue of women's suffrage by looking at when and how American women got the vote. With millions of women in many parts of the world still unable to vote, it's important for kids to be reminded that at one time even in our country, women did not have the right to vote. Even more important, they should know that it was brave women who helped all women gain that important right.

• **Discover the history of suffrage.** A time to start might be around Election Day by simply taking an online tour of the history of women's suffrage on the website of the National Museum of Women's History, a museum scheduled to be built in the nation's capital in the next few years. Meanwhile, find it at **www.nmwh.org**. The online tour explains that in 1848, when the first women's rights convention was held in Seneca Falls, New York, the demand for women to vote was by far the most controversial reform proposed at the time. At the end of the tour, have them take a pop quiz on women's suffrage at **www.nmwh.org/Education/suffragequiz.html**.

• **Read a book.** Ask them to read a biography of one of the leaders of the women's rights movement such as Susan B. Anthony or Elizabeth Cady Stanton. There are several age-appropriate biographies of these women including:

- *Susan B. Anthony: Champion of Women's Rights* by Helen Albee Monsell (Aladdin), ages 9–12
- *You Want Women to Vote, Lizzie Stanton?* by Jean Fritz (Putnam Juvenile), ages 8–10
- *The Ballot Box Battle* by Emily Arnold Mccully (Dragonfly Books), ages 5–8

• **How times have changed.** After reading about these women and the battle for women's rights, spend some time discussing the ways life was different for women of this time. How does it compare to life for girls of today? The women of the suffrage movement were growing up in the middle of the nineteenth century. What were most women's and girls' lives like at the time? How did they dress? What was expected and not expected of them? What opportunities did they have compared with the expectations girls now have for themselves? For a look at women's lives at the time, check out "A Woman's Place in the 19th Century" at **www.fashion-era.com**, a great resource for information on women's lives at various times in history. Most important question to ask: Would any girl today want to have lived then?

• **Watch a movie.** If preteens are interested in this subject, watch a DVD or video about the women's suffrage movement such as *Iron*

Jawed Angels starring Oscar-winner Hilary Swank as Alice Paul, a suffragette or, for older kids, *Not for Ourselves Alone: The Story of Susan B. Anthony and Elizabeth Cady Stanton*, directed by Emmy winner Ken Burns.

- **Have a party.** Women's suffrage finally became reality in 1920 when the Nineteenth Amendment was ratified. But it came down to just one vote in the Tennessee legislature when twenty-four-year-old Harry Burn voted yes. Everyone thought he was opposed to ratification, but he had in his pocket a telegram from his mother that said, "Don't forget to be a good boy and vote for suffrage." He never again won an elected office. So why not celebrate the winning vote with a "We're just wild about Harry party" on August 26th or thereabouts? Have everyone come as flappers, play some music of the time, and serve food that was popular back then. It would make a great girls' sleepover.

DINNER TABLE DEBATE

Harry Burn—A Profile in Courage

Ratification of the Nineteenth Amendment came down to one deciding vote in the Tennessee legislature cast by twenty-four-year-old Harry Burns. Who else in American history has not done what was popular but what he or she felt was the right thing to do? Who is doing that today? Another angle is to ask kids whether a member of a state legislature or a member of Congress is supposed to vote the wishes of his or her constituents or what he or she believes is right. Use the Civil Rights Act of 1964 as an example.

★ ★ ★

Eureka! Great Ideas

Part of the story of America is the story of American ingenuity, people coming up with great ideas that made a difference. An easy way to start talking about great ideas and the men and women behind them is by simply taking a tour around the house and reminding kids that we can thank Thomas Edison for the lightbulb, Alexander Graham Bell for the telephone, and Bill Gates for creating the software that turned the computer into an at-home information tool.

• **Investigate invention.** There are lots of ways to learn about American inventions. One is to ask the kids to choose a well-known inventor, read a biography, and present a short report. Another way is to pick an invention and figure out who dreamed up the idea and how. It could be anything from Double Pink bubble gum (invented by Walter Diemer in 1928) to the steerable skateboard (invented in 1993 by Thomas Welch). There are many good websites out there to find out who invented what including **http://inventors.about.com/library/bl/bl12.htm**, **www.enchantedlearning.com**, and the site of the National Inventors Hall of Fame **www.inventors.org**. You could also make it a little more interesting by cutting pictures of inventions out of magazines or getting them off the Web. Put them in a hat and let each child in turn, without looking, reach in and get his or her invention to research and report back on. There is lots of information available about our most famous inventors. A good site is **http://edtech.kennesaw.edu/web/inventor.html** where kids can visit a virtual museum that gives the history of the invention of the airplane and traces the invention of the telephone as well as presents lively bios of Thomas Edison, Cyrus McCormick, and Samuel Morse.

• **Read a book.** There are also many biographies of our great inventors such as:

- *Thomas Edison: Young Inventor* by Sue Guthridge
- *Henry Ford, Young Man with Ideas* by Hazel B. Aird

- *Wilbur and Orville Wright, Young Fliers* by Augusta Stevenson
- *Walt Disney: Young Movie Maker* by Marie Hammontree

All of these books are published by Aladdin Books in their *Childhood of Famous Americans* series. They can be read aloud to young children and read by themselves by children over age eight.

• **Young inventors.** Learning about our youngest inventors, we hope, might spur a little creative genius in your club or family. And America has produced quite a few of them. They include Louis Braille who invented his ingenious system of reading and writing with raised dots at age fifteen; Chester Greenwood who, at age seventeen, applied for the patent for earmuffs; George Nissan who invented the trampoline at age sixteen; Frank Epperson who invented the popsicle at age eleven; and Taylor Hernandez who, in 2005 at age ten, invented Magic Sponge Blocks. You can find lots of information about kid inventors and suggestions for helping kids become inventors on **www.bkfk.com.**

• **Keep a journal.** So, how can your kids become inventors? They can start by keeping an idea journal. Ask them to write in it every day. They can put down their thoughts as they watch people struggle with a problem and think of ways to help them. Encourage them to record all their ideas for inventions and draw them if they can. Can they come up with an idea for a new toy or a new gadget to use in the kitchen?

• **Fix a problem.** Give them some practice taking an oral history by having kids interview a family friend or relative about "inventioneering." During the interview, they should ask these questions: What problem would you like to see solved? What product or tool does not work as well as you would like? Would a new product or tool help? Do you have any ideas for a new product or tool? Then, let the group brainstorm some ideas. What would Ben Franklin or Bill Gates have done? Come up with some solutions and talk about how to make them work. Then check the ideas by listing why they are good ideas or why they are bad ideas.

• **Competing for ideas.** One way to inspire the group or your child is to encourage them to participate in a contest for young inventors, and there are several. They include the National Museum of Education at **www.nmoe.org**, which gives an annual Young Entrepreneur Award. A recent winner, Kristin Hrabar, invented an illuminated Nut Driver, which has a clear shaft and a light to make tightening nuts in dark places easier. She received a patent for it on her twelfth birthday. The museum also has a monthly "Ideas for a Better America" contest for students in each division (K–5, 6–8, 9–12) for a new product or an improvement for an existing product or procedure. Another great site for budding inventors is BKFK—By Kids for Kids. Find out how to invent and submit an idea, read about great inventors, and even enter new invention contests and earn prizes at **www.bkfk.com.**

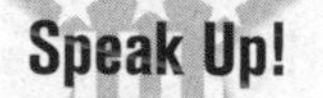

Speak Up!

You know the old saw that "a picture's worth a thousand words." A few hundred maybe. But words—specifically, great speeches—have changed the world. Some of the best were uttered right here in the USA. So make sure your children are familiar with the great speeches that have helped both define and shape the America we know.

• **Pick a speech.** Help your child or the group choose a significant speech, one that changed America, and read it aloud together. First, ask them what makes a good speech? Was it persuasive? What was the most dramatic line? Did it make them feel inspired? Then have the kids research the impact of the speech. What happened after it was given and also ask them what they think might have happened if the speech had never been delivered. How would America be different? For help on finding important speeches in history, former *New York Times* columnist William Safire has written one of the finest compendiums of speeches—*Lend Me Your Ears: Great Speeches in History* (W.W. Norton & Company). It also gives a little historical context to go along with each speech. Online, you can go to **www.surfnetkids.com/greatspeeches.htm** for links to a number of speech sites.

- **Chriss's picks.** When it comes to America's greatest speeches, everyone probably has his or her favorites. Since Chriss was the head White House speechwriter (and first woman to hold the job, by the way), here are her suggestions for speeches to go over with the kids.

  - **A revolutionary opinion: Patrick Henry's Remarks to House of Burgesses, March 23, 1775.** "Is life so dear or peace so sweet, as to be purchased at the price of chains and slavery? Forbid it, Almighty God! I know not what course others may take, but as for me, give me liberty or give me death!"
  - **Our greatest president, our greatest speechwriter: Abraham Lincoln's Second Inaugural Address, March 4, 1864.** "With malice toward none, with charity for all, with firmness in the right as God gives us to see the right, let us strive on to finish the work we are in, to bind up the nation's wounds, to care for him who shall have borne the battle, and for his widow and orphans; to do all which may achieve and cherish a just and a lasting peace among ourselves."
  - **Women—50 percent of America's greatness: Elizabeth Cady Stanton at the First Women's Rights Convention, July 19, 1848.** "The voice of woman has been silenced in the state, the church, and the home, but man cannot fulfill his destiny alone, he cannot redeem his race unaided."
  - **Prescription for a very American style of life: Theodore Roosevelt, April 10, 1899.** "I wish to preach not the doctrine of ignoble ease but the doctrine of the strenuous life; the life of toil and effort; of labour and strife; to preach that the highest form of success which comes not to the man who desires mere easy peace but to the man who does not shrink from danger, from hardship, or from bitter toil, and who out of these wins the splendid ultimate triumph."

* **Shoring up American resiliency: Franklin Delano Roosevelt's First Inaugural Address, March 4, 1933.** "So, first of all, let me assert my firm belief that the only thing we have to fear is fear itself—nameless, unreasoning, unjustified terror which paralyzes needed efforts to convert retreat into advance."
* **A challenge to all citizens: John F. Kennedy's Inaugural Address, January 20, 1960.** "Ask not what your country can do for you; ask what you can do for your country."
* **The conscience of a nation: Reverend Martin Luther King Jr. on the steps of the Lincoln Memorial, August 28, 1963.** "I have a dream that my four little children will one day live in a nation where they will not be judged by the color of their skin but by the content of their character."
* **Answering the most difficult question: President Ronald Reagan on the anniversary of D-day, June 6, 1984.** "You all knew that some things are worth dying for. One's country is worth dying for, and democracy is worth dying for, because it's the most deeply honorable form of government ever devised by man."
* **Today's greatest challenge: President George W. Bush, September 20, 2001.** "The advance of human freedom—the great achievement of our time, and the great hope of every time—now depends on us. Our nation—this generation—will lift a dark threat of violence from our people and our future. We will rally the world to this cause by our efforts, by our courage. We will not tire, we will not falter, and we will not fail."

• **Write their own speech.** It isn't easy to write a speech, but ask a middle schooler to give it a try. Ask children to give a speech about something they think is important. Yes, it can be a protest speech, complaining about something their parents are doing. Remember,

Patrick Henry's speech started with a complaint. Or have them write a five-minute speech they would give, if asked, on a patriotic holiday or about one of the Patriot Projects they have been working on. Let them give the speech to the family and applause, please, at the end.

When Mom and Dad Were Young

History doesn't have to be a hundred years old to be history. Actually, yesterday qualifies, and it's important kids understand that history is made every day. One way to get that point across is to create a Patriot Project that lets them relive with you the important historical events of your life. What year was it when you were the same age as your child is now? Were you growing up during the '60s, '70s, or '80s? What are the historical events you remember?

- **The sixties.** If you were growing up in the 1960s, do you remember the day President Kennedy was assassinated? Even if you were very young, you probably do. Together, watch the breaking news of this tragic event as your family may have seen it, by going to **www.cbsnews.com/elements/2003/11/18/national/videoarchive584325_0_1_page.shtml**. Do you remember the day Neil Armstrong walked on the moon? You can all watch the *Eagle* land once again on the History Channel's website. And what about when the Beatles sang on the Ed Sullivan show? There is a DVD of that history-changing performance, *Ed Sullivan Presents the Beatles,* if you really want to show it to them. But we bet you'll be satisfied with a glimpse of the Fab Four on the History Channel playing "I Want to Hold Your Hand," which was number one on the charts the day the "British invaded." Then, have a Carnaby Street Party.
- **The seventies.** If you were growing up during the 1970s, do you remember when President Nixon resigned? Listen to his resignation speech on the History Channel. When the Vietnam War ended? Check out the *New York Times* coverage of the fall of Saigon at

www.nytimes.com/learning/general/specials/saigon/. When *Roots* was the most watched TV show? The miniseries is still available and still worth watching with the kids. Or when *Saturday Night Fever* was the album and the movie of the year? Anybody still got a white suit to show them? Then, why not have a disco party?

• **The eighties.** If you were growing up during the 1980s, do you remember the explosion of the *Challenger?* On the History Channel, you can watch the loss of the shuttle and listen to President Reagan's moving speech to the nation. The fall of the Berlin Wall? See **www.cnn.com** for videos. When the American hockey team won the Olympics? Watch the movie *Miracle* starring Kurt Russell. USA! USA! Then, have an '80s party including a scavenger hunt. See who can be the first to find a Cabbage Patch Doll, a Rubik's Cube, an original Trivial Pursuits game, a vintage skateboard, and a Crocodile Dundee hat.

• **Personal biographers.** Have the kids become your personal biographers by writing your "life story." Questions they can ask you beyond the basic bio information include: What was your favorite toy when you were their age? Your favorite TV show? Favorite subject in school and teacher? Favorite vacation? How much allowance did you get? How does it compare with what they get now? When you were a teenager who was your favorite celebrity? What did you wear to the prom? What was the first car you ever got? The first job you ever held? How much do they think times have changed? What are the biggest differences? How do they think things are really still the same? This will be a special document years later.

• **Watch a movie.** Spend an evening watching a movie from "your" era. Suggestions:

* From the 1960s: *To Kill a Mockingbird, 2001: A Space Odyssey,* or *A Hard Day's Night*
* From the 1970s: *Star Wars, American Graffiti,* or *Saturday Night Fever*
* From the 1980s: *E.T., Raiders of the Lost Ark,* or *Back to the Future*

DINNER TABLE DEBATE

Are You a Child of Your Times?

A good dinner table discussion might be how you—and your kids—think you were influenced by the times. Did the U.S. hockey team's gold medal victory at the 1980 Olympics make you feel proud to be an American? Did the *Challenger* disaster frighten you? Did the fall of the Berlin Wall inspire you or make you think differently about freedom and democracy? Try to be as open as possible with your kids about your feelings at the time—as a kid like them. Then, ask them what events they think have been the most important in their lives and why.

★ ★ ★

And as for music, we bet they know what you liked then because you are still playing and listening to it today.

- **Get the scoop.** Ask the kids to report on the decade in which you grew up. Then, write a "news story" about one of the big events of the decade including photos or video if available. They should be able to find all the resources they need on the Internet.

Citizenship Central

While working on this book, we spoke to a young man who had attended New York City's best public school since kindergarten, one for exceptionally bright youngsters. He was fifteen, and he said he was very interested in politics. But when we asked him whether he had taken a course in civics, he was confused. He didn't even really know what the word *civics* meant. This young man had taken only one year of American history in fifth grade and admitted he had forgotten most of it. He proved to us that civic education, the teaching of youngsters how to be good citizens and once the primary reason for public education in America, is even more lacking in most schools today that we had believed.

So it really is a good idea to focus one project—or even a series—on getting back to basics: explaining to the kids how our government works and what being a good citizen means.

Start Close to Home

• **Take on city hall.** Or the mayor's office or the county commissioners' for a field trip to see how government works firsthand. Call ahead and ask for you and your child or a whole group of kids to be shown around. While you might get lucky and get a guided tour from one of the elected officials, especially if you've got a good-sized group, a staff member will probably be delighted by your interest and eager to give a tour and explain exactly how your local government works, who does what and why. A good book about electing a mayor is *Vote!* by Eileen Christelow (Clarion Books), ages 8–10, which, with colorful drawings and a lighthearted touch, describes the whole electoral process in an appealing way.

• **Say thank you for the visit.** Here is a great activity for the kids to try and a great way to show their appreciation for the town hall tour. Does your town have its own flag? If not, the kids could design one and send it along with a thank-you note for the visit. They can find out how to design a flag on **www.nava.org**. They might also suggest designing a town flag as a school project, which the local newspaper would probably be very interested in hearing about. If the town already has a flag, how about a town crest or cooking up a town or county slogan?

• **Where do I register?** One of the most important of our many civic duties is voting, of course, but many people never vote simply because they don't know how. Make sure your kids understand that voting is not only a right and a responsibility, it's also easy. The best way to get that message across is to take the group on a field trip to your local elections office. Most election officials would be glad to explain how to go about registering to vote, where you vote, and how votes are cast in their area. Many will have sample machines and ballots to let the kids have a practice session or two. Help dispel the notion that voting is hard (hanging chads notwithstanding) by showing them just how simple it is.

• **Your town's "good" citizens.** From America's earliest days, part of being a good citizen has been contributing to the community through hard work. To help younger children understand that we all have a job to do to be good Americans, give them a disposable camera and send them off to interview a variety of citizens about what they do that helps the community. Almost any hardworking citizen could be a subject—firefighter, teacher, businessperson, nurse, police officer, or doctor. Older kids or teens might try for "leading" citizens like elected officials and other prominent citizens.

The State of Play

When it comes to state governors, everybody knows "Ahr-nold," but could your kids name their governor? Despite courses in state history, most probably couldn't, and they should. They should also have a good idea how their state government works, the type of state legislature your state has, how often it meets, how many members it has, and how it affects their lives. Generic information about state governments is somewhat lacking, so your best bet is to go to your state government's official website, although many of them aren't as good as they should be. A quick link to every state's site can also be found at the federal website **www.kids.gov**. It also has a kids' section with a smattering of history, a guide to places to visit, plus games and activities.

Check out your state's site and see how helpful it is and how it compares to others. Ask the kids to read the governor's bio, usually available on the state website, and find out how he or she became governor.

- **Road trip!** There is nothing like seeing where the action is to help children understand their government. A visit to the state capital to see the state legislature in session, if possible, and the governor's office is a great field trip for a family or a club. Write the governor's office and ask if it is possible to tour the building and whether the governor's official residence is open to the public. Your local state representatives could also help arrange a tour. Planning ahead is crucial. Once again, hand out the disposable cameras and assign each child to write a story as a "reporter" covering a different aspect of the trip: what was going on in the legislature, the history of the capitol building, a story about the governor's office, the history of the governor's residence. Many state historical museums are located in their state capital cities. So make sure to leave time in your day for a stop at the museum to learn a little state history.

DINNER TABLE DEBATE

Talking About "Governators"

Especially for teens interested in politics, a discussion about governorships as stepping-stones to the presidency might be worth a try. See if they can name some of the recent former governors who ended up in the Oval Office (Carter, Reagan, Clinton, and Bush). Do they think being governor prepares a person for the presidency? Ask them what kind of qualifications a governor needs. Then pose the ultimate question: How would they change their community or state if they sat in the governor's chair?

★ ★ ★

State of the Nation

Understanding our federal government doesn't have to be dull. It really doesn't. In fact, there is a nearly endless supply of books, films, websites, games, and activities to keep even the most jaded kids interested. We've talked a lot about the importance of teaching kids the history of our country. But if they are going to be active, involved, and most of all good citizens in the future, they must also understand how our national government works—our unique system of checks and balances that characterizes our three branches of government.

First, here are a few general ideas to kick off your Patriot Project to teach your kids about their government. Then, some specific suggestions follow for each of the three branches.

- **Book it!** There are many very clever and creative books that kids will enjoy—and so will you—that explain how our federal government works. Take a look at:

  - *D Is for Democracy: A Citizen's Alphabet* by Elissa Grodin (Sleeping Bear Press), ages 4–8
  - *House Mouse, Senate Mouse* by Peter W. Barnes and Cheryl Barnes (VSP Books), ages 4–8
  - *The Voice of the People: American Democracy in Action* by Betsy Maestro (Harper Trophy), ages 8–10
  - *How the U.S. Government Works* by Sly Sobel (Barron's Educational Series), ages 9–12
  - *America Votes: How Our President Is Elected* by Linda Granfield (Kids Can Press), ages 9–12

- **How government works—on the Web.** There are also several terrific websites, some created by the feds, which give very good descriptions of the three branches of our national government and how they work. Check them out for lots of information and fun activities at:

Ben's Guide at **http://bensguide.gpo.gov**
C-Span Classroom at **www.c-spanclassroom.org**
First Gov for Kids at **www.kids.gov**
Congress for Kids at **www.congressforkids.net**

For lesson plans, activities, and craft projects that teach children about the three branches of government, try Scholastic's website at **www.scholastic.com.** For two craft projects to start, go to **http://teacher.scholastic.com/lessonrepro/lessonplans/profbooks/branchesgovt.htm.**

• **Respect for our national symbols.** Even preschool children can learn about America's most important symbols and how to treat them with respect. For example, your kids probably say the Pledge of Allegiance in class but go over it with them. Make sure they understand the words and that they are pledging allegiance to the flag because it is the most important symbol of America. They also should know that the correct way to salute the flag is by standing at attention and putting their hand over their heart. Even though the words to "The Star-Spangled Banner" are difficult—we know how many celebs have had trouble with them—they should be familiar with the music by second or third grade and recognize that it is the national anthem. Teach them the words and see how long it takes for them to remember them. And teach them also to always stand up and at attention when the national anthem is played. Other symbols they should recognize even when they are quite young are the Statue of Liberty, the bald eagle, and Uncle Sam.

• **Seal the deal.** The Great Seal of the United States is a symbol many children and adults don't often understand. A good website that explains the importance of the seal is **www.greatseal.com**, especially the words *E Pluribus Unum,* which mean "Out of many, one." Kids should understand that this idea is one of the most profound beliefs that makes us all American. The seal is used two to three thousand times a year on official documents. Now ask the kids if they can find a picture of the Great Seal around the house. And if they are clever enough to find it on the back of a dollar bill, let them have it! At the National Archives in Washington, D.C., kids can actually create their own "seal" onscreen, see it on monitors right there in the Archives, and then print it out to take home. But you can do the same project back home by having kids design their own seal with crayons or Magic Markers. Start by checking out all the state seals for inspiration. You'll find them at **http://civilwarclipart.com/Clipartgallery/usastate.htm**.

The Legislative Branch

• **Start with an overview.** Discovering how the Congress does its job is, we admit, not the easiest of tasks. One website that can help you start the process is "Congress for Kids" at **www.congressforkids.net.** While this site has information about all three branches of government, it has much to teach about Congress through short informational backgrounders followed with *Jeopardy!*-like quizzes, puzzles, and games.

• **Making a bill into a law.** Figuring out how a bill becomes a law isn't easy, either, but **http://clerkkids.house.gov/** explains it well through a cartoon format. The site also gives the family or club the chance to take a virtual tour of the Capitol. And there are also fun games to play on this site for younger kids. They can even change the color of the Capitol dome. Older kids—once they understand the process—can create a law of their own. Or find an actual bill that has been proposed and follow its path through the Congress over the course of time. Assign a couple of kids to "babysit" the bill, create a timeline, and report back to the group periodically on its progress, but make sure it's a bill that will interest the kids.

• **Know your senators and congressman.** Most kids have no idea who speaks for them in the United States Congress. So make getting to know your senators and congressman or -woman a Patriot Project. All have websites that give biographical background, information on issues, and the representative's positions and contact information.

Find links to your senators at **www.senate.gov/** and your congressman at **www.house.gov/**.

• **"Make your voice heard."** This is a good Patriot Project to help children understand that members of Congress represent them in Washington. Have them each write an e-mail and state their opinion on an issue. Make sure they ask specific questions in order to get more than a canned response.

The Judicial Branch

• **You be the judge.** First things first. Kids need to understand that the Constitution and Bill of Rights are the foundation of our nation's laws. Check our ideas for Constitution Day in Chapter 7, but here's a new suggestion for the Bill of Rights. To help kids understand these important amendments, have them find the "missing" Bill of Rights on the Constitution Center's website at **www.constitutioncenter.org/explore/ForKids/index.shtml**.

• **Road trip again!** Most teenagers will never see the inside of a courtroom (we hope), but maybe seeing what *Law and Order* is like in real life isn't such a bad idea. If you've got a friend who is a lawyer, ask him or her to take the group to the courthouse to watch a real trial and explain the proceedings. Then take a virtual tour of the highest court in the land, the Supreme Court, at **www.oyez.com**. Just for fun, see if they can find the "Bill of Rights" tablet in the courtroom (it's on the East Frieze). Then, pick a case before the court and listen to oral arguments. Two of the most popular audios are cases that involved teenagers.

The Executive Branch

Almost every federal agency has a website, and many of the larger ones have kids' pages that are both informative and often entertaining, too. For a list of executive branch kids' pages, check out Ben's

Guide at **http://bensguide.gpo.gov** or "First Gov for Kids" at **www.kids.gov**. While there are plenty of federal websites to interest almost every child, here we're concentrating on the "boss," the president and on one of the best agency websites for kids—the FBI.

- **The president's job.** A very clear description of what the president does and the roles he plays as chief of state, chief executive, chief diplomat, and commander in chief can be found on the Scholastic website at **http://teacher.scholastic.com/researchtools/articlearchives/civics/presres/prsnapsh.htm**. Yes, we know it is a long address! After reading the description of the most powerful position in the world, ask the kids to write a help-wanted ad for the job. What characteristics should a good candidate for president possess? What schooling and work experience are required? What are the demands of the job? Do they think it is the hardest job in the world? In what ways is it the most rewarding? Or you can go straight to the source—the White House and its kids' page at **www.whitehouse.gov/kids/**. There, kids can "meet the presidents" of the past and find out about the current one, participate in polls, take a quiz, or play games. And the site is, of course, "headed" by Barney.
- **The president's secrets.** PBS's "American Experience: The Presidents" website has information about every president. Included is a fun section for kids that includes a "Secrets of the Presidents" page. Kids can read intriguing little facts about each of our leaders at **www.pbskids.org/wayback/prez/secrets**. If you are looking at the website with several children, play a game of "Pass It On" by asking each child to whisper a "President's Secret" to another. See how the "secrets" change in the telling.
- **If you were president.** On "The Presidents" website, kids have also posted their ideas on what they would do if they were president. Ask your kids to write up what they would do. Older kids could also do a plan to accomplish their ideas. And they can play the "If You Were President" game at **www.teacher.scholastic.com/scholasticnews/**

games_quizzes/index.asp and click on "If You Were President." It allows kids to pick their cabinet and even do what few of our presidents ever really manage to do—balance the budget!

• **Go undercover.** While most kids might think the FBI ought to be found on the "judicial branch" of the national tree, it actually belongs in the executive branch—under the Department of Justice. What kid could resist going on the FBI site to check out the "Most Wanted" at **www.fbi.gov/wanted.htm**? But the most fun on this really great website can be found at the FBI's kids' page at **www.fbi.gov/fbikids.htm**. Get the scoop on the FBI's drug-sniffing dogs with pictures and "bios" of these hardworking hounds at, or go undercover at **www.fbi.gov/kids/games/undercover.htm** and create a new disguise for an FBI agent. For older kids, follow a case through the FBI crime lab or investigate a spy. You and your kids can easily spend an hour on this website having fun while learning how the FBI is working to protect all of us—one of our government's basic responsibilities. The Department of Justice also has a good kids' page that teaches kids about the U.S. Attorney system, complete with an interactive cartoon courtroom, at **www.usdoj.gov/kidspage.**

• **Write the president.** Here's our last idea. We told you early on that one of the things that made producer Norman Lear a patriot was seeing his grandfather write the president and always getting a reply. Finding those letters from the White House in his mailbox was the thrill of his young life. Well, ask your kids to write a letter to the president on patriotic stationery they have printed out. The address is 1600 Pennsylvania Avenue NW, Washington, DC 20500. Why not have them tell the president what they think makes a good American citizen and then ask what he thinks? Or they can give their opinion on an issue, offer a suggestion, or just tell the president about their American dream or the Patriot Projects they have been working on and what they have learned about our country. It may take a little time (White House mail is slower because of post-9/11 security), but they will get their letter answered. Being pen pals with the president is a really good way to make them understand that in our democracy the most important person in America is really working for them.

We don't know about you, but we're exhausted after this chapter. Still, we hope it has given you plenty to do for that "hour a week" you've promised. Now, for some final thoughts from us—and we promise to keep it short.

AFTERWORD

SOME LAST THOUGHTS

In his very first State of the Union address, Ronald Reagan spoke about American heroes, but not the heroes of our past. "We don't have to turn to our history books," President Reagan said. "[Heroes] are all around us." He then went on to talk about a young man with the rather unheroic name of Lenny Skutnik.

On a very snowy day in Washington, just a couple of weeks before the president's address, Air Florida Flight 90 crashed into the Fourteenth Street Bridge and went down into the icy Potomac River. Skutnik, a twenty-eight-year-old government employee on his way home from work, stopped to watch the rescue attempts. A helicopter was desperately trying to pull some of the survivors out of the freezing water to safety. Realizing that a woman, clinging to a piece of the wreckage, was too weak to grab the line that had been dropped, Skutnik stripped off his coat and boots and dove into the river. Risking his own life, Lenny pulled the woman, a flight attendant, to safety. She and only four others survived the crash.

Speaking to the nation, President Reagan said that through Skutnik's courageous action "we saw again the spirit of American heroism at its finest." That night, columnist Michelle Malkin, then an eleven-year-old schoolgirl, was sleepily watching the president's speech. But she woke up, she recalls, and was inspired by the tale of Lenny Skutnik's bravery—inspired enough to memorize his story for a seventh-grade school assignment.

"On a chilly night in January 1982, the president ignited a young heart," Malkin wrote. "It was my 'Ronald Reagan moment'—an indelible moment when the exceptional goodness of America, and the boundless capacity of ordinary Americans to do extraordinary things, came alive."

That night Michelle Malkin learned a lesson from the president of the United States. She learned that everyday heroes like Lenny Skutnik embody the very idea of America. In that same speech President Reagan said, "There are countless quiet, everyday heroes of American life—parents who sacrifice long and hard so their children will know a better life than they've known; church and civic volunteers who help to feed, clothe, nurse, and teach the needy; millions who've made our nation, and our nation's destiny, so very special."

Ronald Reagan was an optimist who often said, "America's best days always lie ahead." He maintained that as long as Americans remained inspired by the achievements of our past and the potential of our future, the American spirit would soar and the American dream would never die.

It was our love of America and our belief in its inherent goodness and greatness that led us to write this book. It was also our fear that raising good Americans in today's political and cultural climate is becoming more and more difficult. So we have tried to make you aware of the many forces that are eroding our children's confidence in their future and in their country. We have described those negative influences and have given you some practical solutions to counter them.

But, like President Reagan, we're optimists, too. And, so we've tried to accentuate the positive—the many things you can do to inspire your children and make them hopeful and proud to call themselves Americans. Just raising *your* young Americans will enrich your family, build memories for a lifetime, and be great fun, as well. By taking the Patriot Pledge, by caring enough about your children and your country to do more to bridge the Patriotism Gap, we believe you, too, are one of those everyday heroes President Reagan valued—the ordinary men and women whose hard work, integrity, creativity, and compassion determine our nation's destiny and imbue our children with the potential to be heroic in their turn.

So we close with three last thoughts just for you.

First, don't underestimate your power as a parent.

There's a quote that says it all: "You can't really understand human nature unless you know why a child on a merry-go-round will wave at his parents every time around—and why his parents will always wave back." And it's so true.

Never forget that more than any movie they see or music they hear, more than any celebrity they idealize or any textbook they read, you are the most important force in your children's lives. If you believe nothing else, believe that, and then, use that influence to make them the proud Americans you want them to be.

Second, remember that kids long to be part of something bigger than themselves, something they can be proud of.

That can be a loving family or a strong community or a great nation. We hope, in your family, it will be all three. Actually, a Brit said it best. In July 2003, British prime minister Tony Blair spoke to a joint session of Congress, but, in truth, he was speaking to all Americans. He told us, "Don't ever apologize for your values. Tell the world why you're proud of America. Tell them when 'The Star-Spangled Banner' starts, Americans get to their feet, Hispanics, Irish, Italians, Central Europeans, East Europeans, Jews, Muslims, white, Asian, black, those who go back to the early settlers and those whose English is the same as some New York cab drivers I've dealt with . . . but whose sons and daughters could run for this Congress.

"Tell them why Americans, one and all, stand upright and respectful.

Not because some state official told them to, but because whatever race, color, class or creed they are, being American means being free. That's why they're proud."

Finally, we're especially proud of you.

We really are and grateful that you care enough to commit precious time to such a noble and necessary effort—raising good Americans for America's future. Through the year, there are many lessons you can teach your children to make them the kind of adults you want them to be. But there is no better way for you to express your love of country than to engender the same patriotic spirit in your own children, and, for them, no better gift they can receive from a caring parent.

President John F. Kennedy once challenged us saying, "Ask not what your country can do for you. Ask what you can do for your country." Well, helping your children learn to be proud Americans willing to love, protect, and defend this great country is one pretty terrific answer.

RED, WHITE, AND BLUE GRAB BAG

Here are more books, websites, organizations, contests, even a sample curriculum that, we believe, will be helpful resources for you and your family. Reach in and grab an idea!

Books to Keep in Mind

There are several very good series of books about American history in both fictional and nonfictional formats. They include:

- **The American Girl Series:** The books have as their heroines girls who presumably lived in America at different periods, from Kaya, a Nez Perce Native American girl who lived in the eighteenth century, to Molly, a girl who lived during World War II. Based on the American Girl historical doll collection, there are at least a half dozen books as well as mystery novels about each character and the time in which she lived. There are also games to play about the different heroines, e-cards to send, screen savers to download, and music to listen to on the elaborate American Girl website at **www.americangirl.com.** And, of course, for the American Girl dolls, there are clothing and accessories. The American Girl Places are stores that sell all American Girl products and are fun visits because they include theaters, restaurants, and beauty salons for the dolls. They are located in New York,

Chicago, and Los Angeles. The American Girl collections of dolls, books, and lots more are primarily for girls ages 8 and up.

- **Scholastic Series:** *Dear America,* written in diary form about girls, and *My Name Is America,* written in journal form about boys (both for ages 9–12), are set in different periods in American history. *My America,* also in diary form, is about both boys and girls and is for slightly younger readers. On the Scholastic website at **www.scholastic.com/dearamerica** there are lots of additional activities for readers of these series, including arts and crafts projects. They also offer guides for parents who want to discuss the books with their kids and advice on how to start a mother-daughter book club reading the *Dear America* or *My America* series.
- **Landmark Books (Random House):** This is a nonfiction series that tells the story of prominent people and interesting historical periods. The series originated in 1952 and now has over twenty books, some written by well-known authors. *The Witchcraft of Salem Village* was written by mystery writer Shirley Jackson and *Gettysburg* by MacKinlay Kantor, a well-known historical novelist. In the series is *The Day the Sky Fell: A History of Terrorism* by Milton Meltzer, which has been updated since 9/11. There are books for readers of all ages.
- **Once Upon a Time in America (Puffin Books):** Historical novels set in different periods for readers 4–8 and 9–12.
- **If You Lived at the Time (Scholastic):** Nonfiction in a question and answer format for all ages.
- **A Is for America (Sleeping Bear Press):** A series that includes *D Is for Democracy, M Is for Majestic,* and *P Is for Pilgrim,* alphabet picture books about America and American experiences for ages 4–8.

U.S. Department of Education Recommends

Besides the children's books we've already noted earlier, here is a list of many of the books recommended by the U.S. Department of Education to help your children learn about citizenship and American history. You can find them in their publication "Helping Your Child Learn

History," which is available free on their website **www.ed.gov/parents/academic/help/history/index.html** and also includes activities for children from preschool to around age 10 or 12.

Preschool–Grade 2

AMERICAN HISTORY AND BIOGRAPHY

A Picture Book of Sacagawea (Holiday House)	David Adler
Red, White, Blue, and Uncle Who? The Stories Behind Some of America's Patriotic Symbols (Holiday House)	Teresa Bateman
We the Kids: The Preamble to the Constitution of the United States (Penguin Putnam Books for Young Readers)	David Catrow
George Washington's Teeth (Farrar Straus & Giroux)	Deborah Chandra
America: A Patriotic Primer (Simon & Schuster)	Lynne Cheney
Brooklyn Bridge (Athenaeum Books for Young Readers)	Lynn Curlee
Flight (Smithsonian Institution)	R. G. Grant and John Dailey
Three Young Pilgrims (Aladdin Library)	Cheryl Harness
Great Black Heroes: Five Bold Freedom Fighters (Cartwheel Books)	Wade Hudson
Susanna of the Alamo: A True Story (Harcourt Brace)	John Jakes
Miloli's Orchids (Raintree/Streck Vaughn)	Alisandra Jezek
Those Building Men (Blue Sky Press/Scholastic)	Angela Johnson
The One Bad Thing About Father (Teddy Roosevelt biography) (Harper)	F. N. Monjo

From the Hills of Georgia: An Autobiography in Paintings (Little, Brown) — Mattie Lou O'Kelley
Everything from a Nail to a Coffin (Orchard Books) — Iris van Rynbach
The Story of the White House (Scholastic Press) — Kate Waters

HISTORICAL FICTION, DRAMA, POETRY, AND GAMES

Pearl (Walter Lorraine Books/ Houghton Mifflin) — Debby Atwell
Marshall, the Courthouse Mouse: A Tail of the U.S. Supreme Court (Vacation Spot Publishing) — Peter Barnes
America the Beautiful (Putnam) — Katharine Lee Bates
Sam the Minuteman (Harper Trophy) — Nathaniel Benchley
Smoky Night (Harcourt) — Eve Bunting
This Land Is Your Land (Little, Brown) — Woody Guthrie
Death of the Iron Horse (Macmillan) — Paul Goble
Ox-Cart Man (Puffin Books) — Donald Hall
A Humble Life: Plain Poems (Eerdmans Books for Young Readers) — Linda Oatman High
The Christmas Gift (Houghton Mifflin) — Francisco Jimenez
River Friendly, River Wild (Simon & Schuster) — Jane Kurtz
Little Brother of the Wilderness: The Story of Johnny Appleseed (Holy Cow! Press) — Meridel Le Sueur
Hiawatha (Various editions) — Henry Wadsworth Longfellow
Across America, I Love You (Hyperion Press) — Christine Loomis
All the Places to Love (HarperCollins) — Patricia MacLachlan

A Place Called Home (Sleeping Bear Press)	Janie Lynn Panagopoulos
All By Herself (Harcourt Children's Books)	Ann Whitford Paul
The Flag We Love (Charlesbridge Publishing)	Pam Munoz Ryan
Little Red Lighthouse and the Great Gray Bridge (Red Wagon Books)	Hildegarde Swift
Abe Lincoln Remembers (HarperCollins Children's Books)	Ann Turner
Thy Friend, Obadiah (Puffin Books)	Brinton Turkle
The Sky Was Blue (HarperCollins)	Charlotte Zolotow

Grades 3 and Up

AMERICAN HISTORY AND BIOGRAPHY

Smithsonian Presidents and First Ladies (Smithsonian Institution)	James Barber, Amy Pastan
Kids on Strike! (Houghton Mifflin)	S. C. Bartoletti
Navajo Long Walk (National Geographic Press)	J. Bruchac
A Time for Freedom: What Happened When in America (Simon & Schuster)	Lynne Cheney
Right Here on This Spot (Houghton Mifflin)	J. Clapp
Children of the Dust Days (Carolrhoda Books)	K. M. Coombs
A Bus of Our Own (Albert Whitman & Company)	Freddi Williams Evans
My Brother Martin (Simon & Schuster)	Christine King Farris
The Statue of Liberty (Holiday House)	Leonard E. Fisher
Understanding September 11th: Answering Questions about the Attacks on America (Viking's Children's Books)	Mitch Frank

Shutting Out the Sky: Life in the Tenements of New York (Scholastic Press)	Deborah Hopkinson
We Were There, Too! Young People in U.S. History (Melanie Kroupa Books/ Farrar, Straus & Giroux)	Phillip Hoose
Ellis Island: New Hope in a New Land (Atheneum)	William Jay Jacobs
We Live Here Too! Kids Talk About Good Citizenship (Picture Window Books)	Nancy Loewen
Mill (Houghton Mifflin)	David Macaulay
Coming to America (Scholastic Press)	Betsy Maestro
A More Perfect Union: The Story of Our Constitution (William Morrow)	Betsy and Giulio Maestro
Words That Built a Nation (Scholastic Press)	Marilyn Miller
The New York Times: A Nation Challenged (Young Reader's Edition, Scholastic Press)	New York Times Staff
School Then and Now (Newbridge Emergent Readers Series)	B. Parkes
The American Reader: Words That Moved a Nation (Perennial)	Diane Ravitch
Space Shuttle: The First 20 Years—The Astronauts' Experiences in Their Own Words (Smithsonian Institution)	Tony Reichhardt
How Ben Franklin Stole the Lightning (HarperCollins)	Rosalyn Schanzer
Attack on Pearl Harbor: The True Story of the Day America Entered World War II (Hyperion Books for Children)	Shelly Tanaka
Since 1920 (Doubleday)	Alexandra Wallner
The House in the Mail (Puffin Books)	Rosemary Wells

Uncle Sam and Old Glory: Symbols of America (Atheneum)	Delno C. West, Jean M. West
The Declaration of Independence: Foundation of America (Child's World)	Jon Wilson
Apple Pie Fourth of July (Harcourt)	J. S. Wong

HISTORICAL FICTION, DRAMA, POETRY, AND GAMES

The Struggle for Freedom: Plays on the American Revolution, 1762–1788 (Cobblestone)	Charles F. Baker III
Caddie Woodlawn (Macmillan)	Carol R. Brink
The Oregon Trail (also *Tracks Across America: The Story of the American Railroad, 1825–1900*) (Holiday House)	Leonard E. Fisher
Seedfolks (Harper Trophy)	Paul Fleischman
Cowboys of the Wild West (Clarion Books)	Russell Freedman
The First Decade: Curtain Going Up (Millbrook) (Others in the series about life in the 20th Century: *The Second Decade: Voyages; The 1920s: Luck;* and *The 1930s: Directions*)	Dorothy Hoobler, Tom Hoobler
Across Five Aprils (Berkley)	Irene Hunt
A Patriot's Handbook: Songs, Poems, Stories, and Speeches Celebrating the Land We Love (Hyperion Press)	Caroline Kennedy
Star in the Storm (McElderry)	Wendell Minor
The Story of Divaali (Barefoot Books)	Nilesh Mistry
The Flag We Love (Charlesbridge Publishing)	Pam M. Ryan
The Pilgrims of Plimoth (Aladdin Library)	Marcia Sewall
Giving Thanks: The 1621 Harvest Feast (Scholastic Press)	Kate Waters

The New York Library Recommends: Favorite Books with a Historical Context

These are recommended by the New York Public Library from their pick of the 100 Favorite Children's Books. The list includes biographies, novels, and poetry that are primarily for readers ages 9–12.

Sounder (Harper Trophy)	William Armstrong
Soul Looks Back in Wonder (Puffin Books)	Tom Feelings
Bull Run (Harper Trophy)	Paul Fleischman
A Diary of a Young Girl (Doubleday)	Anne Frank
Eleanor Roosevelt, A Life of Discovery (Clarion)	Russell Freedman
Lincoln, A Photobiography (Houghton Mifflin)	Russell Freedman
Bully for You, Teddy Roosevelt (Putnam)	Jean Fritz
Julie of the Wolves (Harper Trophy)	Jean Craighead George
Charles A. Lindberg, A Human Hero (Clarion)	James Cross Giblin
Letters from Rifka (Puffin)	Karen Hesse
The House of Dies Drear (Aladdin Books)	Virginia Hamilton
From the Mixed Up Files of Mrs. Basil E. Frankweiler (Aladdin Books)	E. L. Konigsburg
Sarah, Plain and Tall (Harper Trophy)	Patricia MacLachlan
Singing America: Poems That Defined a Nation (Viking)	Philip Neil
Island of the Blue Dolphin (Yearling)	Scott O'Dell
The Cricket in Times Square (Yearling)	George Selden
All-of-a-Kind Family (Delacorte Books)	Sydney Taylor
Roll of Thunder, Hear My Cry (Puffin Books)	Mildred Taylor
The Witch of Blackbird Pond (Laurel Leaf)	Elizabeth Speare
Little House on the Prairie (Harper Trophy)	Laura Ingalls Wilder

Prizewinning Nonfiction Books About History

These books are the winners of the American Library Association's Robert F. Sibert Medal and the James Madison Book Award, which was created by Lynne Cheney. They are also for readers ages 9–12.

THE SIBERT MEDAL WINNERS INCLUDE:

Six Days in October: The Stock Market Crash of 1929 (Atheneum)	Karen Blumenthal
Brooklyn Bridge (Simon & Schuster)	Lynn Curlee
The Voice that Challenged a Nation: Marian Anderson and the Struggle for Equal Rights (Clarion Books)	Russell Freedman
Walt Whitman, Words for America (Scholastic Press)	Barbara Kerley
Blizzard! The Storm That Changed America (Scholastic Press)	Jim Murphy
American Plague: The True and Terrifying Story of the Yellow Fever Epidemic of 1793 (Clarion Books)	Jim Murphy
Sequoyah: The Cherokee Man Who Gave His People Writing (Houghton Mifflin)	James Rumford
When Marian Sang (Scholastic Press)	Pam Munoz Ryan

THE JAMES MADISON PRIZE WINNERS

George Washington, Spy Master (National Geographic)	Thomas B. Allen
Photo by Brady: A Picture of the Civil War (Atheneum)	Jennifer Armstrong
Maritcha: A Remarkable Nineteenth Century American Girl (Abrams)	Tonya Bolden
First to Fly (Crown Books for Young Readers)	Peter Busby

Mack Made Movies (Roaring Brook Press)	Don Brown
Ben Franklin's Almanac (Simon & Schuster)	Candace Fleming
Shutting Out the Sky (Scholastic)	Deborah Hopkinson
The Forbidden Schoolhouse (Houghton Mifflin)	Suzanne Jurmain
Duel of the Ironclads (Walker & Company)	Patrick O'Brien
Old Hickory, Andrew Jackson and the American People (Dutton)	Albert Marrin
Built to Last: Building America's Bridges, Dams, Tunnels and Skyscrapers (Scholastic)	George Sullivan
Secrets of a Civil War Submarine (Carolrhoda Book)	Sally M. Walker

The National Endowment for the Humanities: Books on Becoming American

The National Endowment for the Humanities also awards free copies of classic books from their "Becoming American" Bookshelf to libraries throughout the country. The "Becoming American" Bookshelf includes these books.

- **Grades K–3:** *The Lotus Seed* by Sherry Garland, *Watch the Stars Come Out* by Riki Levinson (also in a Spanish edition), and *Grandfather's Journey* by Allen Say.
- **Grades 4–6:** *Immigrant Kids* by Russell Freedman, *The People Could Fly: The Picture Book* by Virginia Hamilton, *Rip Van Winkle* by Washington Irving (also in a Spanish edition), and *In the Year of the Boar and Jackie Robinson* by Bette Bao Lord.
- **Grades 7–8:** *Rifles for Watie* by Harold Keith, *The Glory Field* by Walter Dean Myers, *A Tree Grows in Brooklyn* by Betty Smith, and *Dragonwings* by Laurence Yep.

• **Grades 9–12:** *Death Comes for the Archbishop* by Willa Cather (also in a Spanish edition), *Autobiography of Benjamin Franklin* edited by Louis P. Masur, *Barrio Boy* by Ernesto Galarza, and *Giants in the Earth: A Saga of the Prairie* by Ole Edvart Rölvaag.

Other lists of outstanding and prizewinning books can be found on the American Library Association website at **www.ala.org/ala/alsc/awardsscholarships/childrensnotable**. Find the James Madison Book Award site at **www.jamesmadisonbookaward.org** and the National Endowment for the Humanities' website at **www.neh.gov/wtp/bookshelf/**.

Children's Magazines

• *Appleseeds* at **www.cobblestonpub.com**: Articles, activities, and games that develop skills and interest in various content areas, including U.S. history, ages 7 and up.

• *Cobblestone* at **www.cobblestonpub.com**: Articles and stories about American history, ages 9 and up.

• *Kids Discover* at **www.kidsdiscover.com**: Theme-related articles, many of which focus on events and people in the United States, ages 5 and up.

• *National Geographic Kids* at **www.nationalgeographic.com**: Offers articles, games, and other related activities.

• *Weekly Reader* at **www.weeklyreader.com**: Current events, games, quizzes, and stories about interesting Americans and history.

Our "Top 50" Websites

We know we have given you dozens of websites, and you will come up with dozens more. Here is our compilation of our Top 50 websites to help teach children to appreciate and respect their country and have lots of fun at the same time. Most of the sites are designed for kids or teachers or have kids' pages within them. Others were selected for their focus on patriotic information and activities.

Academic Kids	**www.academickids.com**
American Legion	**www.legion.org**
American Revolution.org	**www.americanrevolution.org**
Apples4theteacher	**www.apples4theteacher.com**
Ben's Guide to U.S. Government for Kids	**http://bensguide.gpo.gov**
Center for Civic Education	**www.civiced.org**
Colonial Williamsburg	**www.history.org**
Congress for Kids	**www.congressforkids.net**
Constitution Center	**www.constitutioncenter.org**
C-Span Classroom	**www.c-spanclassroom.org**
CyberSleuth Kids	**www.cybersleuth-kids.com**
DLTK Crafts for kids	**www.dltk-kids.com**
Early America.com	**www.earlyamerica.com.**
Ellis Island	**www.ellisisland.org**
Enchanted Learning	**www.enchantedlearning.com**
Eyewitness to History	**www.eyewitnesstohistory.com**
Family Fun	**www.familyfun.com**
Family Search	**www.familysearch.org**
FBI for kids	**www.fbi.gov/fbikids.htm**
First Gov for Kids	**www.kids.gov**
Franklin Institute	**www.fi.edu/learn.html**
Gilder Lehrman Institute of American History	**www.gilderlehrman.org**
History Central	**www.historycentral.com**
The History Channel	**www.historychannel.com**
The History Net	**www.historynet.com**
The History Place	**www.historyplace.com**
Historyteacher.net	**www.historyteacher.net**
Kaboose	**www.kidsdomain.com**
Library of Congress	**www.loc.gov**
Mrs. Mitchell Virtual School	**www.kathimitchell.com**
National Archives	**www.archives.gov**

National Geographic Kids	**www.nationalgeographic.com/kids**
National Museum of American History	**www.americanhistory.si.edu**
National Park Services	**www.nps.gov**
NY Times Learning Network	**www.nytimes.com/learning**
Parents Magazine	**www.parents.com**
PBS for Kids, The American Experience	**www.pbs.org**
Scholastic	**www.scholastic.com**
Social Studies for Kids	**www.socialstudiesforkids.com**
Surfing the Net with Kids	**www.surfnetkids.com**
ThinkQuest	**www.thinkquest.org**
US Department of Justice	**www.usdoj.gov/kidspage**
USHistory.org	**www.ushistory.org**
US House of Representatives for kids	**http://clerkkids.house.gov/**
Veterans of Foreign Wars	**www.vfw.org**
Washington Post for Kids	**www.washingtonpost.com/kidspost/**
Weekly Reader	**www.weeklyreader.com/index.asp**
We the People (National Endowment for the Humanities)	**www.wethepeople.gov**
World Almanac for Kids	**www.worldalmanacforkids.com**
The White House	**www.whitehouse.gov**

What They Should Know When: A Sample Curriculum

Although you cannot determine what your children will be taught in school, you might want to know what some greatly respected educators think they should be taught. That's why you might want to familiarize yourself with the Core Knowledge Foundation (**http://coreknowledge.org/ck**), an independent, nonprofit, nonpartisan organization founded in 1986 by E. D. Hirsch Jr., professor emeritus at the

University of Virginia and author of many acclaimed books, including *Cultural Literacy: What Every American Needs to Know* and *The Schools We Need and Why We Don't Have Them.*

The Foundation conducts research on curricula, develops books and other materials for parents and teachers, offers workshops for teachers, and serves as the hub of a growing network of Core Knowledge schools. The Foundation has also developed a Core Knowledge sequence in many subjects from kindergarten to eighth grade, including one in American history as well as world history and geography. Hirsch believes that "knowledge builds on knowledge" and their American history sequence aims to develop in students an increased understanding and appreciation of the complexity of American history.

The school your child attends may not teach in the same sequence and may not, as we know, devote much time to teaching American history. But here is an abbreviated curriculum based, to a large extent, on Core Knowledge that can serve as a benchmark for you to compare with what your children may or may not be learning. A book that includes the entire curriculum, *Core Knowledge Sequence: Content Guidelines for Grades K–8,* is available through their website.

From Kindergarten Through Second Grade

Students should have a very general overview of American history—the most important periods and the most important themes.

Kindergarten

- Very young children should start by learning about a Native American tribe or nation, perhaps about a tribe that lived in a region close to their home.
- They can learn about Columbus's voyage to the New World and the first settlers, the Pilgrims.
- They can be taught about the Fourth of July, the birthday of our nation, and why that day is so important.

• They can become familiar with symbols like the flag and the Statue of Liberty. And learn about our most famous presidents, Washington and Lincoln.

• In a geography sequence related to American history, they can locate the town as well as the state they live in and learn to locate North America and the United States on a map and globe.

First Grade

• The story of the first explorations can be told in greater depth and they can learn that Native American people lived throughout North and South America.

• They can learn about the thirteen colonies and the road to the Revolutionary War with a focus on stories that will interest them like the Boston Tea Party and Paul Revere's ride.

• They can begin to understand the westward expansion, again with an emphasis on stories about Daniel Boone or the Lewis and Clark expedition.

• They can become familiar with important symbols like the Liberty Bell and the Seal of the United States and learn about the current president.

• A geography sequence will help them locate the sections of the country they are studying.

Second Grade

• This is a good time to gently add some civics into second graders' very general overview of American history. A teacher could ask some basic questions such as: What is government? What does it do? It is a good way to introduce an awareness of the Constitution and its importance.

• Students can begin to learn about the Civil War, its causes, and the important figures of the time such as Abraham Lincoln, Ulysses S. Grant, Robert E. Lee, and Harriet Tubman.

• It is also a time when one can begin to discuss immigration and why people have come to America.

• Children can also start to learn about civil rights and the people in our history who worked to extend equal rights to all Americans—for example Susan B. Anthony, Rosa Parks, Martin Luther King Jr., and Jackie Robinson.

• In geography, students should learn about important mountain ranges, rivers, the Atlantic and Pacific oceans.

Third to Eighth Grade

Beginning in third grade, students should receive a more detailed and in-depth chronological investigation of topics that were introduced from kindergarten to second grade. These guidelines are meant to complement locally required studies of family, community, region, or state.

Third Grade

• Children can undertake more intensive study of the earliest Americans and how they arrived in North America and spread out through the North and South American continents.

• Begin study of the early explorers—Spanish, English, and French.

• Far closer examination of the thirteen colonies, how they started and important figures of colonial times, can begin.

• In geography they will learn to locate other countries in relation to the United States such as Canada and the countries from which the early explorers came.

Fourth Grade

• Primarily this is the year to study the events leading up to the Revolution and the war itself.

• It is also the time to study the making of a constitutional government and the meaning of the Constitution in the past and its relevance today. It is the time to make students aware of the uniqueness of the American experiment, focusing on the concepts behind the Constitution and the Bill of Rights and their importance in the past and today.

• They will learn more about the geography of different sections of the country, the mountains, lakes, rivers, and which crops grow in different regions.

Fifth Grade

• In this grade, the focus is on the history before, during, and after the Civil War.

• Students should concentrate on the westward expansion, first the early exploration and concluding this section with the closing of the frontier in 1890.

• The major focus this year is on the "causes, conflicts, and consequences" of the Civil War in all its aspects.

• Another major area of study is Native Americans, their "culture and the conflicts," and governmental policies as settlers moved west.

• Also, it is a time to study the fifty states and their state capitals.

Sixth Grade

• In sixth grade, the focus is on mid-nineteenth-century industrialization and its consequences.

• Students study immigration and urbanization, the growth of big business, and the development of the labor movement in greater depth.

• There is focus as well on late nineteenth-century reform movements, suffrage for women and reform for African Americans.

• By sixth grade, students should have good map-reading skills as well as an understanding of geographic terms and how geography affects economic life.

Seventh Grade

- The year's work focuses on the twentieth century and starts with America's rise as a world power and World War I.
- The Great Depression and its aftermath, including President Roosevelt's New Deal, are examined.
- The rise of totalitarianism in Europe that led up to the Second World War is also studied.
- The Second World War in Europe and at home also is an important part of this year's history curriculum.
- In seventh and eighth grade, students, besides studying geography as it relates to the history sequences, and having a comprehensive knowledge of the geography of the United States, can begin to study the processes that may impact the environment.

Eighth Grade

- Eighth graders are ready to focus on the Cold War and the Vietnam War.
- They should also study the civil rights movement.
- Moving closer to the present, they would study the Middle East and its relationship to American policies as well as the effects of the expansion of democracy throughout the world.
- It is also a good time to have a unit, once again, on civics, making sure students understand the Constitution and the role that the three branches of government play.

Civic Education

The Center for Civic Education (**www.civiced.org/**), which promotes civic and citizenship education, has devised national standards for civics and government for kindergarten through high school. They are based on a series of questions that are answered with increasing depth and complexity through the school years. The basic questions asked are:

- What is government?
- What is civic life?
- What are the values and foundation of the American political system?
- How does the government established by the Constitution embody the purpose, values, and principles of American democracy?

The very comprehensive Standards for Civics and Government can be downloaded at **www.civiced.org/stds.php**.

If you are not satisfied that your child, grade by grade, is discussing these questions in an age-appropriate manner and getting helpful answers, you can get other resource material from the Center for Civic Education—Main Office: 5145 Douglas Fir Road, Calabasas, CA 91302-1440; Washington Office: 1743 Connecticut Avenue NW, Washington, DC 20009-1108.

Homeschooling Programs

There are also many homeschooling programs that offer material that you can use if you wish to augment your children's history and civics education. They include:

- A Beka (**www.abeka.org**)
- Bob Jones University (**www.bjup.com**)
- Calvert School (**www.calvertschool.org**)
- Clonlara School (**www.clonlara.org**)
- K12 Inc. (**www.k12.com**)
- Konos (**www.konos.org**)
- Laurel Springs School (**www.laurelsprings.com**)

Homeschooling curricula are reviewed by Cathy Duffy, a curriculum specialist, at **www.cathyduffyreviews.com** and by Mary Pride, who has written several books on homeschooling, at Homeschool World (**www.home-school.com**).

Civics Organizations

These organizations also supply helpful information and material about civics and history education:

American Council of Trustees and Alumni
(**www.goacta.org**)
1726 M Street NW
Suite 802
Washington, DC 20036

National Conference on Civic Education
(**www.ncoc.net**)
1828 L Street, N.W.
11th Floor
Washington, DC 20036

The Bill of Rights Institute
(**www.billofrightsinstitute.org**)
200 North Glebe Road, Suite 1050
Arlington, VA 22203

We the People, National Endowment for the Humanities
(**www.wethepeople.gov**)
1100 Pennsylvania Avenue NW
Room 511
Washington, DC 20506

The Gilder-Lehrman Institute of American History
(**www.gilderlehrman.org**)
19 West 44th Street, Suite 500
New York, NY 10036

National Council for History Education
(**www.garlandind.com/nche/**)
26915 Westwood Road, Suite B-2
Westlake, OH 44145

Organization of American Historians
(**www.oah.org**)
112 North Bryan Avenue
P.O. Box 5457
Bloomington, IN 47407

Close Up Foundation
(**www.closeup.org/**)
44 Canal Center Plaza
Alexandria, VA 22314-1592

The Concord Review
(**www.tcr.org**)
730 Boston Post Road
Suite 24
Sudbury, MA 01776

Constitutional Rights Foundation
(**www.crf-usa.org/**)
601 South Kingsley Drive
Los Angeles, CA 90005

Freedoms Foundation at Valley Forge
(**www.ffvf.org**)
P.O. Box 706
1601 Valley Forge
Valley Forge, PA 19482-0706

Thomas B. Fordham Foundation
(**www.edexcellence.net**)
1701 K Street, NW, Suite 1000
Washington, DC 20006

Organizations That Care About Kids and Our Country

These organizations all encourage character building, community service, leadership skills, and good citizenship. You can find a local branch through their websites.

Girls Scouts of the USA (**www.girlscouts.org**)
Boy Scouts of America (**www.scouting.org**)
4-H USA (**www.4husa.org**)
Boys and Girls Clubs of America (**www.bgca.org**)
Camp Fire USA (**www.campfire.org**)
FFA (Future Farmers of America) (**www.ffa.org**)
Key Club International (**www.keyclub.org**)
Junior Achievement (**www.ja.org**)
Roots & Shoots (**www.rootsandshoots.org**)
Army Cadet Brigade (**www.armycadets.org**)
Civil Air Patrol Cadets (**www.cap.gov**)
Marine Cadets (**www.marinecadets.org**)
Sea Cadets (**www.seacadets.org**)

All these organizations also have youth activities:
The American Legion (**www.legion.org**)
The Veterans of Foreign Wars (**www.vfw.org**)
The American Red Cross (**www.redcross.org**)
Elks (**www.elks.org**)

These organizations provide civic education and encourage interest in government:

Boys and Girls State (**www.legion.org**)
Boys and Girls Nation (**www.legion.org**)
Junior State of America (**www.jsa.org**)
The Close Up Foundation (**www.closeup.org**)
Presidential Classroom (**www.presidentialclassroom.org**)
Model Congress (held at different universities) Google for "Model Congress"
National Model UN (**www.nmun.org**)
TARS (Teenage Republicans) (**www.teenagerpublicans.org**)
YAF (Young America's Foundation) (**www.yaf.org**)
Young Democrats of America (**www.yda.org**)
YMCA Youth and Government (**www.ymca.net**)

These organizations offer other volunteer opportunities for kids and teens or serve as a clearinghouse for many volunteer opportunities:

Youth Service America (**www.ysa.org**)
Students in Service to America (**www.studentsinservicetoamerica.org**)
Corporation for National and Community Service (**www.nationalservice.org**)
Kids Care (**www.kidscare.org**)
Idealist.org (**www.idealist.org**)
VolunteerMatch.org (**www.volunteermatch.org**)
Dosomething.org (**www.dosomething.org**)

Also, there are numerous religious youth organizations, both local and national, frankly too numerous to mention, that also encourage character building, good citizenship, and community service.

Prizes and Awards

The best way for kids to prove what they've learned about America, its values, and history, and to show off what they know, is by entering a contest, and there are many that offer substantial prizes. They include:

- **National History Day.** National History Day, Inc. is an education organization. Its core program is a national contest for students in grades 6–12. The students conduct extensive research related to an annual theme and present their findings in one of four categories: exhibits, documentaries, performances, or papers. There are two divisions: junior (grades 6–8) and senior (grades 9–12). Students can choose to participate in the contest individually or as part of a group of up to five students. Public, private, and home schools are welcome to participate. The competition starts at a local or district level and progresses to state and national competitions. At the national contest, participants have the opportunity to win national awards of up to $5,000 and university scholarships. For more information contact: **www.nationalhistoryday.org**. Many local historical societies have National History Days that coordinate with this national program or have contests of their own. Also check with your state's historical society.
- **Sons of the American Revolution Essay Contest.** Now called the Knight Essay Contest, this annual competition asks students to examine any aspect of the Revolutionary War, the Declaration of Independence, or the U.S. Constitution in a 500- to 750-word essay. It is open to eleventh- and twelfth-grade students only. Many states have local competitions, leading to state and national competition. Cash awards and publication. Address: Chairman, NSSAR Knight Essay Contest, 1000 S. 4th St., Louisville, KY 40203. E-mail: k2000essay@aol.com. Web: **www.sar.org/youth/knight.html**.
- **American Legion High School Oratorical Contest.** In the American Legion Oratorical Contest, students in grades 9 to 12 compete to demonstrate their knowledge of the Constitution and the

rights and privileges of citizenship in the United States, as well as their ability to speak clearly and intelligently. Qualifying competitions are held at the local and state levels, where they are organized, respectively, by local posts and department (state) headquarters of the American Legion. One contestant per state advances to the national level and automatically receives a $1,500 college scholarship. After the quarter- and semifinals, three finalists compete for awards ranging from $14,000 to $18,000. For more information, go to **www.legion.org** or call your state's American Legion headquarters.

- **Veterans of Foreign Wars Voice of Democracy Contest.** The Voice of Democracy is an audio essay contest for high school students in grades 9–12. The annual contest, which is designed to foster patriotism, allows students the opportunity to voice their opinion in a three- to five-minute essay based on an annual theme. Each state first-place winner receives an all-expense-paid trip to Washington, D.C., plus the opportunity to compete for national scholarships. The first-place national winner receives a $25,000 scholarship. For information contact local Veterans of Foreign Wars posts or **www.vfw.org**.
- **Veterans of Foreign Wars Patriot's Pen Contest.** Patriot's Pen, a youth essay-writing contest endorsed by the National Association of Secondary School Principals, is a nationwide competition that gives students in grades 6–8 the opportunity to write essays expressing their views on democracy. Contestants write a 300- to 400-word essay based on an annual patriotic theme. The first-place winner receives a $10,000 savings bond and an all-expense-paid trip to Washington, D.C. The top national winners each receive a savings bond anywhere from $1,000 to $10,000. For information contact local Veterans of Foreign War posts or **www.vfw.org**.
- **"Idea of America" Essay Contest.** Sponsored by the "We the People Initiative" of the National Endowment for the Humanities, the contest is for high school juniors and asks them to reflect on the "Idea of America." The winner receives $5,000 and the runners-up $1,000 each at an awards ceremony in Washington, D.C. For information contact **www.neh.gov/wtp/essay**.

- **The Gilder Lehrman Prize in American History.** The Gilder-Lehrman Institute cosponsors prizes for the best essays in American history, published by *The Concord Review*, the only journal to publish exemplary historical writing by high school students. The Institute gives prizes of $5,000, $3,000, and $1,000. For information about submitting essays to *The Concord Review*, contact the editor **fitzhugh@tcr.org**. The *Review* itself gives the $3,000 Emerson Prize to students who have published in its pages and also have shown outstanding academic promise in history at the high school level.
- **John F. Kennedy "Profiles in Courage" Essay Contest.** This essay contest for high school students asks them to write a thousand-word essay that demonstrates an understanding of political courage as described by John F. Kennedy in his book *Profiles in Courage*. The winning essayists receive $6,500 in prizes. For information contact **www.jfkcontest.org**.

These are examples of just a few of the many national contests out there. There are also many local contests for Black History Month and Women's History Month. The Girl Scouts, Boy Scouts, Rotary Clubs, Elks, 4-H, Girls and Boys Nation, and state social studies departments all have various essay and art contests. Contact your local branches for more information.

ACKNOWLEDGMENTS

We wish to thank former Speaker of the House Newt Gingrich, Senator Lamar Alexander, former Secretary of Education Bill Bennett, E. J. Dionne, former Under Secretary of Education Eugene Hickok, Michael Medved, Naomi Schaefer Riley, and Rebecca Davis, as well as Chester E. Finn Jr. of the Thomas B. Fordham Foundation, Anne D. Neal of the American Council of Trustees and Alumni, Matthew Spalding of the Heritage Foundation, Victoria Hughes of the Bill of Rights Institute, Barbara Garvin-Kester of the Core Knowledge Foundation, Denise Venuti Free of the Constitution Center, Gilbert T. Sewall of the American Textbook Council, Evelyn Fine of the Character Education Partnership, Ted McConnell of the Center for Civic Education, Lee Ann Potter of the National Archives, Karla Nicholson and April McCauley of the American Association for State and Local History, Richard Pine of Inkwell Management, and Jed Donahue and Mary Choteborsky of Crown Forum for their insights and their help.

A final thanks to both our families for their unstinting encouragement and support.

INDEX

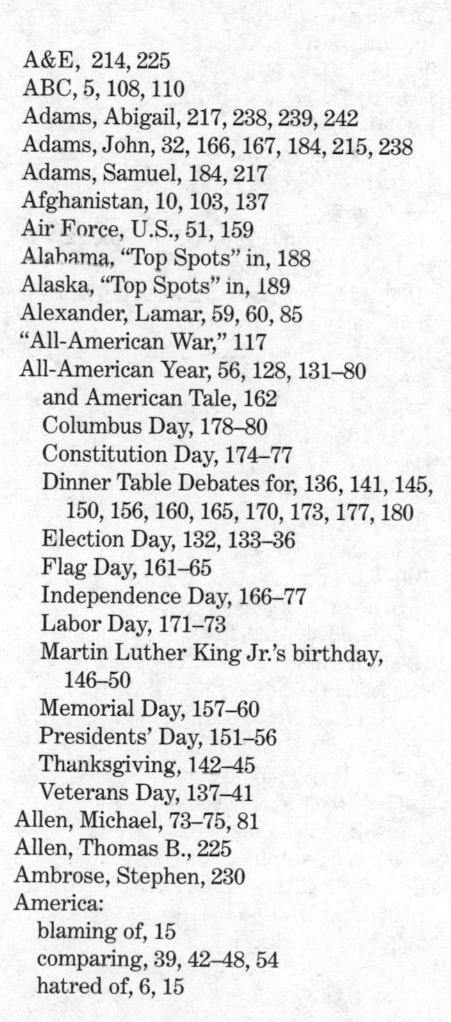

ABOUT THE AUTHORS

MYRNA BLYTH is the bestselling author of *Spin Sisters: How the Women of the Media Sell Unhappiness—and Liberalism—to the Women of America.* The longtime editor in chief of *Ladies' Home Journal* and the founding editor of *More* magazine, she is now a columnist for *National Review Online* and writes for a number of leading publications. Blyth also chairs the President's Commission on White House Fellows and is a member of the Department of Justice's National Advisory Committee on Violence Against Women. She is married, has two sons, and lives in New York.

CHRISS WINSTON was the first woman to head the White House Office of Speechwriting, serving in that position under President George H. W. Bush. The author of several books and a longtime Washington political communications professional, she was also deputy assistant secretary of labor under President Reagan and later served as a senior official at the U.S. Information Agency. She now heads her own consultancy, CorporateWord, which provides strategic communications and writing services and is also a director of the White House Writers Group, a top Washington, D.C., communications consulting company. In 2007 she became a Resident Fellow at Harvard University's Institute of Politics for its spring 2007 semester. Winston lives near Washington, D.C., with her husband and son.